A World of Magickal Help

Most of the few books available on faeries ⟨...⟩
and mythology, with the assumption that faeries do not really exist.
But for hundreds of years, people all over the world have reported
encounters with a race of tiny people, neither human nor divine, who
live both inside and outside of the physical human world. What's
more, our pagan ancestors actually lived, worked, and worshiped
with these elusive creatures on a regular basis.

Today, witches and other magickal practitioners not familiar with the
realm of faery are poorer for not understanding the rich diversity of
beings and thought-forms that dwell there. Even those modern
pagans who work with the Little People relegate them to filling the
role of elemental archetypes—they may call upon faeries to witness
magick and ritual but not to actually participate in these workings.

But *A Witch's Guide to Faery Folk* reclaims this valuable, nearly lost
knowledge as part of the pagan heritage. Whether you are a pagan or
not, if you venerate nature, this book will give you practical help for
contacting these creatures of the wild and will aid your explorations
into the faery realm.

Add a new and exciting dimension to your magickal and ritual workings! This book will lead you through the winding byways of Faeryland and enrich your understanding of this most enchanting part of
the astral realm.

*"The Faerie Realm has often been relegated to fiction and an overac-
tive imagination, but most of what has been handed down to us
through lore has a basis in reality. Edain McCoy presents a valuable
guide to reopening those ancient faerie doorways ... she reveals the
means to re-establishing a magical, working relationship with those
of this realm. Anyone whose inner child still believes in the possibil-
ity of magic will find this book both a joy and a confirmation!"*

— Ted Andrews
author of *Enchantment of the Faerie Realm*

About the Author

Edain McCoy was born in South Bend, Indiana, to parents from diverse ethnic and religious backgrounds, who always encouraged her to explore the history of religious thought. As a teenager, she began seeking the roots of her birth religion. That search, and her increasing feminist outlook, eventually brought her back to the Old Religion. A chance meeting with a hereditary Wittan at a *ceilidh* (Irish dance) in Houston led her to study the Irish Tradition of the Craft. Though she prefers to practice as a solitary, she was initiated into a large San Antonio coven, and has since been active in several other Texas covens, most of them following the Irish tradition. A graduate of the University of Texas, Edain now lives in the Midwest, where she is continuing her formal graduate studies in cultural history. She is also active with the local Irish Arts Association. Her other interests include country decorating, needle crafts, aerobic and Irish dancing, music, and her beloved Shetland sheepdogs.

To Write to the Author

If you wish to contact the author or would like more information about this book, please write to the author in care of Llewellyn Worldwide and we will forward your request. Both the author and publisher appreciate hearing from you and learning of your enjoyment of this book and how it has helped you. Llewellyn Worldwide cannot guarantee that every letter written to the author can be answered, but all will be forwarded. Please write to:

Edain McCoy
c/o Llewellyn Worldwide
P.O. Box 64383-733, St. Paul, MN 55164–0383, U.S.A.

Please enclose a self-addressed, stamped envelope for reply, or $1.00 to cover costs.
If outside the U.S.A., enclose international postal reply coupon.

A Witch's Guide to Faery Folk

Reclaiming Our Working Relationship with Invisible Helpers

Edain McCoy

2003
Llewellyn Publications
St. Paul, Minnesota 55164-0383 U.S.A.

FIRST EDITION
Eleventh printing, 2003

Cover painting: Anna Ferguson
Illustrations: Anna Ferguson, Alexandra Lumen
Book design and layout: Jessica Thoreson

The text of the poems "The Three Wishes" and "The Wee Little Hobgoblin" are used by permission of the author.

Library of Congress Cataloging-in-Publication Data
McCoy, Edain
    A witch's guide to faery folk: reclaiming our working relationship with invisible helpers / Edain McCoy.
        p.   cm. --
    Includes bibliographical references and index.
    ISBN 0-87542-733-2
    1. Faeries.   I. Title.   II. Series.
    BF1552.M37   1994   93-50837
    133.1'4--dc20   CIP

Llewellyn Worldwide does not participate in, endorse, or have any authority or responsibility concerning private business transactions between our authors and the public.
    All mail addressed to the author is forwarded but the publisher cannot, unless specifically instructed by the author, give out an address or phone number.

Llewellyn Publications
A Division of Llewellyn Worldwide, Ltd.
P.O. Box 64383, St. Paul, MN 55164-0383
www.llewellyn.com

Printed in the United States of America

Other Books by the Author

Witta
The Sabbats
How to Do Automatic Writing
Celtic Myth & Magick
Mountain Magick
Magick & Rituals of the Moon (previously titled *Lady of the Night*)
Entering the Summerland
Inside a Witches' Coven
Making Magick
Celtic Women's Spirituality
Astral Projection for Beginners
Bewitchments
Enchantments
Spellworking for Covens

For

Avigail MacPhee
and
Mark Shapiro

With thanks and love

Table of Contents

Why Faeries?

*I*t is nightfall. A howling wind has risen off the sea, battering the thatched roof cottage sheltered in the green hills—hills which now appear as black giants standing as mute guards over the storm-tossed land. Inside, a peat fire burns in the ancient stone fireplace, and beside the hearth sits a small bowl of milk as if in waiting for the family cat. On a heavy, weatherworn chair before the hearth, a woman sits, gazing into the fire's light. All around her, almost imperceptible to the casual observer, is a protective ring of blue-white light. Suddenly the fire leaps joyously, as if in answer to a question. The woman smiles, rises, raises her arms in a gesture of dismissal, and the blue-white circle fades into the ground and disappears. She picks up the now empty milk bowl and goes to bed.

In another cottage far away, a family, all but the mother, is sleeping soundly in their quilt-covered beds. The night is still and cool. Across a night-darkened meadow a small light is seen coming steadily towards the cottage. It is the mother, her lantern held high, casting a circle of golden light around her night path. She reaches home, tired from attending the bedside of an ailing friend whom she believes is now out of danger. Suddenly a low, blood-chilling wail rends the quiet night. The ghostly keening continues for several minutes, and then moves on. The mother shivers and pulls her shawl more tightly around her thin shoulders as she goes to check on her children. She knows now that her friend will not live after all. By morning she receives the not surprising news that her friend has died.

Both of these stories are about faery folk, the Little People who inhabit the astral realm known as Faeryland, a place that is both within and yet outside of our own world. This realm has also been called the astral plane, the inner plane, the ethereal world, heaven and hell, a ghost dwelling, the Land of the Dead, an alternate universe, and a parallel universe. And its elusive inhabitants have been known by many names, among them angels and demons, elementals and imaginary beings, and ghosts and faeries.

Faeries have been believed in and have existed in some form for as long as humans have been here. Seen usually as elemental energies, seasonal helpers to the deities, nature spirits, or as demigods, they have been the subject of much human speculation, fear, and folklore. So pervasive are the legends which abound about them that occasionally their kings and queens have become our pagan Gods and Goddesses.

No anthropologist, ethnologist, or student of comparative religion has been able to find any culture which does not believe in the existence of a race of beings who live in a parallel world somewhere between the realm of deities and that of humankind, a realm which is often referred to as Faeryland. What's more amazing is that modern psychology and philosophy are now willing to give credence (albeit grudgingly) to the existence of this realm. And it may be that the hard sciences will follow suit. The sciences of physics and mathematics have always lagged behind witches and magicians in their acceptance of what these latter two have known all along. But eventually science's hard won formulations back up the intuitive ones of metaphysics.

Physics has already proven what pagans have always known—that all time exists simultaneously. And these same scientists are said now to be only a few steps away from proving that all space also exists simultaneously. If that is so, then it stands to reason that there is an astral realm, or Faeryland, which co-exists with our own world, a world into which we only get occasional and tantalizing glimpses, a world which is separated from our own by only a thin veil of consciousness.

Some occultists, pagans included, often make the mistake of referring to something as being "merely astral," dismissing it as somehow being less than whole, and certainly not "real" in any sense that the human world understands the word. Never make that mistake. Not only will it make any excursions you take into the astral worlds more dangerous, but such an attitude is sure to offend those residents of the astral plane, such as faeries, whom you want to seek out for aid and fun.

The vast majority of our western pagan traditions have made a sad error in relegating faery beings to the role of mere elementals, small creatures who control or archetypally represent the four alchemical elements of air, earth, fire, and water. In the form of the physical directions which they represent, they are called upon to witness our circle magick and our rituals as a courtesy, but they are never asked to participate, nor are they ever approached as sentient, individual creatures. This idea of calling on the elements is a carryover from the days when faeries were asked to come to our circles to participate in the magick. It was once believed that to not at least make the offer was to invite faery ire and retribution, and many legends, both the true and the imagined, abound about families carrying faery curses through many generations because some hapless ancestor inadvertently wronged one of the Little People centuries ago.

And while faeries are, in many ways, elemental beings, they are much more than just that. Faeries have personality and individuality. And though they inhabit a different plane of existence than we do, they do live. They are fully sentient beings with feelings and rights much like our own. Each family or type of faery is unique, and each individual faery has a personality unto itself. Some faeries are mischievous or even dangerous, some are anxious to be helpful, while others may be only thought-form projections of primal human fears created from long ago dangers of the mountains or the seas.

Faeries are as almost, but not quite, as individual as humans, and they each have their own solidity, talents, mannerisms, personalities, and likes and dislikes. They can be solid, appearing almost human; they can be ephemeral whisps of smoky light; they can be simply outwardly projected forms of wish-craft inhabiting the astral plane, or they can be seen openly during meditation or for the short times they manifest on the physical plane. They can be mean or kind, courtly or coarse, and they can fully feel their own pain and anger, and joy and happiness. They can and do function as nature elementals, but they are not merely unthinking representations of those elements, though they can and do live in nature and act upon it in many ways.

Many faeries can, and often will, aid human work, ritual, and magick if approached properly. How to approach them depends entirely on the individual faery and what we ask of it. We can also learn to use magick, meditation, astral travel, wish-craft, and ritual to both meet existing faeries and to create new, fully functioning faery beings to aid us.

Does it sound complicated? It's not. Faeries are all these things, and they function in all these ways. It is we humans who have failed to take advantage of the possibilities inherent in faery-human relationships, just as we have so often failed to see and accept what the animal world has had to share with us. In the past century humans have expected less and less from faeries, even to the point of disbelieving in their existence. And in all but a few magick circles they have been sadly demoted to meaningless roles. It is little wonder that faeries are now rarely seen in a world which treats them so off-handedly. To see a faery one must learn to "see" with the heart and mind as well as with the eyes.

A witch cheats him or herself by not learning all he or she can about these capricious creatures who dance beckoningly on the fringes of our world. This guide is meant to reteach witches, pagans, and others who are interested in these nature creatures about the faeries we have long ago forgotten, and to show how to work with these remarkable beings in a mutually beneficial way. It is also a guide to recognizing those malevolent faeries best avoided, and it will show you how to identify and work with all faery types.

The faery lore of Ireland and Britain is the richest on the planet. These tales have survived largely intact to this present day, and it is these faery forms which take up a majority of the pages of this guide.

The Irish faery lore survived, as did Irish paganism, because of the country's location at the far western end of what was the known world (known to Europeans, that is) until only five hundred years ago. Likewise, the faery lore of the British lands in general is some of the best known to westerners, and because of migration patterns and common language groups it is these faeries which are usually most easily seen by western pagans.

However, faeries are a universal phenomenon, and every land has its faery beings, most of whom easily correspond to the faeries of Ireland and Britain. Only their given names differ, and only a few cultural clothing changes differentiate their physical appearance. For example, the Kolbalds of the Germanic lands can be easily recognized in the Brownies of Scotland.

When dealing with creatures from other planes of existence, humans often express fear or disbelief. Rumors run rampant, and blame is often cast upon these astral beings for all sorts of human failings. No doubt some faery beliefs do stem from ignorance and fear, but these views are easily sifted out from the rest of the world's faery lore, and a thinking pagan can quickly tell what is a faery and what is an astral thought-form created from the depths of ignorance. Pagans must be ever alert to adulterations, deletions, and outright changes to ancient mythology. Fortunately, most of these are easy to spot by their patriarchal morals or their denigration of females. An example of this tampering is seen in a neo-Celtic belief which states that newly married couples should go to bed at the same time because a wife who is up later than her husband can be stolen by faeries. Some version of this piece of folklore may or may not have existed before the coming of the patriarchy, but chances are it was a measure taken by the new religion to control females by fear, and to suppress women's religious cults.

Faery encounters have been well documented, especially beginning in the late nineteenth century when the sciences of the mind began to take their place beside those of the body. From the time humans could write until this very century, many meetings and confrontations, both the beautiful and the profane, have been recorded. These meetings have taken place both on the astral plane and in the physical world suggesting that faeries, like humans, have the mental capacity to project themselves briefly into other realms of existence. Even many modern people who think themselves quite educated and rational see faeries, though they are liable to assume they have merely seen an illusion, a trick of the eyes, or have even dreamed up their encounters with the Wee Folk.

This guide is divided into three major sections. The first will acquaint you with faery lore from around the world, the second will offer practical spells and rituals in which both you and faeries can participate, and the final section will tie all the information together in a Dictionary of Faery Folk of the World.

Yes, faeries do still appear to humans—often, in fact, especially if one learns the best way to seek them out. And no matter how you view faeries—even if you are a skeptic and wish to remain so, or if your views change once you have finished reading this guide—your relationship with them will never be the same again. They are a part of our pagan heritage and, therefore, a part of us all.

Part One

All About the Little People

A guide to the personality of faeries, faery lore, how and where to find them, how to protect yourself, and the truth about the dangers.

Chapter One

The Nature of Faeries

*H*ow faeries came to be, and how they invaded the human mythos, are questions which have never been satisfactorily answered. Ask around and you are likely to get as many different answers as people you ask. Some people believe faeries to be nature spirits, while others believe them to be spirits of the dead caught for unknown reasons on the edge of the earth plane, doomed neither to be in it nor out of it. Some have even claimed them to be fallen angels. But all these hypothetical reasons are as shrouded in mystery as is the answer to the question, "How and why did humans come to be?"

Many theories by leading mythologists and religious leaders on the subject of who and what faeries are have been put forth, dismissed, and often put forth again by the scientific community. These range from insidious and bigoted theories about pygmies migrating from Africa to Europe, to church-generated hysteria about unleashed demonic energies. Faeries have been called angels and devils, fact and fancy, spirits and ghosts, vampires and werewolves, and a host of other appellations which have nothing to do with the faeries known to pagans.

These theories and several others are discussed by mythologist Walter Yeeling Evans-Wentz in his classic work *The Fairy Faith in Celtic Countries*. The book was first published in 1911 and still stands today as a solid and scholarly look at faery beliefs both pro and con.

In the eighteenth and nineteenth centuries, many people in Celtic and Germanic lands likened faeries to the dead, possibly stemming from an older belief that they were human souls awaiting reincarnation. Indeed, there are numerous similarities between beliefs about faery folk and beliefs about the dead. Like the dead, faery folk are believed to primarily live underground, to occasionally attempt to lure humans into their world, to move about mostly by night; they are attracted to burial sites such as raths, cairns, and caves, and—the most significant similarity—they often appear in spectral form.

Folklorist David MacRitchie hypothesizes that our belief in faeries stems from memories of an earlier race of cave dwellers whose existence barely overlapped our own. These would have been a squat, pre-Neolithic, protohuman race who lived underground and hunted with flint arrowheads. This corresponds to the faery lore of many peoples, who believe that their faeries have been among the first inhabitants and still dwell in their earth, and would explain the faery or flinthead arrows often unearthed in Europe.

Some mythologists take the stand that the human belief in faery beings is one erroneously taken from variations in the telling of our own ancient myths, and that these faery tales are just other versions of the same old stories. And certainly this could be true in part. The Arthurian myths, for example, share a great deal in common with faery lore, including similarities in behavioral patterns, taboos, and living arrangements.

A few faeries have backgrounds which must make us suspicious of their mythic origins in light of the mortal tendency to cast blame for our difficulties elsewhere. Certainly some faeries were created in the human mind to explain away the natural phenomena of the earth for which there were once no rational answers. But these faeries are few in number and quite easy to spot in faery lore.

As far away from India and the Middle East as Polynesia and Ireland, the native words for faery echo the linguistic roots of these early cradles of civilization. Whether faeries migrated to the rest of the world with our prehistoric ancestors, or whether humans found them already there and gave them the familiar labels, is likely to remain a mystery.

Modern pagans, on the other hand, have a very different view of faeries from the under-the-microscope one of the sciences. Most pagans tend to take the view that faeries were created by the deities, just as they created humans and other animals. They are a life form which resides in a parallel but unseen world commonly referred to as the astral or inner plane, though they have proven the ability to transcend the plane of their own existence and to travel briefly into other dimensions. They have elemental associations, but they are not raw energy. They are thinking and feeling creatures, and they can and do work with witches for numerous magickal and ritual goals.

Faery interaction with our pagan ancestors was once a common occurrence. Once upon a time, before we humans turned our backs on our intuitive natures, faeries and humans definitely spent much more time interrelating. Pagans once worked with and lived side by side with faery creatures, and legends abound which tell us that the relationships ran the gamut from the blissful to the most difficult. But as time passed and our two worlds polarized, humans as a whole demoted faeries in their minds to meaningless energies, and even pagans assigned them roles in which they were of little or no use as magickal or ritual partners. Misunderstandings and conflicts between our two races became more pronounced, and faeries became more pranksterish, capricious, and jealous as humans sought to exploit them and their gifts, just as we have exploited and misused the other gifts of Mother Earth.

An Irish legend tells us that the Sea God Manann, sensing a hopeless disharmony between faeries and humans, refused to allow the marriage of a faery queen named Fand and her human lover Cuchulain, the Irish warrior chieftain. Manann raised his cloak between them, decreeing that the world of faeries and the world of humans must forever be separated. With that gesture, he erased the memories of each from the other. This legend has echoes in similarly sad tales all around the globe.

To see faeries today one must be open to astral or inner plane experiences, a realm not visible in everyday waking consciousness.

J.M. Barrie, author of the well-known faery story *Peter Pan,* was not far off when he said that to see faeries you "have to believe."

Today there remain fragments of faery lore which echo a time when making these shifts in consciousness was as easy as blinking. These stories concern human beings in voluntary or involuntary trance states frolicking with faeries in those inner plane worlds from which they were reluctant to emerge. Someone in such a trance was thought to be in Faeryland, and if they had trouble leaving that magickal realm or dreamily pined away for it, they were said to be pixy-led. All these tales may be metaphors which attempt to explain astral travel.

Very young children still can and do see faeries with remarkable ease. They have not yet been taught to close down the active psychic centers we are all born with, and they have not been taught the difference between real and unreal as defined by western culture. Children often speak of faery encounters only to be either ridiculed or patronized by adults. Eventually they are taught that to believe in faery folk is silly at best, and a sign of mental derangement at worst.

As a child, I was fascinated by the faery world. I collected picture books of faeries and I even chose a faery name for myself. I had a faery costume, and wanted someone—anyone—to make me some wings. I loved spring, a time when I believed faeries, sent by a loving deity, came to earth to bring new life to the land. I truly believed that I could catch a Leprechaun and claim his gold, and I was sure that if I could only find the right place I could disappear into the faery world, sprout gossamer wings, and become one of them.

Of course my religious leaders and public school teachers, and even my usually open-minded parents, turned my mind away from such beliefs, trusting that they were doing what was best for me. They stood by proudly as I grew up and, as the New Testament teaches, "I put away childish things." Theirs was not a well thought-out campaign. It just happened. A reproachful word here and there, pressure to mimic adults, a subtle transfer of patriarchal values, and soon I, like other well-acculturated young people, saw faeries no more.

For many years I thought those creatures I had seen were the product of a child's overactive imagination. It wasn't until many years later, when I first found my way back to the Old Religion, that I realized those faery beings of my childhood had been quite real indeed. But because of my socialization, it was a long time before I could begin to see again the barest trace of some form of faery life.

Those who would have us forget our faery neighbors can offer some convincing arguments, but they are nothing we pagans can't counterbalance with a little rational thought. Separating fallacy from fact where faery folk are concerned is a matter of degree. One must look at the practical side as well as the spiritual. For instance, one of the many ways in which faeries were said to punish humans who displeased them was by pinching, biting, or kicking. Occasionally the human victims threw fits and reacted with horror at the prickings they felt. One theory is that these sensations were caused by ergot poisoning. Ergot is a disease of grain crops which undergo a season of excessive moisture and not enough heat. Persons who consume the infected grain often react as if they have ingested a hallucinogen, and the effects of the poisoning are most keenly felt by children and the elderly—the same persons most often prone to faery attacks. Some scholars believe that ergot poisoning was partially responsible for the witch-hunting hysteria in Salem, Massachusetts, since in the early 1690s weather conditions were right for producing ergot.

So the question remains: did people through the ages who were claiming to be attacked by faeries really have ergot poisoning? And even if they did, might it be possible that since faeries are nature spirits, that they use that which is in nature to cause their harm? Therefore, is it reasonable to assume that faeries can cause ergot poisoning if they wish?

There are no clear-cut answers, only things which pagans must consider and weigh carefully.

Similar arguments can be made about changelings, human babies exchanged in their infancy with faery children. Some would claim that this charge was made in cases where children failed to thrive or were consumptive. At one time anyone who simply wasted away in plain sight of all was thought to have been taken by faeries. However, since we are dealing with an astral or ethereal realm into which one can obviously not go in human form, it is logical to assume that first the heavy human shell would have to waste away before a permanent entry to the faery world could be made. So did these children deliberately shed their mortal shells to venture into the faery realms, or did they die and go to the patriarchal heaven?

What are the answers? Just how much does the faery world overlap our own, and just how much harm or help can faeries cause? Perhaps no one knows for sure, but those of us who have sought to restore faeries to their former place of prominence in magickal life are just now starting to understand how much they can do for us, and just how much they have been blamed for things they did not or cannot do.

As pagans we should also keep in mind the Pagan Rede:

As ye harm none, do what ye will.

This charge implies an assumption of self-responsibility. We cannot blame other beings for our own failings, no matter how tempting it may be. To do so puts us in danger when we consider the one pervasive pagan law, the Threefold Law, which states that energy sent forth from us will return to us threefold. If we go blaming others for our shortcomings, we will in turn bear the brunt of someone else's misplaced blame.

Witches were always thought to be on good terms with faeries and were frequent visitors to their burghs, the grassy hillocks under which faeries are said to live. Accusing someone of such an alleged visit was considered proof of guilt during the Burning Times, the years of European and North American witch persecutions and murders. Throughout this period faeries were considered by mainstream society to be dangerous creatures, the spawn of the Devil himself, and only a true witch would be brave enough to consort with them, knowing he or she was protected from harm by Satan.

But in truth, witches must be as cautious in their dealings with the Little People as anyone else—maybe more so. After all, witches are trained to see into astral realms, witches can feel and sense these other beings around them, and witches have developed powers which many faeries also have and may jealously guard. And witches know how to banish faeries, and how to destroy them and their world. And faeries know witches when they see them, too, and they in turn know how to help or harm a witch.

What are the truths about the dangers of working with faery beings? Even pagans who have believed in faeries as something more than elemental representations have often shied away from trying to build a working relationship with them. They regard faeries as too capricious or too dangerous to trust in a working relationship. And there is a bit of truth to that viewpoint. But faeries are each different, just as people are different, and there are some faeries you want to avoid, just as there are some people you want to avoid. But just as you don't turn your back on the whole human race due to a few bad apples, you needn't turn your back on the faery races, either.

There are numerous faery types one should probably not attempt to seek out. But on the other hand, if you should run into them while travelling in the realms of Faeryland, there is no need to flee in terror. You may either pass on by with a mere nod of acknowledgement, or, if you are the brave type, you can attempt to draw them into a conversation which is apt to be bizarre at best. The last thing you should ever do is run. This will only inflame their interest, just as it did to that bully who used to chase you home from kindergarten. Remember the old saying, "If you don't run, you can't be chased."

As you begin opening doors to the faery world you may occasionally find a faery or two who tries to thwart your progress with any number of fear tactics. This is a jealous reaction, an emotion based in fear and in a sense of territorialism. Contrary to the beliefs of many, you will always be in control of any faery encounters, and in this book you will be taught how to protect yourself from this type of faery and even how to banish it, if need be.

Working with faeries can be a tricky relationship fraught with problems, but it can also be a rewarding one, well worth the effort it takes to gain faery trust. But before we seek to reclaim this part of pagan heritage and practice, we must first understand some of the basic generalities of the faery nature.

Faeries are very sensitive beings. To say this is almost an understatement. Their feelings are hurt most easily, and that is the chief reason for the platitudes we use in reference to them such as the Wee Ones, the Little People, and the Good Folks. When you are working in a shifted consciousness, you need to be aware of faeries, look out for them underfoot, and do not hurl out off-handed remarks which they might view as insulting. Many cultures also have folklore which tells of certain prohibitions of physical world actions, such as that against discarding water out a window after dark for fear of hurting a faery and bringing their wrath down upon the entire household. These folk beliefs grew out of inner plane experiences with hyper-sensitive faeries.

What do faeries look like? The answer varies drastically with the type of faery you are dealing with, but they are generally small, from several inches to about three feet high. There are, however, a few faery spirits who have the ability to take temporary human form and size, and there are even faeries classified as giants.

Almost universally faeries love nature, music, hunting, dancing, horses, and teasing and spying on humans whose follies and foibles never cease to puzzle and intrigue them.

Games, particularly contests of skill, are popular faery pastimes. Irish lore tells us that the High Kings of Ireland often engaged in hurling matches with the faeries of that land. If you would seek faeries out for such sport be aware that they play roughly, though they always play fairly, and always insist on a weighty wager. In his marvelous book on the Druidic tradition, *The 21 Lessons of Merlyn,* Douglas Monroe attempts to recreate authentic Celtic Druidism for the reader, and in doing so offers us an ancient exercise called "The Wild Hunt" which pits a witch or magician against the elemental forces of nature. The prize for the contest is the ultimate elemental control of the area where the game is held. His teaching scenario, vividly depicting the vital power in the unleased forces of nature, demonstrates just how seriously faery folk take their games.

Some faeries, such as seasonal helpers, actually do have work or other work-like tasks to do, but most have little to do but play and pull pranks on hapless humans and farm animals, especially those of us skilled at travelling in the astral realms. They rarely play pranks on wild animals whom they befriend and mutually assist, though there are numerous faery types who loathe all other living creatures, even their fellow faeries.

The reason for the proliferation of faery pranks on humans may be traced to jealousy. While faeries live in a beautiful astral world which is as fluid as thought, and have long lives, they lack many of the joys of human existence such as romantic relationships, creative endeavors, a full spiritual dimension, and sometimes even sexuality and children. Faeries live on the perimeter of these things, vicariously experiencing them by mimicking humans, but never fully experiencing these emotions which characterize the ups and downs of human life. This is one reason why they are willing to aid us in magick and ritual in order to feel connected with this part of existence. While we both envy a part of the other's world, faeries know we, even with all the world's faults and pitfalls, have the better deal.

Faeries are also jealous of the physical world which contains the living, breathing trees and plant life they love and have so carefully reproduced in their own world. Our cavalier and often callous treatment of nature angers them, this anger again manifesting in pranks and distrust.

Faeries love music and number among themselves some of the finest musicians ever known. It is also said that a goodly number of these faery musicians are former humans who were spirited away for their talents. If we note the preponderance of fine musical talents who die (or transform, as pagans prefer to think of it) at a very young age, we have to wonder. Could it be that Mozart and Gershwin are living it up in Faeryland?

Faeries also love to dance, particularly the native folk dances of the lands they inhabit. But who has copied the dances from whom is a question no one has yet ventured to answer.

The Wee Ones love beauty and luxury, and the tales of their rich stores of gold and precious gems have not been exaggerated. After all, they live in a world where thought is action, and creation is as easy as daydreaming. Most people know the tales of the Leprechauns' crocks of gold which they jealously guard, and most cultures have their Leprechaun figure. But be warned that any gift from a faery, especially if it is a gift of value, is likely to be illusory and will vanish when the enchantment is gone. The mountain of gold coins heaped on you in Faeryland will be nothing but grass or air when you return to the earthly world. Part of the reason for this is that it is difficult, and usually impossible, to take items from one world into another. Just ask any witch who has tried to manifest a prosperity spell. This has led many mythologists to believe that these riches are metaphors for spiritual enlightenment, a view most pagans share. For after all, the crock of gold is a cauldron, the ancient symbol of the Crone Goddess who has the power of life and death. To gain possession of her crock would be to gain her powers.

There does exist an intriguing old occult myth attributed to the alchemists which says that there is an herb which will allow you access to the gold inside the crock, but no one has yet discovered it, and it is doubtful they ever will.

Faeries may only guard this cauldron of golden enlightenment, but never possess it for themselves; this may be just one more reason why they are often jealous of humans and choose to mislead them or play nasty pranks.

Are faeries immortal? It is believed not, for there have been numerous sightings of faery funerals. Proponents of the belief that they are immortal claim that such faery displays are merely the mimicking of human ways, a not uncommon faery pastime. But the grief seen and felt at such funerals has been very real, say observers. As near as can be surmised, faeries live anywhere from 400-1000 years. If they reincarnate, and in what form, is a mystery we may never solve.

Faeries are fascinated with human beings and love to discover all they can about us. Often they will appear unknown to us in shapeshifted forms, particularly in the guise of friendly domestic animals. And their mischievous nature makes playing pranks on hapless humans an irresistible delight.

Many faery types are excellent shapeshifters, though they can only remain in their altered form for a limited time, just as we can only maintain illusions of ourselves for short times when we are in the astral world. Friendly faeries often ride along with travelling animals rather than using the excessive energy it takes to assume an animal shape of their own. In eastern Europe, dogs with white rings around their necks are said to be faery dogs who carry the Wee Folk around the earth by night.

Faeries not only live on the astral plane but can also live on the edge of that world anywhere within nature, and they are often classified according to the places which they choose to inhabit as much as by their appearance or friendliness towards humans. Some are sea dwellers, and others live below ground. There are even reports by sailors of faery islands. These semi-solid isles rise out of the mists at dusk and then vanish again at twilight. Occasionally they take a sailor into this hidden realm with them, and occasionally a faery comes out of the faery world and sails with them.

Other than the traditional faery burgh, it is believed that faeries on the edge of our two worlds can inhabit human homes, trees, woodland groves, mushroom clusters, root systems, and underwater kingdoms. Those humans who violate the sanctity of these dwelling places after they have been clearly warned away suffer the consequences which are as varied as faery life itself.

Faeries are often divided into two broad sub-groups: those who work and live together in groups, called "trooping faeries," and those who are solitaries. Trooping faeries tend to be among the most friendly and helpful to humans, while the solitaries are often, but not always, less approachable.

Trooping faeries are the ones best known to humans because their spectacular processions have been frequently seen and reported. These processions are called Rades, and in Ireland, Britain, Germany, Norway, and Russia there have been numerous sightings of these. While on Rades the faeries wear their finest garments, whether they be of foliage or costly cloth, and they decorate their small horses with the bounty of nature.

The best recorded Rade in history was written down by a Scotsman almost two hundred years ago and is part of the story "Nithsdale and Galloway Song" in which he describes the pageantry of the procession, the fine clothing, the superb miniature horses, the jingling of the gold and silver tack, and the mesmerization he felt at watching this incomparable parade. The faeries carried with them huge stores of precious gems, and they drank from silver chalices as they rode along.

Trooping faeries' social and political organization is not like any known to our human cultures. In Ireland and Scotland, the Tuatha de Danann and the Gnomes have a hierarchy of kings and queens, but most faery bands seem to rule by consensus, if there is any rule at all. It is more likely that faeries live in a state of anarchy. This is not the anarchy that modern societies fear in which there is mass mob rule and violent deviations from accepted norms. That is not anarchy, but chaos. Anarchy simply means "without law," and in no way does it imply living without conscience or self-responsibility. Faeries living in this manner have evolved far beyond human beings. Each one accepts this tenet, aids other faeries, and is able to live in a faery community without the faery police hiding behind each elm leaf looking out for violators of arbitrary and controlling policies. Nature

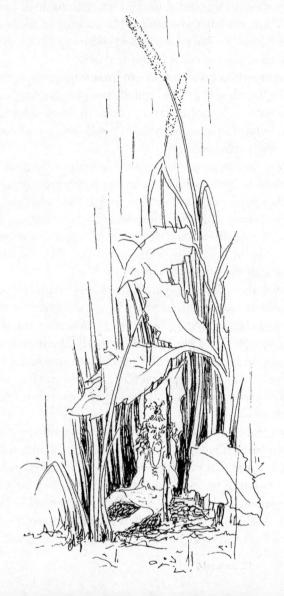

spirits just could not live that way, and maybe we will someday see that humans cannot live that way, either.

Other faery ethics are something which no human can fully comprehend. On one hand faeries will sometimes steal or seek to cause humans harm, and yet they seem to loathe human greed and injustice and will occasionally make their displeasure known to the perpetrator of these offenses.

Faeries almost to a one love horses, and they are the only animal of which no faery lore or legend in the whole of the world tells of being harmed by them in any way. In fact, it was the Leprechauns' love of horses which first caused the horseshoe to be adopted as a symbol of luck. Lady Wilde, who chronicled much Irish folklore in the late nineteenth century, described the faery horses belonging to the Tuatha de Danann as perfect miniatures, a breed "unsurpassed in the world."

Most faeries hate profuse displays of "thanks" from humans whom they have helped. It is best not to utter thanks at all, but to leave out extra portions of milk, butter, or bread for them by way of showing your appreciation. These offerings, whether they are done ritually or mundanely, are called libations, and are often a part of Sabbat observances.

Faeries like to adorn themselves with pretty things, just as humans do. They will use foliage, flowers and other greenery, or sometimes jewels and gold from their treasure hoards. They are said to have a particular fondness for toadstools and mushrooms of any kind which they often wear as headgear, and toadstool rings are said to mark the circles of faery rings where the Wee Ones dance and do their own magick.

Wednesday is their day of rest, a kind of sabbath on which they do not work magick, steal, or travel, and on which they take a break from making mischief. Some faery lore says they hibernate on this day, from sundown Tuesday night until sunset Wednesday evening.

Ragwort, the weed which causes much human misery in the form of hayfever, is a favorite herb of faery creatures. Often they bury their treasures in a ragwort field and many people have seen them riding the stalks. One Cornish legend tells of a man who rode a ragwort stalk into Faeryland and was fearful that he could never leave. But when he again mounted the ragwort he found he was instantly home.

Do faeries have gender, and if so, how do they view sexuality? That is one of the hardest of all questions to answer about them. Even in the astral it is believed that it takes a male and female principle to reproduce anything which will be of more than a transient nature. And yet many faery types appear to have only one sex represented among their species. But this may be due to our perception of them and not to any oddity on their part. Probably the most prevalent belief about faeries among pagans and other occultists is that faeries are completely androgynous and only appear to have a discernible gender either because that's how we want them to appear, or because that is how they wish to appear to us.

But the astral plane is not a place devoid of sexuality. Many people claim astral sex is the greatest single event they have ever experienced. However, it is suggested that if you court this experience, you use caution regarding whom you pick as a partner. The Succubus and Incubus, faeries which sexually assault humans, also live on the astral plane. Those courting astral sex should try using an incense of valerian, rosemary, and hibiscus to facilitate such encounters. The valerian induces astral travel, the hibiscus is an aphrodisiac, and rosemary is a strong protective herb which is also used in many love spells.

Just how smart are faeries? Egocentric humans—pagans included—tend to believe that any creature not human must be innately stupid, or they swing the complete opposite direction and are just as sure that any being which does not inhabit the earthly plane must possess vast knowledge of the secrets of the universe. It is because of these two overly pat and misguided beliefs that for centuries fraudulent mediums have been able to make a fat living off the gullible.

Some faeries may indeed have vast knowledge, others may know no more about spiritual attainment than any human, and a few others are not thinking creatures at all. Keep in mind that, like humans, each faery has its own abilities and talents.

The eight Sabbats of western paganism have much faery lore inherent in them. These Sabbats are the Winter and Summer Solstices, the Spring and Autumn Equinoxes, and the four crossquarter days of Bealtaine or Beltane (May 1), Lughnasadh or Lammas (August 1 or 2), Samhain (October 31), and Imbolg (February 2). Each Sabbat has its own faeries which are most active at that time, and each has a set of dos and don'ts in regard to the treatment of those faeries.

In Ireland, the Tuatha de Danann are active just before Samhain and will bless your home for a small portion of your harvest. But any crop left unharvested after sundown on October 31 is taken by the Phookas, baneful faeries who render the crop unfit to eat. Spelled Pwca in Wales, these baneful faeries remain active until spring.

In Scandinavian countries, faeries are most active at Ostara, the Spring Equinox, when they come to collect a portion of the Sabbat feast. If they are denied this they will cause much havoc until Midsummer when the payment of food can be doubled, or again ignored, in which case more trouble will ensue until next Ostara.

Midsummer is the Sabbat which probably has the most faery lore attached to it. At this time it was thought wise to leap the balefires (ritual bonfires) and drive herds through them for protection from the Little People. It was also a time when one could most easily venture into Faeryland, and the night when the burghs were opened to human visitors.

Faeries love spring as much as humans do, and they revel at the spring Sabbats in a way that makes us seem almost dour in our expression. On the Bealtaine Sabbat faeries seek to steal ritual fire and the fresh butter made for the celebration. Therefore it is better to just leave out a portion of butter for them to maintain their good will. But never give away the Sabbat fire, or you break a taboo which folk legends tell us could cause your enslavement in Faeryland.

On Imbolg the faeries pause to rest and honor the Goddess just as we pagans do. If you fear malevolent faeries, this is a good time to ask for your patron Goddess's protection.

To ensure faery good will, especially as you start to seek them out more and more, it is an excellent idea to leave the last fruit of any harvest out for the faeries, and also a small portion of any of your Sabbat feasts. It is also traditional in many pagan sects to leave left over food from the Esbat (full moon) feasts to the faeries. Other pagan traditions go even further and decree that *any* food left out at night cannot be eaten by humans or animals and should be regarded as a gift to the faeries. The libations we make to our deities and to the directions at a circle's closing are a carryover from these traditions.

Pagan Goddesses and Gods are closely associated with faeries, and many of our deities belong in some ways to the faery races. Some faeries are the handmasters and handmaids of various deities and are much beloved by them. But there is perhaps no deity more closely associated with faeries than the Great Horned God, that omnipresent God-form of western paganism. Several ancient drawings depict him frolicking at the Sabbats, playing his pan pipes, his faery legions and animal friends dancing in tow.

Chapter Two

The Faery Experience Around the Globe

There has been no culture on the planet which does not have some pantheon of elementals or nature spirits whom we can call faeries. The many faeries of the world share striking similarities, even though they may be native to cultures on opposite sides of the planet. The only thing that significantly differs among cultures is the way in which various peoples relate and have related to these beings, and how much of the native and ancient faery lore has been preserved and accepted by them.

Celtic Beliefs

Faery beings play a large part in the belief system of the Irish people past and present. More than in any other western pagan tradition the Irish one utilizes, acknowledges, and works with faeries on a regular basis. A strong belief in faery life existed all over Ireland until well into this century, and is still surprisingly prevalent in the west country. County Donegal's poet laureate, William Allingham, also known as the Bard of Ballyshannon, wrote these lines only a century ago:

> ... *Up the airy mountain,*
> *Down the rushy glen,*
> *We daren't go a hunting*
> *For fear of little men ...*

In the Irish language the word for faery is *sidhe* (shee), derived from the Hindustani word *siddhi* meaning "something which controls the elements." Various euphemistic names are used in the Irish vernacular to refer to faeries. Among the most popular are Wee Folk, the Little People, the Wee Ones, the Gentry, the Good Folk, Them Who Prowl, and the Blessed Ones. They are also called Daoine Maith—the Good People, and Daoine Sidhe—the Faery People.

Irish mythology tells us that faeries were once much more involved with the human world than they are now. In County Roscommon where documented faery sightings are numerous, there are accounts of faeries seeking human physicians and wise women for healing, and asking for food and shelter in winter. Queen Maeve of Connacht had good relations with the faery folk of her region, and she was rewarded for her kindness towards them with healing powers and travel spells. Etain, the Queen of the Tuatha de Danann, was once a human woman wooed into Faeryland by her future consort, King Midhir.

In the Irish myth cycles the earliest invaders of the island were faery races. The most famous were the Tuatha De Danann (People of the Goddess Dana), who were said to have ruled Ireland for nearly a thousand years. After their defeat by the Milesians, a cousin race of the Celts, the Tuatha stayed underground to become the faeries and Gnomes of Ireland.

Most Irish faeries are thought to live in burghs, underground dwellings beneath grassy hillocks. Many of the modern versions of faery burghs sound suspiciously like the Christian Hell. Unfortunately much of this description is taken as gospel (no pun intended) in Ireland, and has been since St. Patrick began demonizing pagan ways, with many people there believing faeries to be spirits from purgatory, a way station for souls on their way to either Heaven or Hell.

Throughout Ireland are earthworks properly called tumuli, though they are popularly referred to as raths or forts, and are a type of faery burgh. Raths are circular ditches which enclose a small field. Most Irish will not dig in them, as to put a spade in them is to invite terrible luck. When Shannon International Airport, Ireland's largest, sought to expand some of its runways, it was discovered that the original plans called for destroying a nearby rath. All the workers hired for the project quit en masse, and airport officials were forced to reroute their expansion project.

Some Irish faeries live off the coast of Ireland on faery islands which can appear and disappear again in the blink of an eye. Several tales from sailors and some mythology tell us the fate of those who step onto these nebulous lands. Some disappear forever when the island vanishes, and some, like the minor Irish chieftain Teigue, are welcomed by the reigning faery royalty. Teigue returned to tell of his adventures, and with him he brought the faery queen's gifts of exotic birds and an emerald chalice which had protective powers.

In Ireland many of the faery rulers have become minor deities in the pagan pantheon. Among the best known are Finvarra, Faery King of Connacht; Fiachra, King of Western Sea Faeries; Nuala, Queen of the Munster Faeries; and Etain and Midhir, last rulers of the Tuatha De Danann, who are viewed as the High King and Queen of all Irish faery folk.

The Isle of Man in the stormy Irish Sea is rich with faery lore, much of it shared with Ireland and Scotland even though the island is retained as part of Great Britain. Even the island's name is intimately tied up with Irish mythology. Man was named for Manann, the Irish God of the Sea. The Isle was said to have been created by the Giant-God of Ireland, Finn MacCool, who, with his massive hands, scooped out Lough (Lake) Neagh in northern Ireland and hurled the land into the Irish Sea.

Faery sightings on the Isle of Man are still very common, and virtually no one who visits this mist-shrouded island of mystery comes away a nonbeliever in the little folk whom the natives refer to as the Little Fellas, Themselves, the Middle World Ones, the Good Folk, or the Natives. The Manx people always refer to faeries with great respect, mostly because the Little Fellas have earned it.

Strange, nonhuman singing and music is often heard from the Manx glens at night, and natives dare not venture there. Some have claimed to see faery footprints in the light of day where the music was heard the night before. On Dalby Mountain, if you put your ear to the ground you can hear what natives call Sheean-ny-Feaynid (Sound of the Infinite), believed to be the voices of underground-dwelling faeries.

The great Irish bard Carolan deliberately slept on a Manx faery burgh one night, and forever after had faery tunes running through his head.

Herbalism is a specialty of Manx faeries, and some of them can be induced to lead humans to cures. The Manx cat, with the strange pointed ears which resemble those of many faeries, originated on the island, and some folklore says this cat was bred by the faeries.

Most of the Isle's faeries are either very ugly and go nude, or are beautiful and enticing. They are both baneful and good, and there seem to be few native Manx faeries who are not of one extreme temperament or the other.

It is said that Manx faeries like to churn butter.

Close behind Ireland and the Isle of Man in the sheer richness of its native faery lore are the Celtic lands of Scotland and Cornwall.

Scottish faeries resemble Irish ones in both manner and appearance, which should not be surprising because of the shared history, culture, language, and migration patterns of these two countries. In Scotland the word for faery is *sith*, and is pronounced "shee," the same as in the Irish language.

The word sith is occasionally found among old Scottish place names, and probably began being used in this way because it was once believed that this respectful remembrance of the native faery folk would cause them not to blight or wreak havoc on the so-named places.

Scotland has numerous sites where faery music is frequently heard. Near Portree on the Isle of Skye is a burgh called Sithean Beinne Bhoidhich, meaning "fairy home on the bonnie hill." Those who pass it at night will usually hear the music, though no one has ever been able to pinpoint the exact spot from where it emanates. And if one stands beneath the arches in Fraisgall Cave, similar tunes are heard. Near the town of Tiree are two separate burghs from which faery music comes by night, complete with bagpipe accompaniment. Many disbelievers have gone there to debunk the myths only to come away stumped.

And lastly, the faery music dubbed the sweetest in Scotland comes from a burial cairn near Glen Elg where the noted family of pipers, the MacCrimmons, lies buried.

The pagan Scots, like the pagan Irish, were known for giving obligatory libations to their faery folk during their rituals. A libation of milk poured on stone for them in Scotland was called Leac na Gruagaich (roughly, "Milk to the Hairy Ones") and was a traditional must on Samhain night. To forget this minor ritual was to risk finding your prized sheepdog or your entire herd dead and rotted in the morning.

Faery paths in Scotland were places where one did not risk building or creating any form of obstruction. When this breach of sacred faery space was discovered by the Wee Folk, homes and barns were shaken, pounded, and nearly torn apart until the offending portion was removed. In rural Scotland it is still traditional to build one's cottage with the back and front doors directly opposite each other to allow the faeries to pass through on their Rades.

Scottish faeries are broadly divided into two well-known opposing categories, the Seelie Court and the Unseelie Court. Seelie is roughly translated into English as "blessed," and unseelie as "damned." These trooping faeries fly on their Rades rather than parade, and have a vaporous physical form reminiscent of ghosts and other discarnate spirits. The howling Rades of the Unseelie Court were feared throughout the Highlands, where the populace believed them to live under the huge, stony bens (mountains) which cover much of the land. They were hideous to behold, so much so that folklore tells us that those who came face to face with this evil host were most often struck dead from fear.

In contrast, the Seelie Court was made up of the most benevolent faery spirits, and was most often felt to be present at the changing of the seasons. Through the air the Seelie Court ride their beautiful white faery horses, and the most ancient Scottish mythology tells us that these blessed ones and their pets were among the first inhabitants of Scotland.

As in Ireland, Scottish faeries live in burghs, which in Scots Gaelic are called *sithean* and *bruthain,* or as they are more commonly known, "bowers." Other places they are often sighted are near stone burial cairns, castle ruins, streams and lakes, and at the rocky seashores.

Scottish faeries without wings of their own are known for transporting themselves on ragwort stalks, much as witches were once depicted riding on broomsticks. Flinthead arrows, called faery arrows, are found all over the Highlands and were believed to be ancient faery tools because they bear no resemblance to those used by humans.

According to Celtic musicologist and historian Avigail MacPhee, many of the Scottish faery names share a root with the names of very old families of Scotland. It could be that these old families took the faery's names to enhance their status and reputations as the oldest families in Scotland, or perhaps there was intermarriage between them which caused these names to be adopted by the various clans.

Euphemisms for faeries in Scotland include the Still Folk, People of Peace, The Silent Moving Folk, Pixies, The Wee Ones, and Prowlies.

Off the north coast of Scotland lie the Shetland and Orkney Island groups. These northern islands have some native faery lore of their own, but they share much of it with the rest of Scotland and also with Scandinavia, a region which repeatedly conquered the islands from 700 to 1100 CE.

The Hebrides, a massive island chain off Scotland's western coast, is another area where there are still prevalent beliefs in the faery folk. Here the old Gaelic language is still spoken, and the people have not sought out many modern "necessities" such as electricity and television, hallmarks of civilization which destroy the ability to easily slip onto the inner planes.

Cornwall, another Celtic land, is that peninsular part of southwestern England which sticks out like an elongated triangle with the English Channel on one side and the cold North Atlantic Ocean on the other. The Tamar River divides Cornwall, once an independent duchy, from the rest of England. The region is rife with the remains of its ancient history, and the names of Cornish cities include ones familiar to readers of Gothic mysteries.

On the north coast of Cornwall near the village of Camelford sit the ancient ruins of Tintagel Castle, the reputed birthplace of the legendary King Arthur. Sadly, so many of the Arthurian myths underwent drastic alterations during the medieval period that the original faery mythology of Cornwall is sometimes hard to uncover amidst all the newer legends.

Cornwall's faeries share more in common with those of Wales than of anywhere else, partly because these two areas have the distinction of sharing the Arthurian myths. But while the people of Cornwall are distinctly Celtic in their history, culture, and mindset, the people of Wales have come over the centuries to more closely resemble their English neighbors, whose folklore they have largely adopted as their own.

The faery lore of this peninsula is very much concerned with the proper way to treat and show respect for faery folk—called the Pobel Vean, or the "Small People," by the Cornish—and deals in depth with planes of existence for faeries and humans and attempts to explain how they overlap. For example, a unique bit of faery lore from Cornwall surrounds shapeshifting. It is believed that each time a faery chooses to manifest in the physical world he must come in an increasingly smaller form due to energy lost in making the transfer. There was a prevalent taboo in Cornwall which was widely accepted until the early Victorian period against stepping on ants and small insects lest you be crushing friendly faery folk.

In the middle ages, the Cornish Christians frequently saw faeries and even documented their encounters. To explain them away, they were said to be the souls of Cornish pagans who were not so bad as to need Hell, but neither were they "fit" for Heaven. Early priests in the region helped lure the Cornish away from their native religion by telling them that faeries were the condemmed souls of the Druids who would not give up their idolatries for Christianity.

The deep mines and caves and the expansive moors of the region are places where faeries still dwell. Faeries are very active around the many tin mines and at the ancient stone ruins and megaliths which densely cover the region. The Cornish have always held their dangerous moors in awe and respect, and much faery and spirit life resides in these desolate and lovely places.

Cornish pools and lakes also conceal faery kingdoms. If you would have a glimpse of them there, look into them with the light of a full moon reflected off their surface.

The Unseelie Court of Scotland is also a part of Cornish faery lore, a court they believe travels with a host of vicious bodyguards which they call Spriggans, faeries who can call up any illusion to frighten away intruders of their profane frolics.

Brittany is and was the one stronghold of the old Celtic Empire still remaining on the main continent of Europe. Brittany's customs, music, and traditional dress reflect its Celtic background. From Brittany much folklore and many faery forms were taken to Britain and Ireland, but Bretons refer to faeries by the generic French word *Fees*.

The Welsh and English Experience

Though Wales has a Celtic history, it has over the past few centuries become very much like its parent nation of England. Welsh and Old English are both part of the Brythonic language group, which enables them to more easily share their cultural heritage and folklore. But Wales' Celtic past does preserve some faery lore which was lost in England, a land which more keenly felt the invasions of both the Romans and the Normans.

In Wales there are many tales of human entrapment in the faery realms, especially if this was accomplished by means of dancing. And there are many tales of intermarriage between faeries and humans, and much advice on how to make sure you have obtained a fully human mate. For example, a married couple cannot touch one another with iron if one is a faery, or they will both turn old and fade away. The Welsh remain true to their character in being determined to see the good in all sides of an issue, and their views on these mixed marriages are no exception. Marriage in Faeryland can be good or an enslavement. Most assuredly you never see family again, and may even forget your human existence, but if you are happy, then the Welsh wish you well.

Wales, like Cornwall, is a land abounding in the lore of the Celtic King Arthur. They even relate Arthur and Queen Guinevere to their faery lore. Guinevere literally means "white phantom," and many Celtic scholars believe her abduction by Arthur to have been an abduction by the faeries of whom Arthur was then king. She was captured as his bride in May, a month when humans thought it unwise to marry, which links both Arthur and Guinevere to the pagan belief that deities, as well as nature spirits, mate at Bealtaine. Guinevere often had her knights dressed in green, the traditional color of the faeries in Celtic lands, and they were all superb horsepeople, another faery trait. Morgan LeFay, Arthur's sister, was said to have lived underground, perhaps in a burgh.

This is not an interpretation of the Arthurian legends you will get from medieval writers such as Mallory, someone many people mistakenly believe has the final word on these myths. If you wish to study the Arthurian tales in depth, ask for books at your local college library which will explore their many unique perspectives, or check the bibliography in this book for suggested titles.

The Land of the Dead in the Welsh Arthurian tradition is called Avalon, and descriptions of it parallel the faery world. It is a place where one never grows old, where needs are fulfilled by thought, and where rebirth is always at hand.

Welsh faeries are generally depicted as having a courtly, rather medieval appearance, and, like their Irish cousins, they love horses. They are also exceptionally fond of stealing human babies and love to lure hapless human mates into their world.

Welsh folklore tells us that red and white are the colors of the faery folk, colors which are repeated in the faeries' choice of dress and in the color of the pets they keep. In Wales, white dogs are strictly faery animals. Red and white are two of the three colors of the Triple Goddess, reminding us just how closely the lore of faeries and that of our pagan deities is intertwined.

Welsh euphemisms for faeries are the Fair Folk, the Night Walkers, and Them Who Be.

In England, where the old ways were more harshly stamped out than in other parts of the British Isles, most of the faery and pagan lore was forced into hiding among faery tales and Mother Goose rhymes. English faeries share much of their form and content with those of the legends of both the Celts and the Germans. Among the English faery legions we see the Germanic Bogies and Bogeymen, the dangerous shapeshifting goblin, the Buggar, and also the Gnomes and house Brownies of neighboring Scotland.

In the very late Middle Ages belief in faeries was still common, even among well-educated people in high places. King James I, a native Scot who reigned in England from 1567-1625, wrote a book called *Daemonologie* in which he equates faeries with demons and blames them for much human misfortune. He further encouraged everyone who had a faery in their home to rid themselves of it even if it was "doing no evil."

A good deal of English faery lore surrounds prehistoric sites, particularly the megalithic standing stones such as Stonehenge. These structures, whose origin and purpose are clouded in the mists of the pagan past, are sites where faeries are often seen and heard, especially around the Sabbats.

Wassailing the apple trees was an old Celtic and English custom which involved going out to the oldest tree producing the juiciest fruit in the orchard, and singing its praises while passing around a cider jug. This was originally a ritual of health and protection which later became the Christmas custom of caroling. In the nineteenth century guns without shot in them were taken along on the wassail and fired into the branches to frighten away owls, faeries, and other haunts. Owls got thrown into this group for two reasons. It was a feared bird, sacred to the Goddess who had been well-demonized and nearly forgotten by this time, and also because owls were often thought to be shapeshifted faeries.

Well-dressing to honor the spirits and deities of a well was another custom practiced throughout England and the Celtic countries, one still practiced in rural areas at the Midsummer Sabbat. The wells are dressed with flowers, garlands, ribbons, and other finery. This was done to appease the spirits of the well, who are also faeries, so that the water will run fresh and clean for another year.

English faeries are believed to steal shadows which will render the victim weak and eventually kill. It was further believed that if you could steal a faery's shadow, that he or she owed you a favor. Recall the story of *Peter Pan* by the English writer Sir James M. Barrie in which Peter meets the Darling children when he comes sneaking around, searching for his lost shadow. In repayment for Wendy Darling's kindness of sewing it back on for him, he takes her and her brothers to a place where one never grows old, an idea echoed in many tales of Faeryland.

English euphemisms for faeries include the Little People and Pixies, though the latter is actually a specific faery type.

The northernmost region of England is called Yorkshire, an area which borders the Scottish Lowlands and shares some of its faery lore with both countries. But Yorkshire has one of its own curious trademarks in the case of faeries—they have more faery mythology concerning Giants and Ogres than any other part of the world. Other slang names for Yorkshire faery folk are Addlers and Menters, whose linguistic derivation is lost to us.

Yorkshire faeries crave fresh milk, and many legends abound there of faeries who come to nurse at a new mother's breast.

Germanic and Nordic Faeries

The Germanic faeries include those native not only to Germany, but also to Austria and parts of Switzerland, Czechoslovakia, and Hungary. Germany was not a united nation until the middle nineteenth century, and throughout its turbulent history contained as many as 240 and as few as 30 independent principalities.

Germanic faeries are well-known to westerners largely due to the efforts of two brothers named Grimm. *Grimm's Faerie Tales*, a compilation of 242 Germanic faery stories, were collected orally by the brothers in the late eighteenth century. These stories are still being translated into many languages, and collections of them are nearly always in print. When reading with the idea of gleaning from them useful information, pagans must remember when and where these stories were gathered. The oral tradition of Germany had undergone profound changes since these faery tales were first told, and their alterations towards blatant misogynism and anti-Semitism sadly foretold the course of Germany's future.

Faeries with dragons as pets are common in German faery folklore, as are faeries with densely hairy bodies.

Germany has a host of enchanted faery forests into which only the most intrepid travelers will venture at night. These dense woods are populated with guardian faeries who are not disposed to act favorably towards humans who trespass in their world. One such place is the famous and beautiful Black Forest, where the trees are said to become animated at night and walk about.

Also popular in Germany are water spirits called Nixen which guard the rivers, especially the Rhine, which they hold sacred.

Scandinavian or Nordic mythology divides elves, their most numerous faeries, into light and dark elves, terms which have less to do with personality than appearance. Light elves are pale and can fly and are usually, but not always, good. Dark elves, called Huldrafolk, live below ground, are dark and land-bound, and are more often, but not always, bad-natured.

The Old Norse world for elf is *alfar,* from which our English word is derived. This is also the generic word for all faeries in Scandinavia, suggesting just how prevalent these dwarf beings are in that region.

Faery islands play a large part in Scandanavian faery lore, so much so that where the Norse went, the lands they conquered grew corresponding legends of faery islands. If you wish to see these mystic places, the Norse say to look out over the ocean at the setting sun and you will see the islands rising for the night.

Greece, Italy, and the Iberian Peninsula

Most people are familiar with the mythical beasts and deities of ancient Greece and Rome. These were archetypal nature spirits, many of whom were devalued to elemental status when the Christian religion gained predominance there. Many of their Gods were shapeshifters, a power usually reserved for faeries, such as the God of Gods, Zeus. And like many of the Greek deities, the Greek faeries have a very sexual nature.

Fauns, Satyrs, and other mythical beasts of Greek mythology are faery folk, too, and are written about as extensively today as they were when Homer wrote his famous *Iliad* and *Odyssey*.

Likewise, the Italians had a lot of faery folk fall from their old pantheon of deities. But with the faery-rich Alpine Mountains nearby, Italy was spared a total purging of these beings from the popular mind.

The Italian word for faery is *Fada* from the Latin *Fatum,* which means "fate." This is a direct reference to the belief that these faery beings were once demideities who controlled the fate of human kind.

On the Iberian Peninsula, which comprises modern-day Spain and Portugal, most of the faery lore was lost through the terrible Spanish Inquisition which began in the late fifteenth century. This was during the middle of a dark period in pagan history known as the Burning Times, when pagans and other non-Christians were tortured, burned, and/or forced to convert to Catholicism. Faeries, considered demons by these fanatical churchmen, were virtually wiped off the peninsula. To display any knowledge of or belief in these beings was tantamount to confessing one's self a witch, which carried the penalty of death.

Of all the known Spanish folk tales only one pertains to faery beings, "Tonino the Hunchback and the Faeries." From this story we learn that Spanish faeries are partial to olive trees, but we also get the all-important message that the one-time leaders of Spain wished us to have—the irrefutable knowledge that Sunday is a holy day, a name which faeries cannot even hear pronounced, and a time when they have no power. Though we now know such information to be spurious, we can count ourselves fortunate that any faery lore survived in Spain at all.

Asia, Africa, and the Pacific Islands

In Polynesia, faeries, called nature spirits, are known in minute detail because the indigenous population of these south sea islands has never fully lost its ancient pagan ways. The most popular faeries are the Menehuna, Leprechaun-like elves in native Polynesian dress who aid the lost and grant wishes.

There are also nature spirits of the many volcanos which shape the islands, and another pantheon of storm and typhoon faeries. The force and unpredictability of the volcanos allowed them to become a central part of Polynesian worship. Their nature temples, called *heiaus,* were constructed of lava rocks.

Treasure hoarders are also a part of Polynesian faery lore, but one must be willing to follow these faeries into their own world and be willing to forever remain there in order to gain the booty.

Because of their off-handed treatment by westerners, the native Polynesians have been understandably loathe to relinquish to us a lot of their pagan and faery lore, but slowly, we as fellow pagans are forming relationships with them and learning each other's ways.

In Egypt the general name for faery is transliterated as Hathor. This name links them to the Goddess Hathor Tiamet, Goddess of copper and other solar-related metals, and of the Underworld where these faeries make their homes. Unlike most other faeries, the Hathor do not find metal, or even iron, taboo.

Despite the rich information on pagan deities we have from Egypt, there is very little faery lore. The predominant Egyptian religion—Islam—has purged many of the old beliefs out of existence. But it is likely that they shared much in common with the Persian and Hebrew peoples of the Middle East, of whose faery lore we still have fragments.

The predominant religion of India, Hinduism, does not reject the spiritual forces of nature entirely and has always allowed a native faery belief to remain, if not to flourish. The very word Hindu was derived from the Sanskrit word *sindhu,* which means "power of the river." There are striking similarities in India to the faery beliefs of the Celts, which may eventually prove the anthropological theory that the Celtic people originated there.

Hinduism allows its worshipers to choose where in nature they want to pray, and they can address their petitions to a mountain, lake, or stone knowing that the nature spirits within these objects will carry their prayers to the deities.

Small, quick-moving, winged faeries with pointed ears are sometimes seen near the Hindu holy days, and their playful nature makes them a delight. Small children are often encouraged to search for them, at which time the faeries are offered libations of food.

Africa's faery lore is part of an abundant oral folk tradition of which little has been recorded. Elves, seasonal faeries, and other nature sprites are common in their pantheons. They are seen on a regular basis and are even sought out for aid in much the same way as the pagans of Europe used to do.

Like the nature spirits of the Native Americans, African nature spirits also take animal forms. For example, instead of personifying death in human form as was done in Europe, death in West Africa is symbolized by and embodied in the tiny chameleon, which represents the ever-changing cycle of reincarnation. Hence, chameleon-shaped faeries would be sought out to aid in the understanding of the cycles of life, death, and rebirth.

Hopefully someday we will have written records of the African faery beliefs before the encroachment of modern civilization destroys them forever.

Russia and Asia

Russia and the Balkans are rich both in faery legend and in legends of wild, half-human creatures of the night, such as vampires and werewolves. These are not faeries in the classic sense but instead are classified with magickal beasts such as the unicorn, dragon, and firebird.

Dairy products are a staple of the diet in this region, and there is a correspondingly large number of faeries who spitefully enjoy spoiling milk, ruining butter, and stealing cheese and yogurt. Seasonal faeries, especially ones which are out and about in winter, are also popular in Russia.

In Russia the word for faery is Domovoi, and it is usually attached to the full name of a faery form and denotes its habitat. For example, a Gnome is called an Domovoi Djedoe, which roughly translated means "earth faery."

In east Asia evil spirits, particularly of discarnate humans, are more prevalent than faery spirits. The major exception to this rule is in Japan where the indigenous faith, Shinto, still honors the forces and spirits of nature much as it has for centuries.

Shinto means the "way of the gods," and its roots date from pre-history. For a long time it had no fixed writings, books, dogma, or morals, and was allowed to flourish uncorrupted. But over time it has been patriarchalized, and its treatment of women shows this all too clearly. Even the principal nature spirits and faeries have taken on decidedly masculine personas.

Shinto's vast pantheon of nature deities are called kami, and they rely heavily on elemental beings—faeries—to aid them. In the oldest of Japanese faery legends we are told that the kingdom of the faeries lies underwater and is defended by an ancient sea deity. The Japanese used to regularly make sacrifices to these faeries in exchange for the protection of their island. So strong was this belief in that protection that for centuries Japan thought itself impervious to invasion. Indeed, it was not until the disastrous dropping of atomic bombs in 1945 that Japan's shores were finally breeched.

China has a long belief in house faeries whose energy, called *chi,* must not be impeded. The Chinese will go as far as to rearrange their furniture if they feel the energies of their house spirits are blocked in any way. This usually means changing the interior decor to avoid any sharp corners and harsh lines, and avoiding beams and posts in the direct center of the rooms or over sleeping places.

Faeries in Latin America

Mexico and South America have two sets of faery lore, one from the Native Americans and one from the sparse remains of those tales which came from Spain and Portugal during the time of the Inquisition. But there remains in this region a profound belief in and acceptance of the power of nature's forces and of the occult, which includes elemental beings and other faeries, and dead ancestors. World-renowned Chilean author Isabel Allende incorporates many of these native beliefs into her books, most notably *The House of Spirits.*

Curanderos and Curanderas are Mexican shamans who are sought out for spellwork, advice, and healing. These dispensers of folk wisdom practice not only in Mexico, but also in Central America and in the American Southwest. They rely heavily on ancient divinatory tools such as the talking board and Tarot cards, are usually very adept at astral travel, and have an amazing track record of accuracy and successful healing. But because of strong Catholic influence in this region, the Devil and Death are the major faery forms.

The religions of the Native South Americans did not last long against the Catholic conquistadors. What remains of their nature spirituality has been grafted onto Christianity so well that it is hard to separate the two.

North America, Australia, and the Native Americans

Native North Americans still see and work with their rich pantheon of nature spirits, faeries, deceased ancestors, and totem animals. These beings are usually contacted during a vision quest or journey which requires several days of fasting, prayer, and travels on the inner plane.

Animal totems, or familiars, are seen as nature spirits by the Native Americans, the best known of these being the coyote, the archetypal Trickster. Other popular totem animals are bears, snakes, jaguars, and wolves. These animals perform a role somewhere between that of deity and faery and offer guidance and wisdom from the animal world to those who seek them out.

The Native Americans further believe that all things, living or not, have an inherent spirit called a Manitou which can express joy or displeasure on an elemental basis. Each season and each act of nature also has its own spirit, spirits which are prayed to as deities rather than approached as raw elemental forces.

The only known anthropomorphic faery of Native America is a small elf-like male, somewhat like the Menehuna of Polynesia, who wears native dress and usually carries with him a prophetic message.

In Australia the indigenous people known as the Aborigines have faery forms in native dress which control weather and provide oracles. Theirs seems to be a cross between Polynesian and South African beliefs. Some Aboriginal faeries are evil, but most are neutral, neither liking nor hating humankind, nor being good nor bad. It is up to the person seeking their aid to decide if they will take away with them the good or the bad energy which is inherent in all things.

The large Anglo-Celtic populations of Australia, Canada, and the United States claim the faery lore of their British, Irish, and German ancestors. Because these areas were settled by Anglos long after faeries were largely banished from the human psyche, no faery forms are known to these nations which were not imported or familiar to the Native Americans.

Chapter Three

How and Where to Find Faeries

*M*uch of the confusion in folklore concerning finding faeries is the result of popular misconceptions about where and how these creatures live. Faeries are residents of the astral world. It is only when your consciousness has deliberately shifted, when you slow your mind and focus your thought processes inward and outward, that you can place yourself into the astral realm. This is where faeries are most likely to be found. A faery is not apt to aid or harm you while you are sitting at your dinner table having a pleasant conversation with your family, but one may show up when you do your next ritual, spell, or meditation, and especially when you astral project.

Sometimes we hear the question that if faeries are of the astral plane, then why do persons who are clearly functioning in concrete earth consciousness occasionally see faeries? Planes of existence co-exist, separated merely by veils of consciousness, and we, and other thinking creatures, are able to temporarily gain entry to these other worlds. For example, people who have seen a ghost have seen a manifestation of an otherworldly form which has gained temporary entrance to our world. And we know through experience that we can travel to the astral plane and beyond. It is the same with faeries.

Other faery stories have been told about humans who fell into the faery world by accident, as did Alice in Wonderland, either through a stream, a well, a burgh, or down a hollow tree. These are part of recorded faery tales and often tell of experiences which took place while the traveler was asleep, or were written to explain an experience for which the person who had undergone it had no other explanation. Others are archetypal images which have a deeper meaning than is at first apparent. For instance, someone who falls down a well and into another world may be symbolically returning to the womb.

To find and communicate with faeries you must open your mind as well as your heart and call upon all your talents as a witch.

The Shifted Consciousness Methods

Whether you are in a magick circle or in a city apartment, or wandering through a secluded wood, your best chance to see faeries is to shift your consciousness to enable you to peer into the astral world where these beings live. By shifting your focus you will slow the frequency of your brain waves, and your mind will expand so that your consciousness can traverse other realms of existence.

Fortunately this is not nearly as complicated as it sounds, though it does take practice to get it under control. Such changes happen naturally during the course of every 24-hour day, usually without your consent or knowledge. You fall into a light trance every time you read, watch television, sleep, or even daydream. A trance state differs from sleep in that in a trance state you seek to control your brain waves and direct the course of your thoughts. Other terms for an altered state of consciousness are meditative state, astral sleep, lucid dreaming, trance state, going out, going within, out-of-body experience, and shifted consciousness. All describe the same process and all are acceptable synonyms for each other.

There are several methods of shifting consciousness. Every witch has his or her own favorite, and none is better or more right than any other … just different.

Scrying is one of the easiest of the shifted consciousness methods to learn. Scrying is the act of gazing gently into some reflective surface such as a lake, a candle flame, a bowl of water, or a mirror in order to slow and focus the mind and bring about visions. This has been a popular method of divination for centuries because it requires nothing more than the witch and some commonly found item.

To scry, form in your mind that which you want to see or know; in this case, faery contact. Then gaze, but do not stare, into your chosen scrying aid, all the while concentrating on viewing Faeryland. Don't force your mind to cooperate, but try to keep gently focused. If your thoughts wander, simply bring them back and continue. With practice this becomes easier. You might also try scrying into a particular element associated with a faery you especially want to contact. For example, try scrying into a golden surface for seeing a treasure-hoarding faery, water for a water sprite, misty air for a winged faery, or a handful of rich, dark earth for a Gnome.

Meditation, particularly guided meditation (sometimes called pathworking), is probably an even easier method of contacting faeries because when you feel dreamily carried along with a guide, you are immediately able to allow your noncritical, subconscious mind to do your thinking. Following Chapter 4 is the complete text of a guided meditation which can be used to facilitate faery contact. This meditation carries the witch into the astral realm of Faeryland and allows meetings with four faery forms who are known to be friendly toward humans.

In other forms of meditation one systematically slows and focuses their thoughts until they have no thoughts at all, or until they are concentrating solely on one thing. In this case you would concentrate on faery contact. To practice this type of meditation, simply spend time concentrating solely on one object, such as a flower or leaf, to the exclusion of all else. You can do this with your eyes open or closed. Practice increasing the amount of time you can spend on that object without your mind straying. Later you can put this exercise to practical use by focusing on finding faeries and seeing Faeryland.

Astral projection, or lucid dreaming, is another very good way to find faeries, because with this practice you go immediately into their world. However, astral projection can be difficult for some people to learn. Many books have been published on the topic and each writer has his or her own method for proceeding.

Astral projection is defined as consciously sending forth a part of yourself to another place or time. Many persons mistakenly believe it is the real you, or the soul-matter, which is expelled. Rationally this is an impossibility. The essence which is you cannot leave its physical shell without causing death. It is your deep mind which journeys forth, your deep mind which can turn so far in on itself that it goes out of itself, and which has the ability to contact any and all other intelligences and planes of existence. Because the astral plane is in the mind, it is synonymous with the term "inner plane."

Our pagan ancestors were well aware of the power of the inner plane, and that all things were possible there even though we may not always be able to achieve them. When darkness came and they gathered around their hearths for protection and warmth, they would tell the old folk stories and reach deep into these other realms of existence. The last lines of the nursery rhyme "How Many Miles to Babylon" clearly illustrates their beliefs about these worlds:

… If the darkness fall about me,
Can I get there by candlelight?
If your heels are nimble and light,
You can get there by candlelight.

No doubt this poem was a veiled way of saying, yes, anything is possible when the mind is quiet and you make an effort.

Years of hiding witchcraft from the authorities behind metaphors has caused many witches who have not yet achieved success with this practice to believe astral projection to be something that it is not. Many expect to feel shot out of their bodies as if from a cannon; others feel like they should be flying. But the whole process is really as simple as learning lucid dreaming. Once you feel your consciousness to be elsewhere other than in your own head—as in a dream—but at the same time you manage to have conscious control of it, you *are* astral projecting.

The method I recommend for learning to astral project is one of simply inducing a meditative state by whatever means you prefer while remaining perfectly still physically. With your eyes closed, concentrate on one object or phrase to the exclusion of all else. Eventually, usually after about 20 minutes, your body will go numb, your mind will tire, and it will automatically send itself outward in self-defense. You can help it along by having been thinking all along about where it is you want to go. Those interested in other methods for astral projection can check the bibliography for suggested books on the topic, or you can use the astral state induction from the guided meditation in this book.

Be sure that when you use meditation and astral projection as methods for faery contact that you double your normal protection. Witches have always thought it best to work inside a carefully drawn circle and/or carry protective herbs or talismans when doing any shifted consciousness exercises. Chapter 4 gives numerous ideas for such talismans.

In-Nature Methods

Faeries love nature as much as witches and will occasionally manifest in it, though their ability to stay there is as limited as our ability to remain long in the astral. And because of the deep archetypal association of faeries and nature, many witches new at faery contact find that a natural setting better facilitates faery sightings and contact whether in a shifted or normal waking state of consciousness.

Shifted state contacts with faeries are often easier in these natural surroundings because this is where both your conscious and subconscious minds have been conditioned to believe you will find them. But remember that if you are disturbed while in a meditative state, you will probably be unpleasantly jolted back into yourself—a metaphor for a quick return to waking consciousness. This will not cause you any harm, but such interruptions repeated over time can cause your subconscious to become leery of the process, making it harder for you to achieve the state of mind you seek.

*Look for faeries in natural, unspoiled settings on both
the inner and the outer planes.*

Wide-awake faery sightings are much harder to achieve even by those skilled in the art, and you will have better success if you use a light, eyes-partially-opened trance. Remember that the Little People, like woodland animals, have every reason to be distrustful of human motives and are not likely to just walk up to you.

To successfully find faeries in natural outdoor settings, one must first find a quiet and secluded spot to relax and where few other humans are likely to be at the time. Next, you must find the sort of places where faeries are expected to be found. Finally, you must offer some sort of inducement for them to manifest in the physical world, such as a bowl of milk or a bit of fresh butter. The first two of these things have a profound effect on how, and how well, your mind is programmed for faery sightings, and the last is just common sense.

Faery mounds, sometimes called raths or burghs, are traditionally the homes of faeries throughout much of the world and would be a good place to start your in-nature search. The best time to approach a burgh is at Midsummer while wearing protective charms. Faeries are very active at this time and are known to revel for days just prior to and just after this Sabbat. To see a faery at Midsummer, go to the burgh and, if it is possible, place yourself in a light trance. Tap on the side of the mound lightly three times and request it to open for you in the name of the Goddess. Then stand back and see what happens.

Faery rings, faery trails, and faery islands are other popular faery sites, but they are ones which are reputedly fraught with danger. However, a little common sense can untangle many of these murky legends for us.

A faery ring is a dark ring of grass, perfectly round and distinctly deeper in color than the grass which surrounds it. This is another of those freaks of nature which no scientist has ever been adequately able to explain. Pagans have long believed them to be the faeries' magick circles, and numerous reports of faery rituals and revels within them have been chronicled. If you are in normal waking consciousness there is little to fear from stepping into one of these rings. But if you are in a contemplative or ritual state of mind, beware. Pagans and non-pagans have been known to become stuck in the rings when the faeries are there, but this may be a metaphor for being "stuck" in a trance state, something which will we later discuss at length.

A faery trail, or path, is like a faery ring except it is a long trail of dark grass rather than a circle. Often the trail goes on for miles, and again, science can offer no explanation for this phenomenon which follows an identical pattern year after year. These trails are believed by pagans to be the paths taken by trooping faeries on their Rades.

If you would see faeries in a faery circle or on a faery trail, sit at a respectful distance and slow and focus your thoughts. You might even request aloud to be permitted to see the faeries if they are there. Announce yourself as a fellow worshipper of the Old Gods and Goddesses, and as a friend who intends them no harm. To help things along, try this exercise at the full moon or just before sunrise.

Misty faery islands such as Avalon or Anglesey of England, Gresholm of Wales, and the Isle of the Blest of Ireland abound with faery legends. Sailors have reported faery islands which on one voyage are there, and on another have vanished. Near these islands the sailors were most cautious. Here abounded Merpeople and other water spirits, both friendly and dangerously malevolent. Ghosts of drowned sailors and their ships traveled the seas near these islands and are still seen by those who make their living on the oceans.

Contact with these vanishing islands has never been thought to be a good idea, even if you could get close enough to actually get on solid ground before they vanished again. These islands may be explanations of or metaphors for the experiences of people who began to astral project, got scared at what they saw, and snapped back again witlout ever really knowing what happened to them. The result? Legends of disappearing faery islands.

If you are interested in faery islands and the faery legends native to them, it would be worth your while to make a trip to the Isle of Man in the Irish Sea, which was once thought to be such an island, and is a place where faery lore is still abundant.

Woodland streams are another likely spot to faery hunt. Sit a ways back from the stream, slightly shift your consciousness, raise a circle around you, and focus your attention softly at the edges of the stream.

Stone heaps near old ruins (except for those which are burial cairns) are very sacred and private faery dwellings and should never be disturbed. This is simply a matter of respecting the privacy of the faeries, who are not obligated to be at our beck and call.

Faeries at Your Circle

A circle is the sacred space in which witches have worked for thousands of years. It offers both a space of protection and a place to store raised energies until they are needed. By casting a circle you state your intention to leave the solidity of the earthly world and the boundaries of your normal consciousness behind you. In a circle you are on the edge of all worlds—the physical, the astral, the spiritual, and probably ones of which we as yet have no knowledge. At the edge of your circle all things, all time, and all places meet, and it is here that faeries can easily come to watch, aid, or participate in your worship and work.

Remember that faeries as a whole cannot be summoned at will, nor controlled by egotistical magicians. They are sentient, living beings who are extremely sensitive, and they deserve our respect. When you are in the protection of your circle, try calling on faeries while keeping their individuality in mind rather than thinking of them as merely elemental energies. (You can and should certainly keep in mind their elemental associations, but try to divorce them in your mind from being only such a representation.) Invite them with the same respect with which you would offer an invitation to a cherished friend.

Different pagan traditions have various rules or guidelines for casting circles, and a set of prescribed rituals to do in them before any magick or ritual can begin. If you are used to these proceedings, it is perfectly all right to keep following them. In fact they may even help you see faeries, for your deep mind is already conditioned to these preliminaries and is being signaled that you are about to enter another world.

To summon faeries to the circle, turn to the four directions and invite—never demand—the faeries' presence. Your invitation might sound something like this, as you face each direction in turn as your tradition prefers, saying the following at each one:

> *Hear me now, oh powers of the (direction). With an open heart I invite all the friendly spirits and faeries of the (direction) and of (element associated with the direction, usually air for east, fire for south, water for west, earth for north) to come to the edge of my circle, this sacred space, to witness and participate in the worship of our cherished Goddess and our blessed God, and to joyfully work towards our goals for the good of all. Come join me (or us), if you will. You are welcome here. You are wanted here. Blessed be all who come in the name of the Bounteous Lady and the Gracious Lord.*

If your tradition calls for bells to be intoned as the directions are invoked, you must avoid this if you wish to bring faeries. Bells have long been used as a deterrent which frightens them away. Also, any sharp sounds while you are in your circle, including hand clapping and whistling, will frighten them off, leaving you only the mere raw energies of the directional elements. Remember, your goal is to get the input and assistance of a whole being for the duration of your ritual. For example, if you were frightened enough to flee from a sacred place, a part of your energy would undoubtedly remain behind (this is, in fact, one explanation of a haunting), but the real you, the part capable of thinking and acting, would not be there and therefore could not fully interact with others.

When you first begin contacting faeries, *always* stay within the protection of a circle until you get a feel for their intent towards you. If you feel faeries are indeed present you should not break the circle for any reason until the circle has been grounded, at which time most entities who were attracted to it will disperse.

If you cannot see the faeries at the perimeter of your circle, try to sense their presence. But even if you do not see or feel them, do not repeat the invitation to them. Be assured that it was heard the first time, and to press the issue could be construed as demanding or rude. You are, after all, about to enter another dimension of reality, and you do not want to drag into it negative feelings of any kind which might be magnified by the energies you raise in ritual.

Tips Which May Help

When you're willingly dealing with any psychic phenomenon such as faeries, you must be prepared to do things which will enhance your chances of interaction. Faery lore contains some of the oldest folk beliefs recorded, much of it taken from an even older oral tradition, and therefore there is much written about how you can aid your contact with the faery realms.

The flowering herbs primrose and cowslip were long thought to be the source of the faeries' invisibility. This idea no doubt grew out of the fact that when these flowering herbs were brewed and drunk as a tea they were found to open human eyes to the astral plane. In the Middle Ages primrose was believed to cause madness, which may have been what some persons thought of those who claimed to see faeries. The English saying, "Dancing down the primrose path," no doubt grew out of the belief that this herb caused persons to disconnect with reality. Today these same teas can help pagans step into Faeryland.

Magickal teas have a long history in pagan circles, and many of them will help open your psychic centers which will naturally assist you in seeing faeries and any number of other astral beings. To make the teas strong enough to work, you will need to have about two tablespoons total of dried herbs per cup of tea you wish to make. You can place the herbs in a tea ball and pour boiling water over them, or if you have an automatic coffee maker you can use this instead. Simply place the herbs in the filter as you would your coffee grounds and turn on the machine.

Before ingesting any herb you have never used before, you will need to be sure of two things: that you know exactly what it is you are taking—no guesswork; and that you know if you are allergic to the herb or not. You can be sure of what you are drinking by buying the herbs through a reputable company or through your local health food store. And you can test for allergic reactions by rubbing some of the

Faeries love the wild flowering primrose.

herb on the soft skin on the inside of your arm, or by drinking no more than one strong quarter-teaspoon full. Wait 24 hours and then try another small dose to judge if you have a reaction. People do not react on the first exposure to a substance. The first dose will only sensitize you to it, whereas the reaction, if there is to be one, will come later. Common signs of allergic reaction are runny nose, raspy breath, rash, itching, vomiting, diarrhea, exceptionally slow or rapid pulse, falling blood pressure, paleness, cold sweats, and swelling, particularly of the throat and lips. If any of these begin to become severe, head immediately for the nearest emergency room for treatment. This severe but rare allergic reaction, known medically as anaphylaxis, can be life-threatening.

Try any one of these tea combinations for opening your psychic centers, or mix and match them to taste. If you like sweeteners in your teas, try using a natural one such as raw honey or rice syrup rather than processed sugar or artificial sweeteners. Be sure to empower the teas by visualizing what you want them to do as you are brewing them.

Valerian	Catnip
Peppermint	Eucalyptus
Echinacea	
Hawthorn berries	Catnip
Spearmint	Mugwort
White oak bark	Wintergreen
Witch hazel bark	Cinnamon
Ginger	
Peppermint	Willow
Valerian	Valerian
Goldenseal	
Sassafras leaf	Damiana
Chamomile	Valerian
Ginseng	Eyebright

*Gather your own herbs from wild, natural places
whenever possible.*

Burning jasmine incense has helped many people induce an astral-level trance, and others swear by jasmine tea. Faeries love the smell of jasmine. Use it to facilitate contact.

Another incense made of the herbs Dittany of Crete, sandalwood, and wormwood is said to facilitate both astral projection and other psychic visions.

Lilac bushes and pussywillows are nearly always mentioned in children's stories and poems about faeries, and yet in no extant compilations on faery folk is there any mention of these being favored plants. But because of the instinctive associations we make between these bushes and faeries, it is a safe guess that these are favored vegetation. Plant them around your home to attract faery life.

Mistletoe, foxglove, and poinsettia are also popular faery herbs, but be warned that they are quite poisonous. If you have young children and animals around, you should look for other herbal ideas.

Japanese faeries inhabit sacred bonsai trees.

Faeries also love certain stones, especially shiny ones such as marble or tiger's eye, or any which have been processed so that they are smooth. They are also said to be attracted to staurolite, lava, fluorite, peridot, and jade. But their most sacred and favored stone is the rich, green emerald. Carry one of these with you when faery hunting, or consider offering one as a gift.

Most of the trees associated with faeries in western folklore are the same trees which were sacred to the Druids, with thorn trees, elder, birch, willow, oak, and rowan being the most popular. In North America, tulip and birch are also popular with faeries. The Wee Folk are also attracted to felled oaks, and to hazel and elder trees. Willow trees are said to harbor Dryads. If any of these trees are on or near your property, they would be good places to start looking for faery life.

Hawthorn bushes are mixed in history. Some witches plant hawthorn hedges near their homes to protect them from a number of psychic problems, faeries included. Other sources claim faeries love hawthorn and are highly attracted to it. It might be safe to say in this case that only the most beneficial and friendly of faeries seem to be attracted to hawthorn, especially white hawthorn.

In the Middle East cypress trees harbor faeries, and in Asia they live in specially cultivated dwarf trees, many of which are erected in their honor. In Greece, olive trees are the ones where faeries are most likely to be found; in Polynesia one should look for them in date palms, but never in coconut trees, which they abhor. In the Caribbean they inhabit palmettos at the edge of jungle clearings.

In Japan, bonsai trees, the diminutive bush-like trees, stand in honor of the many nature spirits of the Shinto religion. Look for faeries in their tiny boughs.

Trees with spiky projections on them, whether caused by the natural growth of the tree or by an illness or fungus, are also said to be favored faery homes.

The herb mugwort is often used in herbal recipes for travelling spells in the physical world, but many witches have found the herb

Trees with spiky projections usually harbor malevolent faeries.

works equally well when travelling in the non-physical. Try making it into a small pillow or burning it as an incense to release its powers.

Oak, ash, and thorn are the trees of Celtic lands which, when found all together, form what is called the Faery Triad. These groves are sacred to faeries, especially the tree faeries known as Dryads, who were supposed to have instructed the Druids in the use of sacred tree magick. The Druids cultivated clusters of oak, ash, and thorn, and these ancient groves can still be found today throughout Celtic countries.

In North America, it might be more efficacious to seek faeries in the trees and sacred lands of the Native Americans. Look for faeries in tulip trees, birch, giant redwood, cypress, magnolia, and maple. Also watch for them in sacred spots such as Enchanted Rock in southern Texas, the red rock canyons in northern Arizona, and in the wild, natural places beloved by the Native Americans, which have become our cherished national, state, and provincial parks.

Remember that you need not physically visit any of these places; they can all be recreated on your inner planes, and doing so will make faery contact much easier because you are meeting them halfway between their world and your own.

Farmers who have had faery encounters say faeries like to play in straw. Straw is related to the herb called broom (European broom, not the North American kind which is poisonous), which has long been associated with witches' reputed flying abilities, an obvious mis-understanding of astral projection. You might try carrying or burning broom or straw to aid faery contact.

These same farmers say that faeries love strawberries with a frenzied passion. Try setting out a few as an offering while you are trying to contact them.

When faeries are known to be most active is the time when they are most likely to be found. Usually these times are at the Sabbats and the Esbats. Other faeries have their own preferred times for being active. Look in the dictionary section of this book for specific information on any faery you hope to find. In general, try hunting for faeries a few nights prior to the Sabbats. By doing this you take advantage of the waxing energies naturally being raised by pagan anticipation world over, energy which you can tap into to make your search easier.

Green is the faeries' traditional favorite color in many lands, probably because it is the prevalent color of nature. Use lots of greenery in your garden or windowbox, and maybe burn green candles as you try to contact faeries. But don't actually wear the color green. Some faery lore tells us that faeries regard this as their own private clothing color in much the same way as royalty used to regard purple.

Faeries love music, and many popular folk tunes have been attributed to faery composers. If you would have faeries come to you, then play the folk music of their native lands or, better yet, learn to play the music yourself on folk instruments. One of the easiest folk instruments to learn to play is the pennywhistle, popular in Ireland, Britain, and northern France for two centuries. Another idea is to play a recorder, which is similar to the pennywhistle though slightly more expensive. This instrument was well-known throughout Europe and the Middle East as long ago as the late Middle Ages. Folk instruments run the entire range of the spectrum both in difficulty and in price. Check with local ethnic cultural societies for instrument prices and the availability of lessons.

Another way to explore the subtle world of faeries and learn more about them is by reading faery tales which feature them. Some of these are "Rumpelstiltskin," "Sleeping Beauty," and "The Three Billy Goats Gruff." Much pagan lore, especially concerning our deities, is also hidden among these old tales and legends.

And one last tip … faery lights, commonly known as Will-O'-the-Wisps, those elusive flickering spots of gold which dance just out of reach in the night, might entice you to give chase, but don't bother unless you are looking for a mere diversion, one which may grow frustrating. No one has ever made contact with these or even been able to explain them.

Keeping Faeries Around

Once you have discovered faeries, you will have to do some special things for them which will keep them around. While you can draw on raw elemental energy at any time, you can't always draw on the extra power of faery energy unless you remain on good terms with these sensitive creatures.

Above all else, show them respect. No one likes to be belittled, ridiculed, slandered, or taken for granted. Never forget to invite them to be a part of any magick or ritual you do, even if they have been invited only as spectators. Think of the perimeter of your circle as any other religious center, as a place where all who share your love of the deities are welcomed.

Faeries, like other beings, need food for sustenance, and in faery lore around the world the common thread of nourishment is prevalent. Leaving out food for the Little People is as common a practice in some pagan circles as is setting out bird feed in winter. Clean water, butter, cakes, wine, honey, and bread are the most commonly sought-after foods, and their favorite is fresh, creamy milk. In Cornwall and in Russia it is a folk custom never to scold a child who has spilled milk, for this should be seen as a gift to the faeries and scolding would make it seem as if it were given grudgingly. This is probably the origin of the popular doggerel, "Don't cry over spilled milk."

Traditional faery libations include milk, bread, wine, and butter.

Formal libations to faery folk can be performed in place of simply leaving out food and drink. A libation is a ritually given portion of your food or drink which is offered before you partake of it. For example, if you wish to offer your resident faeries a bit of your wine, raise the glass and say so, then pour out a portion on the ground or put some in a small bowl which will later be set out for them. Do this before you drink. Or break off part of your bread or cake and set it out in a wild place where it can be found. Never toss a faery offering out haphazardly as you would for a wild animal. Faeries consider this very disrespectful.

Respect for faery dwelling places both in the physical world and in the astral is also a must. Do not march into the astral realms as if you own them, and do not go there making demands of the creatures you meet. In the physical world do not do things which contribute to the pollution of our planet, and do not desecrate faery mounds. Legends abound of families still reeling under the curses of indignant faery folk who were provoked in this way by some ancestor long dead.

Put out the plants they love, whether it is a full garden or only a planter in a small apartment. Trees which the faeries love to inhabit can be planted on your property, or a start of one can be brought into a small home or apartment.

Always be honest about your faery contacts, or risk losing them. Faeries do not like being gossiped about any more than humans do, and to lie about magickal workings violates pagan ethics. At best they will shun you in retaliation, and at worst they will be a nuisance during every altered state you enter.

In the first two decades of this century it became a fad among occultists to claim faery contact, and several elaborate hoaxes were staged for the public. The most famous was the Cottingly Grove hoax in which two young girls were photographed frolicking with faeries. The "faeries" turned out to be cut-out drawings taken from children's books. However, at the time many persons were fooled, and flocked to Cottingly, England, to see the girls and talk with them about the faeries. Unfortunately, this hoax rang down the curtain on modern faery belief in all but a few pagan circles. Among modern pagans, the full dimension of faery life is only just now being rediscovered.

A Brief Word About Ethics

There have from time to time been cases where persons believed they have captured faeries, and they have shown their catch to others. These may have been cases where an astral being was temporarily "stuck" in our world, just as we occasionally hear stories of humans who are "stuck" for a time in the astral world. These are merely temporary mental blockages which can be overcome with concentration and relaxation. In any case, the faery eventually makes good his escape, and the poor folks who tried to hold it against its will pay dearly for their cruelty.

Never forget the Pagan Rede when you deal with faeries. This Rede applies to a witch's dealings with all living creatures—astral beings included.

Chapter Four

How to Protect Yourself From Faeries

While it is true that whenever we deal with astral plane phenomena it is necessary to take certain precautions to protect our physical and psychic selves from harm, it is not necessary or healthy to live our lives in fear. Most of the inhabitants of the astral world are delightful creatures, and only a few have other agendas. It is also true that the very act of consciously shifting our focus into that of another realm of existence can leave us somewhat vulnerable, but we can compensate for this with a little common sense and a bit of magick.

Most old magickal faery protections stem from a time long ago when mainstream society taught us to have an exaggerated fear of faery folk. Blame for all sorts of human misfortunes was left at their feet, even though they were largely blameless. Except in rare cases faeries have no ability to harm us, though they can appear very frightening or intimidating if they choose.

Read through these ancient prescriptions while keeping in mind that they need not, and should not, all be used at once. Take from them what you feel will work best for you, and relegate the rest to your storehouse of magickal knowledge.

Faery protection lore from around the world shares startling similarities, though some tales are admittedly confusing for the reader who is unsure whether the legends are referring to astral or physical experiences. In the past such protective charms were probably used in both worlds, and we can use them that way also.

Traditional Methods of Protection

The most pervasive legend about faeries is that the metal known as iron is their worst enemy. Most faeries cannot come into physical contact with it without being banished or rendered powerless. In northern and western Europe there are tales still told of mothers who place needles or pins on a sleeping baby's clothes which, to a small faery, resemble iron bars.

If you wish to guard your sleep from faery intrusion, you might place a small bit of iron in or near your bed. Any iron will do. The iron most easily found is probably in the form of a cast iron skillet available at most kitchenware stores.

Another protection associated with iron is to carry a nail in your right pocket. The right side of the body is usually seen as the side which reflects energy, while the left absorbs it. Place the nail in your right pocket to form a protective barrier around yourself.

Scythe blades and other metal farming tools have also been used against faeries. In Russia, it was customary to hang a scythe over the doorway to a home at night to prevent faeries from entering.

In Ireland it is said that a four-leaf shamrock will break any faery spell or power over the human possessing it. Carry one in your right pocket to keep faeries far away.

Using metal horseshoes as a symbol of protection was an idea taken from the Leprechauns of Ireland, who love horses to distraction. The difference is that while Leprechauns hang their horseshoes with the opening down, humans hang them with the opening up so the luck won't run out. No one has adequately explained why the metal of horseshoes can be handled by some faeries with no ill effects. It may involve the affinity faeries have for horses.

Besoms, or witch's broomsticks, are also good sources of general protection. Besoms were traditionally left by the hearth in western and northern Europe, a custom which may have grown out of a desire to protect this opening, since faeries and other uninvited spirits were often thought to gain entrance to homes through chimneys.

Another method of protection associated with the fireplace involves the ashes of a spent fire. Pagans have always thought that ashes contain magickal properties. Ashes are the transformed bodies of logs which may have been burned to perform magickal functions such as spellwork, or the simple magick of transforming raw food into a warm meal. Ashes can be placed in bottles and set in windows, barns, or homes. They can be scattered around the home to create a protective barrier, or tied into small bags to be either hung up or carried as talismans.

It is known that faeries like fire, but they dislike excess smoke. In Ireland and Wales clay pipes were often smoked as protective devices, and they were used similarly among Native Americans and Polynesian islanders.

From Scotland and northern Ireland come numerous folk songs having to do with night protection which are to be sung over smoored (banked) peat fires. These songs are still used in rural areas where peat remains the most common source of heating fuel. As the flames died to trails of smoke, women would cast protection spells which they believed worked in two ways. First, they believed that the smoke carried their prayers to the ears of their deities in much the same way as incense is used in churches today; second, that the presence of the smoke itself would help drive away faeries and unwanted spirits. The most famous of the these songs is the chant-like "Peat Fire Smooring Song" from the Hebrides. A lesser-known smooring song, called "Baloo Baleerie," is specifically designed to protect one's children from faeries who roam the night. The following is an encapsulated version of the repetitive lyrics:

> *Gone away, peerie (very small) faeries,*
> *Down come the bonnie (pretty) angels,*

Sleep safe, my baby.
Away be to Bugaboos (bad faeries and spirits),
Smoke shrouds the inner room (sleeping in a windowless
room was considered faery-safe),
Sleep safe, my baby.
Smoor the peat fire,
Gone away, peerie faeries,
Sleep safe, my baby.
Gone away, peerie faeries,
Gone away, night stealers (perhaps those faeries looking
for changelings),
Sleep safe, my baby.

If you have pagan children and are looking for a pagan-style bedtime prayer for them, you may wish to adapt one of these ancient peat smooring songs for them. Public libraries, college musicology departments, and many music stores can assist you in finding these songs either in print or on recordings. Check the resource guide in the back of this book for some addresses to help you get started.

Broken mirrors, thought by superstitious Europeans to be bad luck, can also be used to protect a home from unwanted faery beings. Place the fragments in a glass jar and set it on the sill of the main window of your home. Visualize the pieces as having become millions of smaller mirrors reflecting away all uninvited guests.

Faeries love to look at their reflections in pools of natural water, but they hate manufactured mirrors. Placing mirrors near the entrances to your home or near your bed will protect you from them. To give a mirror an added boost, draw a pentagram across its back and empower it with your own energy.

A classic protection known as a Witch Bottle can be specifically directed towards faeries. Witch Bottles are containers, usually of glass, which hold rather unpleasant items such as nails, pins, broken glass, urine, blood, salt, ash, or herbs which have all been empowered and buried near your home. Items specifically used to deter faeries can be added in place of any or all of the above mentioned items. A traditional Celtic Witch Bottle for faery protection contained nine shoots from the roots of an ash tree, or three each of rowan, oak, and ash. A simpler and just as effective Witch Bottle can make use of rue, garlic, and cloves on a bed of ashes and salt.

Be creative and add the things which to your own mind signal protection, for these are the only things which can truly shield you. Empower the Witch Bottle by visualizing it doing its job of reflecting away from you all faeries who seek to enter your home. When you feel it has absorbed as much energy as it can hold, you should bury it near your home. It is traditional to bury the bottle at midnight during a waning moon, but anytime the protection is wanted and needed is the best time.

An excellent way to turn faeries away from your home is to get a cat. Cats, long identified as the traditional familiar and helpmeet of witches, are very psychically sensitive and will see and chase away faeries. Dogs, on the other hand, seem to get along well with most of them. In some countries, particularly in eastern Europe, white dogs are thought to be the familiars of faeries.

There are a number of herbs whose lore comes down to us with instructions for their use against faeries. Queen Guinevere of the Arthurian legends collected white hawthorn on Bealtaine as a protection against faeries.

Tying up twigs from the trees of the Faery Triad—oak, ash, and thorn—is a faery protection only if they are bound together, and only if they are carried with you. Leaving them loose is an attraction. These bundles are traditionally bound with threads of white, red, and black, the colors of the Triple Goddess.

Garlic or rue hung over a crib will protect a baby, and purslane under the pillow will prevent faeries from invading your dreams or bringing you nightmares.

In Wales, gorse hedges are planted around houses for protection, and in Scotland, heather is brought into home to ward off faeries and other uninvited astral presences.

In Mexico, Curanderas (Mexican shamans) instruct mothers to lay rosemary in baby's cribs, under their own beds, and in windowsills as protection. And carrying rosemary to a wedding will protect the couple from faeries and ensure their happiness until their first anniversary.

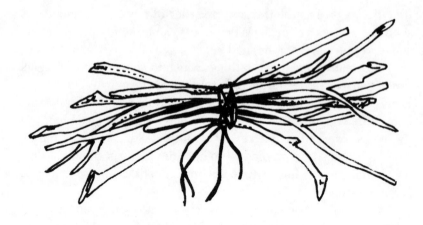

Twig-tie bundle.

Other protective herbs which are especially good for repelling or protecting against faeries are clove, bay, blackberry (which invokes Goddess protection in Ireland), mistletoe (remember, it is toxic), lilies, sandalwood, black pepper (excellent!), frankincense (when burned as an incense), witch hazel, wintergreen and all the other mints (especially when taken as teas), St. John's Wort (very effective, but very toxic), linden, garlic (well known from vampire tales), mandrake (a toxic protective amulet used for centuries by witches), and tomatoes. Faeries will not enter a garden where tomatoes grow.

Gather protective herbs into bundles and place them around your home, especially over doors and windows, and in the area where you do most of your meditation or astral projection work. Or tie them into small pouches which you can carry with you. There are two simple ways to do this. One is by placing the herbs in a plain piece of cloth and tying a string tightly around the opening. The other is by cutting two identical squares or circles from a piece of fabric and stitching them together, leaving one side or a small section open.

Turn the piece inside out, stuff in the herbs, and stitch together the opening with a needle and thread. Be sure to clearly visualize your goal through every step of this process in order to empower the talisman.

Rowan sprigs collected on Bealtaine and hung over doors, food lockers, and cribs will protect until Samhain when new cures must be found. At Samhain try hanging up dried apples or dried heather in place of rowan.

Yew bushes are often the homes of faeries who are not predisposed to humans. These poisonous bushes—whose needles have been sometimes associated with negative magick—and their inhabitants can be neutralized by tying nine small, white strips of cloth on the needles in the name of the Goddess.

If you fear faeries may harm your family, remove any lusmore, a poisonous plant, growing near your home, because it is said to be used by faeries to produce sickness in children. Lusmore is an herb whose scientific name has been lost. It was probably named for an Irishman who was thrown out of a faery party for his rude and loud behavior. An educated guess equates lusmore with yellow oleander, also known as Be Still, which is what the faeries asked of old Mr. Lusmore.

The smell of burning leather or rubber is an odor most faeries find repugnant, and they will permanently avoid any place where these things have been smelled.

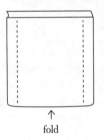

Step One:
Take a small square of felt or another heavy fabric and fold it in half. Sew up the two sides.

↑
fold

open end
↓

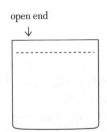

Step Two:
Turn the pouch inside out and place the herbs inside. Then sew up the remaining open end.

An herb pouch and an herb tie-bag.

Salt is another ancient protective device. In western Europe, salt was flung on the earth before sowing crops to keep faeries from blighting them.

Amulets of ashes, kelp, and sea salt are an ancient protection against drowning by water faeries, and they also protected travelers going where water sprites were known to be. Sailors usually did not venture to sea without their own talismans and amulets at hand. They especially liked wearing necklaces made of pink coral which they collected themselves during their voyages.

From England come several unique faery protection charms. These include the washing of hair in sage, putting ashes from a Midsummer balefire in your shoes, and tying an equilateral cross made of rowan sprigs above your front door. The English also believed that the planting of a mulberry tree would offer protection. They would dance around the tree at Midsummer and Yule to summon its protective powers. The old English nursery song "Here We Go 'Round the Mulberry Bush" was probably used at one time as a chant while dancing counterclockwise around the tree to banish faeries.

One of the most well-known protections is also an ancient one, and that is to discover a faery's true name. Recall the German story of Rumpelstiltskin, the baneful faery who wished to take the son of a queen whom he had helped, or of the English Tom-Tit-Tot, who cheated a miller's daughter. When the heroines of these stories discovered the true names of their tormentors, the earth opened up and swallowed the faeries. The belief that knowing someone's true name will give you power over them goes deep into pagan history. It is still customary for pagans to adopt a "craft name" when one comes of age or is initiated, and to keep it held secret from all others, with the possible exception of a trusted coven. This custom was in common use in many parts of Europe until early in this century.

If one fears he or she is being pursued by a faery, or any illmeaning spirit, one should cross over running water. The water acts like a grounding element and diffuses the baneful power. This popular prescription is rehashed every Halloween in the Washington Irving tale *The Legend of Sleepy Hollow*.

Sharp noises, especially ringing bells, snapping fingers, and clapping hands, are said to hurt the Wee Folk's ears and they will flee from the sounds, especially if the faeries are in an unfamiliar place. The more recent custom of tolling a church bell at a funeral was derived from this belief. The bells worn on the heels of the English Morris dancers on Bealtaine are also a faery protection, since faeries are especially active then.

Just before Samhain the final harvest had to be gathered in. Whatever was left in the fields after this time would be taken by malevolent faeries. But just in case some of these creatures wished to jump in early, bells were often tolled all during the day of October 30, the last day of the harvest, to ward off encroaching faeries as the work was being done. An old Mother Goose rhyme reflects this ancient custom with the words, "The boughs they do shake and the bells they do ring, So merrily comes our harvest in ... "

The decorative door harps of the Middle East and Scandinavia are also bells, and act as protective amulets for homes. These small, hollow, stringed instruments are attached to the outside of doors. On their front sides are wooden pegs suspended on wires which bounce

Bells, often used in pagan rituals, will frighten away faeries.

A door harp.

against the harp strings when the door is opened or closed and make a musical sound intended to frighten away faeries who might try to sneak in when the door is opened. These are now reproduced as folk art pieces readily found in country stores or at craft fairs.

In Celtic countries, similar harps made of willow wood were believed to render not only protection against faeries, but to increase one's magickal and sexual powers.

Windchimes are popular decorative items in many modern homes, but few realize their magickal significance. Windchimes originally functioned in much the same way as the door harp. When placed up where they can catch the wind, the chimes, made of bamboo, ceramic, or metal, clang gently together, producing a bell-like musical sound which was intended to frighten away faeries and evil spirits. Windchimes originated in China, where they still serve ritual and magickal functions.

Faeries love milk, and milk is often used to lure faeries and keep them around. But if you wish to banish them—especially the faeries who steal milk—then lace the milk with mothan (also called Pearl-Wort), for this combination renders the faery powerless over a human. Mothan is also called Moan in Scotland, where it has found its way into poetry about faery life, such as this bit from the "Flora Scotica:"

... So long as I preserve the Moan
There lives not on earth
One who will take my cow's milk from me.

Butter is another commodity which the faeries seek from humans. In many parts of Europe it was once believed that faeries would steal or spoil butter if the process of making it was not protected, especially if the butter was being made for a ritual occasion. The remedy was to toss a hot coal into the butterchurn.

The Bealtaine and Midsummer Sabbats are times when faeries are believed to be especially active, and many charms have grown up around these two holidays. Daisy chains made at Bealtaine when worn by children render them protection, as do the aforementioned bells on the heels of Morris dancers. Driving children and animals around or over the Midsummer balefire was also thought to offer

Cast a hot coal in your butterchurn
to protect the butter from faeries.

protection, especially to animals whose meat and milk might be soured by mischievous faeries.

White and gold are traditional colors of protection. Burn white or gold candles around your home while visualizing their glowing circle of light chasing away any harmful or unwanted entity which may be lurking in the shadows of your home. You may even wish to anoint the candles with a protective oil. Cinnamon, clove, and bay smell terrific, have wonderful protective energies, are easy to come by, and are relatively inexpensive. You can also carve a pentagram or a Brigid's Cross (an equilateral cross) or other symbol of protection on the candle to enhance the defensive energies. (Caution: never leave a burning candle unattended for any reason!)

The robin was a sacred bird to pagans in Ireland and England, and no malevolent faery could shapeshift into its form. In fact, faeries are reported to be somewhat fearful of robins. Faeries commonly shapeshift into birds of prey, such as vultures, or into the shapes of ravens and crows. Set out seed or do spells to attract robins to your property to chase away unwanted faery life.

Wearing one's clothes turned inside out, especially when abroad in the night, was a popular faery remedy from medieval England, where it was believed that a dirty sock under the bed would protect a sleeper. This latter notion may have been made up by someone too lazy to clean their room.

Other Things to Watch For

Faery rings, the dark green circular areas of grass which stand out clearly against lighter grass, have long been regarded as sacred areas where faeries cast their magick circles and dance and worship. These are also places that can trap humans in the faery world. The remedy? A glove tossed in the ring is thought to make it safe to enter.

Faery trails or paths, like faery rings, are areas of green grass, but these run in long strips along the ground. They are believed to be the ancient paths on which trooping faeries travel. In much of Europe it was believed unlucky to build homes or outbuildings across these paths. Many Scottish and Irish cottages are designed so that the front and back doors are directly opposite each other to allow the faeries to pass through unhindered, just in case an unknown path was built upon. The Wee Folk can bring a house down if it crosses their pathways, and there are documented cases of such things happening. As with the faery rings, a glove tossed across the path will allow a human traveler to pass through unmolested.

To hear a flowering bluebell ring means malicious faeries are near and you should get away. Bluebells traditionally adorn a witch's garden because they are friendly to witches and warn of all sorts of approaching trouble. This was a popular bit of folk knowledge which at one time made growing bluebells a dangerous prospect, for it could be used as evidence against the gardener at a witch trial.

Shapeshifting faeries often make mistakes as they shift into their own version of an animal or person. Look for flaws which may give a faery away. The advantage is working with you in this case, for any creature which travels into a realm not its own can only remain for a short while.

A faery ring: a dark circle of grass within a field of lighter green.

In general, baneful faeries are more active during the last quarter of the waning moon, and helpful faeries are more active at the waxing. Inland water faeries are generally friendly, while sea faeries are usually more malevolent, a concept which no doubt grew out of the dangers of sea travel. Good faeries are commonly most active from Bealtaine to Samhain, and the more mischievous ones from Samhain to Bealtaine.

Never take an offer of faery food or drink while in the astral, for that can lead to enslavement in the faery world. It is best if one avoids all physical contact, especially as romantic touches or kisses can lead to captivity. And never, ever begin to dance with faeries in the astral, no matter how hauntingly compelling their music, as one can dance one's self to death. If someone is dancing uncontrollably inside a faery ring he or she can be removed by three friends. Two hold onto the dancer with one hand and the third rescuer with the other. The third rescuer keeps both feet firmly outside the faery ring, and the three of them pull the dancing friend away.

On the other hand, faery lore tells us that payment is steep for refusing faery hospitality while we are in our own physical world. If you are on your own territory, meaning in the physical world, and you are offered faery food and drink, you must accept them or risk the consequences of slighted faery feelings. But don't look for a faery to come knocking on your door bearing gifts. The offer can come in unexpected forms. For instance, if you are searching for water in a dry area, express a wish for it, and feel led to it, chances are you were aided by a friendly faery being.

Faery music is beautiful, and many ancient airs are said to have been gifts of the faeries, including the popular "Londonderry Air." Many humans have followed entrancing music which seems to come out of nowhere, and have stumbled upon a faery band at their revels. And some people have been deliberately lured into dangerous situations by sounds so fair they demand attention. If you hear these enticing strains and wish to follow them, exercise caution. Do not allow the music to persuade you to remain in the faery realms longer than you intended.

Avoid elder wood if you wish to avoid faeries. This is their most sacred single tree and they are believed to jealously guard it. Elder wood was never used to make cradles in most of Europe for fear that a child would be stolen by the faeries if they slept in an elder bed.

The folklore of much of Europe also states that the third meeting with a faery or third trip to Faeryland is one in which one must be especially cautious. It is this meeting or trip which will set the tone for your dealings with faeries or their world for all time. Be extra careful of entrapment and of manipulation. But you can also forge lasting relationships with the Wee Folk if you appear honest, fearless, and sincere in your seeking.

About Changelings and Faery Entrapment

There are two faery legends which are often confusing, even for the witch who is readily able to separate the astral from the physical world. These two legends are that of faery changelings and of entrapment in the faery world.

Belief in faery changelings is older than recorded history. Basically, this is a concept which accepts that faeries, in order to strengthen their gene pool and resuscitate their dwindling race, steal human babies and leave in their place a wizened, sickly faery child. This bit of lore was probably an explanation for the failure to thrive syndrome which still affects infants today. A child who fails to thrive grows weak and wizened for no apparent reason until it just fades away.

Watching this type of slow death which seemed painless and for which there was seemingly no cause might easily have seemed to our ancestors to be the same as seeing someone fade into Faeryland. After all, they knew what the astral plane was, and they knew that it was that same painless, dreamlike state which took them there in dream or trance. And no doubt there were precedents to further this belief, such as stating that someone who had died in their sleep had died during an "out-of-body experience."

No one can say for sure that the baby's "soul" was not taken into Faeryland, but if we believe in the evolution of the soul through the metaphor of reincarnation or in the oneness of the human spirit, this would seem to rule out any acceptance of changelings.* Today, many pagan parents practice some of the old infant protections more to honor the old ways rather than from any real fear.

Folklore from around the world offers us numerous ways to protect babies from faery snatching, with nearly all cultures having their own peculiar charms which were thought to be effective. These usually involved secret names, the use of native herbs, or using smoke to purge the area, as aversion to smoke is a theme in faery lore from around the world.

The most popular method stems from an old belief that knowing someone or something's true name provided power over that person or object. This conviction was prevalent worldwide, particularly among Celtic, Semitic, and Polynesian people. Parents who feared faeries would not use their child's real given name until the child was at least three years old, or even as old as five, at which point the danger was believed to have passed.

Placing garlic or dill weed under a baby's crib is a remedy used in the Mediterranean area, and placing iron (the metal, not the hot household appliance) under the bed is a practice from western Europe.

More numerous in folklore are methods for causing the changeling to leave the body of the child, replacing itself with the proper owner. Most of these techniques are very dangerous to the

---

*There is one documented case from turn-of-the-century England which bears mentioning. Two siblings, a boy and a girl, were found in a dense wood by hunters. They were small for their ages, and had an unexplainable greenish cast to their skins which was apparently quite pronounced, and they spoke a tongue no linguist could decipher. Even though it was the dawn of the twentieth century, the children were immediately dubbed changelings and taken to a village in Suffolk where it was hoped their families could be found.

When it came to meals, the children only wanted milk and wild greens. No amount of persuasion would make them eat anything else. Finally it was decided that the diet of greens was causing the unnatural green pallor, and a diet heavy in meats was ordered. The children cried and nearly starved themselves before finally eating the meats. As time went by the greenish cast faded from the children, and they readily ate meat and learned English, but many of the villagers still eyed them with suspicion and caution, quite sure that the children were changelings who had somehow escaped their fate. While there are enough holes in this story that one could offer several logical and scientific explanations for what happened in Suffolk, it is nonetheless an interesting tale to ponder.

child, and definitely constitute child abuse by today's enlightened standards. No doubt many a suspected changeling died because of well-meaning but ill-informed parents who adopted these practices. These practices are presented here for *historical interest only, and should never under any circumstances be tried:*

Filling the infant's room with smoke.

Allowing the baby to "smoke" a pipe.

Starving the faery out.

Threatening to prick the child with a pin, especially one made of iron. Metal scythes were used for this purpose in Russia and eastern Europe.

Feeding the child a drink of hen's blood at midnight.

Cajoling it into speaking its native faery tongue.

Throwing the child toward the fireplace, or holding it over the fire on a shovel.

Provoking the child to sneeze three times in a row.

Denying the child fresh greens or dairy products, feeding it only a diet of meat.

Tying up a white feather and the hair of a black cat with a red ribbon as necklace to be worn by the child for a year and a day. (If this idea appeals to you, then hang the charm in the child's room. *Do not place anything around an infant's neck for any reason, ever!*)

The other confusing faery legend is that of the entrapment of humans in the faery world. Such actions as accepting food and drink while in the astral or dancing with faery folk were said to imprison humans in that world.

The idea of this sort of entrapment may simply be a metaphor for a worsening of the astral phenomena known as time distortion. The astral world sits just outside of the normal boundaries of the physical world, and it is a fact of modern physics that time does not exist outside of our universe. In the astral world time has no meaning, as many have discovered who have been meditating, thinking only a few minutes have passed, then awakening to find an hour or more has gone by. Accepting food or drink or joining in dancing while in the astral seems to worsen that effect. The reason for this may be as simple as that you're just having too good a time to leave.

Some have experienced or read about people who have become "stuck" on the astral plane and unable to return to their bodies. In general, this doesn't happen because you are not out of your body, only your consciousness is elsewhere, and since consciousness is controlled by you, you always have a choice of where to take it. Being stuck "out" is a merely a metaphor for a mental blockage caused by one's own fears, a blockage which can almost always be overcome by relaxing and simply thinking yourself back into yourself in rather the same way that you force yourself to awaken from a bad dream.

For those who have a sincere fear of not being able to handle such a situation on their own, I suggest you practice projecting with a friend nearby. If you express an inability to return, all your friend has to do is "come in" verbally and take you back with him or her. This is done by talking to the one who is "stuck" and telling him or her that you are coming, following the same path, and that you now see the individual. Ask the person to take your hand and then "return." This is a method used by hypnotists who are faced with subjects who will not snap out of their trances, and it is virtually 100 percent effective.

Protection Spells

Pagan history is packed full of rites of protection, and we still use these rites today, or similar ones, to increase the psychic barrier which we set up around our homes and selves.

Protection rituals are usually very simple. The only thing really required from the witch is a heavy investment of personal energy. The simplest method is to take an incense traditionally used for protection—such as frankincense, basil, pepper, sandalwood, cinnamon, or clove—into every room of your home. As the smoke fills your home, visualize all negative energy and all uninvited entities being neutralized and turned away. See the smoke from the incense literally pushing them out. As you go you might chant something like this:

By this smoke and by my will,
Peace and safety be where I dwell.
No astral being nor faery folk
May enter where these words are spoke.

Another method would be to visualize a bright white-gold beam of light surrounding your home. Think of this as the divine light of the deities which makes an impenetrable shield around your home and repels any negative beings with which it comes into contact. Then mentally set up a pentagram, the five-pointed star that symbolizes paganism, on each side of your house. Visualize each one as a fiery blue-white, the same color as your magick circle. Persons psychically sensitive enough to actually see the energy of these pentagrams and circles report that this is the color in which they appear. And always see each pentagram with its apex pointing up. The pentagram is an ancient symbol of spirit over matter, and the inverted version has been adopted and perverted by persons on very negative paths.

Make all these visualizations real, and see them pulsating with protective energy. It is a good idea to renew these energy barriers at least once a month. Doing this on the new moon is a good way to remember.

You can also tie up small bags of protective herbs in little circles of white or gold fabric and put them up in discreet corners of your home. Use clove, bay leaves, acorns, frankincense, garlic, cinnamon, valerian, basil, blackberry, mints, pepper, sandalwood, ashes, cactus needles, pine needles, lavender, mandrake (toxic), broom (toxic), heather, or rowan. As you place each herb in the cloth and proceed to tie it up, visualize the herbs repelling any faery being who tries to enter your home. Remember that visualization and desire are the key elements to successful magick.

As you hang the bags up in your home repeat a chant such as:

Bag of cloth and herb and oak,
As ye do hang, hang bane to choke.

You can create you own spells with any of the protection methods listed above by empowering them with your energy and ritualizing them. Appendix Two in the back of this book contains a detailed outline for spellcraft.

Exorcism of Faeries

Occasionally witches feel their protection rituals have not been strong enough, and they feel plagued by astral beings. Astral creatures are naturally drawn to the energies produced during spellwork or rituals. Usually they depart when the circle is grounded, but occasionally they hang around. Anyone who has experienced this invasion knows it can be very disconcerting. You see these things race across your rooms out of the corner of your eye, your pets are startled by them and shy away from them, and they want to put their curious noses into your life at the most awkward moments—such as when you are bathing. I had one such invader who was wildly attracted to my vacuum cleaner.

The only answer to dealing with these beings, faeries included, is to exorcise them out of your dwelling and out of your mental world.

Exorcism or banishment rituals differ from protection rituals because in protecting yourself and your home you are seeking to prevent unwanted beings from entering. In exorcisms, the beings are already there and you need to get rid of them.

Fortunately for the faery seeker and the Faeryland traveler, much lore exists on how to banish unwanted or malevolent faeries form your home.

Again remember that we as modern pagans have to sort out the hidden meaning in this lore. In many cases we are speaking of astral or thought-form acts rather than physical ones. Only you can decide for yourself which it is to be. Spells to dispel general negativity are not usually very effective against faery folk unless the spell specially asks protection from both physical and astral sources. Even though all magickal energy must first pass through the astral realms before it returns, none but faery magick originates there. In the case of asking for protection from faeries in both worlds you are doubling your chances of having a successful working. If you use no words or chants with your banishment acts, be sure to visualize this dual world protection. Some witches prefer to do these rituals in both the physical and the astral just to be sure all bases are covered.

If a faery you don't want around and who doesn't live with you makes an appearance, you can sometimes get it to leave by chanting this common nursery rhyme which is really an ancient spell of faery banishment:

Ladybug, Ladybug,
Fly away home.
Your house is on fire
And your children have gone.

Hazel wands will banish faeries. Irish legends state that it was a staff of hazel wood which St. Patrick used to drive the snakes out of Ireland. Carry the wand from room to room, wave it in a counterclockwise direction, and say something like this:

By the waving of this wand,
Faery folk shall now be gone.
From the planes of earth and mind,
No more faeries will I find.

You can also try an oak, willow, or pine wand if hazel is not available. The only catch here is that the wand must be cut on Bealtaine.

Frankincense is an excellent banishing incense and is readily found in stick or cone form at many gift and import shops. For centuries this herb has been used in the Middle East and India to banish negative influences and raise positive vibrations. As with the wand, take the burning incense from room to room and picture the faeries fleeing before it. As you go you might chant something like this to help you focus your energy:

Gone from dreams and from my earth,
Gone be faery folk from mind and hearth.
As I fill this place with fragrant wood,
Faery folk now be gone for good!

Feeding faeries from an eggshell is a French method of gaining control over a faery. Once the faery has drunk from the shell, you can tell it to leave and it must obey.

In Scotland it is believed that ash tree wands give power over faeries and you can tell them to leave.

If you have been putting out food to entice faeries to your home, try putting pepper in the food. This is said to drive the faeries far away. Of course they will become enraged once the peppery taste is out of their mouths and may come seeking revenge, so fortify yourself and your home with extra protection.

If you can lure them into metal rings they will disappear forever—at least from you. In this case, the rings are acting like the magick circle which protects witches and magicians during rituals. But the Celts warn us not to use gold or silver rings for this experiment, or this magick can backfire. Just how it does this is not spelled out, but it is probably good practice in this case to follow the old wisdom.

The inverted white light tornado is my own creation for banishing anything unwanted from a dwelling, and works just as well for faeries. The way this works is for you to lie down somewhere where you can have 15 to 20 minutes of absolute peace and quiet. Lie back, close your eyes, and relax yourself as much as possible. Then call upon all your reserves of power to call down from high above you a white inverted tornado, large enough to encompass your entire property. It should be spinning in a counterclockwise direction. This is the direction pagans have always called upon to banish or decrease anything. (If you ever forget which direction is which, just envision the destructive counterclockwise movement of cyclonic storms seen on weather radars.)

See its energy grow, and its vortex gather speed and strength. As it descends on your home, see it gathering up in its powerful suction all negative influences and uninvited beings. See them being stuck in the tornado as it slowly goes down, on past your home and into the ground, where it harmlessly unleashes the things it has taken away.

Then see it rise again, clean and fresh, ready to make a second sweep of your home. See it rooting out all the uninvited energies and guests that hid from it the first time, and watch them too being sucked into the ground.

Then do it one more time. In my tradition three is the number of completion, and no spell is finished until it has been done three times.

The inverted white tornado is a powerful cleansing tool, and it has never failed yet.

The Native Americans of the Midwest used peony roots to exorcise unwanted entities, including beings which appear to be the

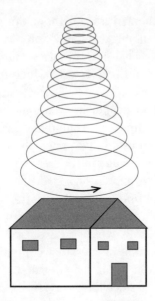

The inverted white light tornado.

Native American version of faeries. Burn the roots as an incense, or create a wand of the plant stems to banish the faeries. Then bury the used plant, and carry a fresh one with you for renewed protection.

A more ritualized exorcism ceremony can involve the traditional elemental tools which are really not a part of paganism at all, but adaptations which came to us through ceremonial magick during the late Middle Ages. To do this ritual you will need protective incense, a candle (of any color, but white or gold is best), a stone or bowl of salt, and a cup or chalice of some kind.

These four tools represent the four alchemical elements of water, air, earth, and fire which pagans regard as the basic building blocks of all matter. And since faeries are elemental beings, this ritual can act on their most basic make-up to drive them away.

In the center of your home, or as close to center as you can get, set up your altar or a small table or platform. You can use anything for this, even a box or a stack of books. You want it just high enough to be comfortable for you to reach from a standing position, and wide enough to hold all your tools. If you do not already have ritual tools, you can improvise them. Just run them through some water and smoke first to purify them. Again, any water and smoke will do. The important thing is to visualize the tools being cleansed of any other vibrations and psychic influences with which they might have come into contact.

Set your tools on the altar in accordance with their traditional directions. Place the cup (representative of water) in the west, and the stone or salt (representative of earth) in the north. Put the incense (representative of air) in the east, and the candle (representative of fire) in the south. Your own tradition may have a slightly different version of east and south. It is perfectly all right, and even encouraged, that you use a wand or athame (ritual knife) for either of these directions, if that is what you are used to using. Modify the words of empowerment as needed to accommodate your changes.

Bells are traditional altar accouterments and should definitely be out during this ritual since their very presence can help drive away unwanted faeries.

It is also necessary to cast a circle around yourself for protection. If you have never cast a circle before, it is as easy as using your mind to daydream. But don't be misled into thinking that the circle is not really there, because it is. Its strong protective energy will both

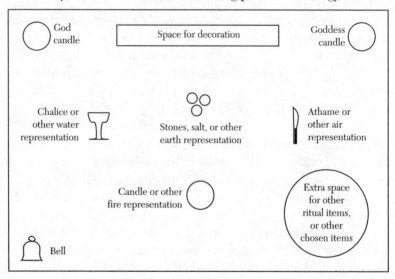

A standard altar layout.

keep your raised energy contained until you are ready to use it and keep entities and other negative influences out.

To cast a circle you may use virtually any magickal tool you possess, but the most commonly chosen ones are the wand, the knife or sword, or your own forefinger, which all symbolize projected and directed power. Starting at any directional point you choose draw a circle around you and your altar while staying within it, moving from left to right in a clockwise motion. As you go, visualize the circle rising around you in fiery blue-white light. Feel its energy and know you are safe inside.

You may begin the body of this ritual with any direction you like, and again this may be dictated by your tradition. The following words of empowerment begin with the west because that is where my tradition usually begins a ritual.

Stand on the west side of the altar facing it. In your power hand (the dominant one), raise the cup high over your head. Begin to feel the power you are raising filling your circle, feel it radiating out of the cup like a protective ray of sharp, unyielding energy. Say:

Cup of water and the west, banish from this place all creatures of water and spirit who dare to enter here uninvited. All those who invade both my dwelling and my dreams now be gone. Drown their power to harm. Take them far from this place.

(Note: The words "my dwelling and my dreams" are merely a poetic way of saying that this spell covers both astral and physical invaders.)

While still holding the cup walk counterclockwise (the traditional direction for banishment magick) around the altar, all the while feeling the energy from the cup and from yourself building, pushing at the perimeters of the circle, bulging it, wanting to get out and banish the faery folk. When you reach your starting point again, set the cup back down in its place.

Move to the north. Take the stone or bowl of salt in your power hand and raise it high above your head. Again, feel the energies in it build around you. Say:

Bowl of salt of earth and the north, banish from this place all creatures of earth and spirit who dare to enter here uninvited. All those who invade both my dwelling and my dreams now be gone. Ground their power to harm. Take them far from this place.

Walk counterclockwise around the altar while you visualize the energy building, wanting to do its job, aching to be released. When you reach your starting point, lay the stone or salt bowl back down in its place.

Now move to the east and raise the incense high above, in your power hand. Say:

Incense of air and of the east, banish from this place all creatures of air and spirit who dare to enter here uninvited. All those who invade both my dwelling and my dreams now be gone. Blow away their power to harm. Take them far from this place.

Walk counterclockwise around the altar while still holding the incense, and when you return to your starting point, set the incense down.

By now you should have no trouble visualizing the power in your circle. It should be crackling in the air around you with a tangible electricity, like dry hair on a winter night.

Move to the south and raise the candle, the final object, with your power hand, over your head (watch out for falling wax!). Feel it adding its power to the already barely containable force.

Candle of fire and of the south, banish from this place all creatures of fire and spirit who dare to enter here uninvited. All those who invade both my dwelling and my dreams now be gone. Burn away their power to harm. Take them far from this place.

Walk counterclockwise around the circle one last time. When you return to the south, set your candle down in its place.

Pick up your bell and ring it loudly for a few moments, allowing it to drive away as much unwanted faery life as it can. You can walk around the perimeter of your circle with it if you like. When you are done, replace it in its spot.

Stand quietly for a moment in front of your altar and feel your own power as you contain and control the throbbing energy about you. You are about to release it to do its job. When you do, you should visualize it bursting forth from the circle like an explosion, hurtling through your home, drawing, grounding, blowing, and burning away all unwanted entities. See them being hurled far from you, their power gone. Know they are gone; your home and your astral travels are now safe from these creatures.

To prevent reinfestation of your home or your astral projections, it is necessary to follow up all exorcisms with steady doses of increased protection.

After you conclude your banishment ritual, try never to think about the negative entities or energies again. By not giving them the power of your thoughts, you rob them of the very energy they need to live. If at any time you find your thoughts steered towards them, don't worry about it; just say aloud the words, "Go away." And say it in the same tone of voice as you would speak to an annoying younger sibling. And like a pesky younger sibling, if the negative energy can't get a rise out of you it will see no point in continuing the game.

Guided Meditation into Faeryland

*T*he following guided meditation (for use after reading Chapters 3 and 4) is designed to help you reach the inner plane known as Faeryland. It is a straightforward text which induces relaxation, takes you to the astral or inner plane, and returns you to your normal waking consciousness.

This meditation can be read for oneself while awake with minor success, but will work better if it is tape recorded or read to you by another witch so you can allow yourself to fully concentrate on focusing your thoughts inward and outward. The idea is to immerse yourself as much as possible in the astral world—not impossible to do with your eyes open, but significantly harder.

The first part of the meditation is an induction which is designed to slow and focus brain activity. The deeper you are in trance while still maintaining your ability to consciously think and react, the better your faery contact (or any inner plane work) will be. Keep in mind that my method of altered state induction is only one of many that are equally workable. If you have a method of inducing these states that you prefer, feel free to substitute yours for mine. In most cases they will work better for you because your subconscious is already cued to working with that particular method.

No matter what method you choose to enter Faeryland, you should take that same path out, retracing each step. The conscious mind, which is along on this journey, has a desperate need for order and logic, and will be much happier if you follow the same trail both ways. The meditation written here will provide that continuity.

In the main body of this guided meditation you will meet several faery types, all known to be friendly towards, or at least accepting of, humans. They have been chosen from Celtic and Anglo folklore because these are ones which are among the easiest for western people to comprehend.

The excursion takes you to all four corners of the faery realm in search of the elusive crock of gold. The Leprechauns and their crock is a legend which is as well known outside of Ireland as within. There are few people, even in these modern times, who have not heard that if they are able to capture one of these slippery little tricksters, they will be given the crock of gold and three wishes.

The crock is a cauldron, and the cauldron is symbolic of death and rebirth, the Goddess, and spiritual attainment. Modern persons, driven by greed, have mistaken the reason that we seek the crock to be one of material gain. The crock of gold was pursued by our pagan ancestors because the person who found it would then possess some of the Goddess's power over life and death. That is the crock's appeal, and it remains so for we pagans who seek it today. Those who, in an altered state, actually get hold of this crock/cauldron should count themselves fortunate because it symbolizes that, even if only for a moment, they have connected with the universal Goddess power sought by humans for countless centuries, not only as the Leprechauns' crock, but also in the form of the Arthurian tradition's Holy Grail. Archetypally it represents a high level of spiritual attainment, legitimacy of any rulership, and understanding of the doctrines of reincarnation, and it should signal to the finder that his or her mind has moved beyond the mundane to a point where the person cares about and understands both humanity and larger concerns.

If at any time during the guided meditation you feel uncomfortable, nervous, or frightened, try increasing the protection around your physical body with a strong white-gold light energy. The key is to work through each blockage and each fear by realizing that your quest is more important than any petty anxiety manufactured by the human mind. If you are still not comfortable, it is probably best that you return to full waking consciousness, or what some would term "returning to your body." You should then attempt to analyze just what it is that disturbed you so much and then try again later.

You will be in control through the entire journey and fully able to return to your normal waking consciousness at any time you choose. Trigger words for returning will be given in the induction.

You are reminded that the rules of hospitality in Faeryland include one against accepting any form of food or drink or dancing with them in their revelries, even though they may invite you to do so. Also, remember that faeries hate profuse displays of gratitude and demand respect. In the mid-nineteenth century, folklorist Thomas Keightley wrote a book called *Fairy Mythology* in which he states that faeries are bound by a rule which says that they must exchange with you any item you ask for of theirs with one of yours which appears to be of equal value to the one you want. Be careful with this last one and remember that these gifts will be spiritual ones at best, for inanimate objects cannot travel from one plane of existence to another.

Before you begin this journey you will need to find a place where you will not be disturbed. Most witches have such a place they can go where they regularly practice meditation, astral projection, and spellwork. If you have no such place, it is time you decided on one. The best choice is a comfortable corner of your home at a time when you are alone. You may either lie down or sit, whichever you prefer. If you choose to recline, make sure you are able to stay awake during the entire exercise. Falling asleep will cause no ill effects, but your conscious mind will lose all the benefits of the inner plane exercise, though your subconscious will probably continue until the end of the meditation.

If you wish, you may burn incense or play some "New Age" music softly in the background. These things aid concentration for many and can certainly help to drown out the sounds and smells of the mundane world.

You will also need to have on your person some symbol of psychic protection. This is a standard practice in nearly all traditions when one is attempting psychic work. The protection can be a talisman such as a piece of pentagram-shaped jewelry, or some protective herbs tied together in a colorful pouch. Do whatever signals protection to you. Other protective visualizations will be provided for you in the text of the meditation.

An example of a good protective talisman would be to tie up three protective herbs or stones in a white or gold cloth. Choose any three herbs which have protective energies. Some suggestions are cinnamon, thyme, hyssop, thistle, heather, valerian, bay, blackberry, mints, pepper, sandalwood, frankincense, acorns, rosemary, gold, bloodstone, or pyrite. You might substitute mugwort for any one of these. Mugwort is the herb which protects travelers and is supposed to aid in astral travel as well. Put the talisman together by clearly visualizing the desired protection.

As you tie up the herbs in the bag (see the previous chapter for ideas on how to tie the bag), be sure to keep up your visualization. As you do this you might wish to chant a charm to help you concentrate. Try something like this:

Charm of herbs, of stone and earth,
Guard my self, and my home and hearth.

Or you might chant something specifically related to astral travel:

Protective charm with energy bright,
Be my guardian while I'm out tonight.

If none of the above methods appeal to you, then look over Chapter 4 for more ideas on magickal protection.

There will be a short pause in the middle of the text as you are guided to a scrying pool which—hopefully—will give you some indication of the state of your spiritual growth or some commentary on the path you are on. This information may come to you in different ways. You may see an entire scenario played out before you, you may be spoken to by some other entity, or you may only see symbols, ones which only you will be able to interpret. Keep an open mind regarding how you receive this message or you might be tempted to dismiss some very important piece of knowledge.

The scrying portion of the text should be given at least five minutes of uninterrupted silence. If you finish before this time is up, just sit quietly reflecting on the information you have received until the voice of your reader takes you on along your journey. This portion will be marked off with parentheses ( ), as will other portions of the text. These indicate instructions to the reader and should not be read aloud.

Faeryland is a seductive place, as those who have ventured there will tell you. Of all the astral worlds you will ever visit, Faeryland will be the hardest one to leave, and the one most tempting you to return. But keep in mind that faeries are notoriously capricious creatures, some of them are quite mischievous, and still others do not like humans. As long as you stick to the guided path no harm will come to you. The faery beings you will meet in this working are not malevolent, though sometimes they will seem indifferent.

Slightly more than halfway through the text the Gnome King will offer you a chance to leave Faeryland if you wish. The choice will be yours to make. Some people feel they have absorbed as much as they can or should by this point and will wish to come back, while others will be eager to go on. If you do choose to come back at this point or any other, you will probably feel compelled to complete the meditation at some later time. Faeryland is a seductive place, and this may be the root source of the Scottish proverb, "For those who enter Faeryland there is no turning back. One must continue on and go through it."

After this point you will venture into the darker reaches of Faeryland, the area ruled by the Crone Goddess. Some occultists have suggested that these dark images are best avoided, but that only seeks to perpetuate the destructive myth that old women are somehow repulsive and dangerous. The Crone is part of the Triple Goddess, and to get to know, love, and be comfortable with her is every bit as important as knowing and loving the Maiden and Mother forms. They are all a part of the whole, and we must explore each one if we are to become whole ourselves.

Once you become comfortable with this venture into Faeryland try adding to, subtracting from, or modifying this guided meditation into more advanced forms. Add places where you can stop to do divinations and rituals, or where you can contact other faery life forms. Then try venturing off the path on your own Faeryland adventure and see who you can meet and what you can teach each other. Before you do this be ready to carry extra protection, and be sure you are adept at returning to your normal waking consciousness without any aid or hesitation.

With practice, you will learn that you can quickly find anyone or anything in Faeryland. All you have to do is either ask someone, or else will yourself to be in the presence of those whom you seek. As stated earlier, if you find yourself facing a faery you would rather not be in contact with, just nod a greeting and continue on. There is no reason to fear. Remember, you are in control.

This guided meditation is only a place to begin—the possibilities in Faeryland are literally endless.

Pronunciation of words in meditation:

Gruagach (grew-g'ac)   Beansidhe (ban-shee)

Bealtaine (beel-teen)   Lughnasadh (loo-nah-sah)

Samhain (sah-vain)   Satyr (sait-er)

Cead Mile Failte (kee-ah meel-ay felt-chay)

Close your eyes and begin breathing rhythmically and deeply. Slow your thoughts. Quiet your mind. Center your spirit and feel your body begin to relax. Relax and let go. Focus inward, shutting out the physical world. You are slowing your mind, relaxing your body, going inward.

With each breath you draw in, your mind slows itself more and more, falling inward. Falling, falling, going inward, reaching outward. Slower and slower. Deeper and deeper, into itself. Slower and deeper. Continue to relax.

Now inhale deeply—as much air as you can take in (pause). Hold it (pause). Now exhale, very slowly, feeling your body relax as you do, all your tensions draining away. And you relax even more. Your mind is quiet and your spirit calm.

Inhale again, very deeply this time. Hold it for a few seconds (pause). Now exhale, very, very slowly. All the tensions of your physical body have fallen away. You are relaxed and growing less and less aware of your physical shell.

One more time—inhale as deeply as you can and hold it (pause). Now exhale, slowly, allowing the last hold to your physical consciousness to slip away with it. Your mind is quiet and reflective, your body still and relaxed. Release it all. Relax, go deeper.

As this last breath leaves your body you notice a tingling of energy deep within you. It is not a remnant of tension from your physical life which begins to stir within you, but an energy which is new and exciting, as if ignited by a divine source. Suddenly you feel yourself surrounded by this energy. It is the protective energy of your Goddesses and Gods which now surrounds your body in an egg of golden light that throbs and sparkles about you as if kissed by the sun and blessed by the full moon. This egg of protective energy is born of the divinity that has always been within you and will never desert you. In times of stress or fear it will only glow brighter, its defenses stronger. It is all-knowing and far-reaching. It will protect your inert body as you travel to the astral realms, and it will also go with that part of you which is now ready to journey forth. It will guard and defend.

You have no fear because you know that you are always in control. You know that if for any reason you wish to return to your body and to your normal waking consciousness, you can do so by saying to yourself the words "I AM HOME." The words "I AM HOME" will tell both your subconscious and conscious minds that you wish to return immediately to your normal consciousness—and it will immediately happen. You can then open your eyes and go about your daily life unharmed. The words "I AM HOME" will always bring you home.

You are relaxed and you have no fears, no worries, no concerns outside of your pathworking goal. So feel yourself relax and go deeper … deeper … deeper into a meditative state. Feel yourself sinking—sinking so deeply into yourself that you feel you can fly. So deep that you know you will not much longer be attached to the physical world. You have never felt so relaxed or so peaceful.

Now become unaware of your physical shell. For one last moment know it is a part of you, and then let it go. Release it. It is not needed now. Become unaware of your legs (pause). Become unaware of your arms (pause). Become unaware of your back and stomach (pause). Relax your neck and shoulders and then become unaware of them. Feel them fall away from you like old clothes, and relax even more (pause).

As you feel yourself sinking deeper and deeper, you are ready to call upon your deities for the extra protection you need as you traverse the astral realms.

With your mind call out to your Goddess and ask her blessing upon your venture as you seek entrance to the astral world (pause). Feel her approval. Accept her blessing. Feel her protective energy come to you, as sure and as safe as the arms of a loving mother. As if in answer to your plea you notice above you a large pentagram. It blazes strongly with a blue-white flame. It is impenetrable to any but yourself, and with that knowledge you are able to relax even more … even more.

Already the veil which separates your everyday world from the astral plane is blurred, and you can feel the astral coming closer and closer. You sense its subtle energies.

You know you will be there soon and you relax even more … more.

With your mind call out to your God and ask his blessing upon your venture as you seek entrance to the astral world (pause). Feel his strength and his assurance that you are safe and well, and that your journey is blessed. As if in answer to your plea you notice that a bright shield has been raised over you, glowing golden like the sun. On the shield are carved intricate knots and pentagrams, and animals of strength and courage, the same ones that have protected seekers of old. Ancient energies of protection and power are now with you.

With the glowing shield of the God, the pentagram of the Goddess, and your own protective energy pulsating around you, you feel warm and very sleepy, and yet incredibly energized. You know you are safe and protected, and you know that soon you will step from inside yourself into the mysterious and ethereal astral realm—a plane of existence in which anything is possible.

Suddenly you realize that your physical body is completely numb. You are now so deep in trance that you can no longer feel any sensations of your physical body—it has no connection whatsoever with you. That mortal shell is now completely forgotten, and your separation from it is nearly complete. You are so deep into yourself that your mind is reaching outward, stretching toward new worlds and new experiences. And you feel yourself begin to sway. That part of you which is able to go forth and travel unhindered by your physical being is anxious to begin the journey. It wants to leave. As you sway you feel a sense of lightness and buoyancy which draws you closer to the astral world.

As you continue to sway you feel a weightless sensation in the pit of your stomach, and suddenly you find you are no longer part of that heavy shell. You feel light and free and you move slowly upward, out of and away from your physical self.

You travel out a few yards and find that you are above your body, looking down at it. You see that it is safe and protected and will remain that way until you decide to return.

The astral part of the talisman you brought along on the journey is safely with you, and the egg of protection still surrounds you, giving you a bright, otherworldly appearance. You are ready to go now.

You turn and fly through your ceiling, feeling happy and carefree. You rise up and up and up, flying free, and the air becomes thinner and thinner. You are now in a whitish mist which you know borders the entrance to the higher astral world. As you think to yourself, "the astral world of Faeryland is my destination, the astral world of Faeryland is my destination," a swirl of rainbow-like colors begins dancing around your flying form as if wanting to play.

You slow your upward flight and float gently along as you watch in fascination while the rainbow colors begin to come together to form the bottom of a beautiful astral rainbow. The rainbow rises from you so high into the mist that you cannot even see up to where it begins to arch. The colors are vibrant and the rainbow sparkles beautifully as if it is a living thing. All your hopes and dreams and aspirations are a part of this beautiful swirl of colors which can lead you anywhere you wish to be in time or space. This rainbow bridge is your passport and pathway to all that ever was, is, or will be.

A joyfulness overtakes you, and you began to fly again and follow the beckoning rainbow which rises up high into the white mist. Up and up and up you fly until you reach the rainbow's apex. Like a playful child you sit on the rainbow and start to slide down the other side. It is a long way down, but the ride is fun. You are so light that you feel like you are riding on air. The soft wind blowing in your face is exhilarating; you feel energized by it.

As you slide down further you notice a world forming below you, and you are coming closer and closer to it. You know this is a part of the astral world, the higher astral world where the beings and experiences you wish to contact reside, and you are about to step off the rainbow bridge into this mysterious and magickal world.

As you near the end of the rainbow, you can see that the world beneath you is a beautiful land with lush green trees and blooming flowers. It is that magickal part of the astral world known as Faeryland.

Looking down, your eyes seem to be playing tricks on you. Just before reaching the bottom of the rainbow bridge you notice a very large, heavy, black cast iron pot. It is a cauldron, and it is filled to overflowing with silver and gold. The surface is so bright it is blinding, and you can barely make out the colored lights of precious gems within the crock. As you slide down you are sure you are going to land right in that cauldron, and a joy like you have never experienced before seizes you.

Then just as you are about to slide into it, it vanishes. The cauldron has faded and you slide off the rainbow and step lightly on to the beautiful, verdant green surface of Faeryland.

As you look around and take stock of of the environment, you feel a great peace. This is a place you might never want to leave. The part you have landed in is a land which is always spring. Several gardens near you have flowers in full bloom swaying gently in the light spring breeze. There are so many colors—many of them colors you have never seen before. And each flower is more beautiful and more interesting than the one beside it, as if they each have their own personality. The trees are a soft green, some of them flowering with white buds. In their heights brightly plumed birds sing sweetly under the sparkling blue, cloudless sky.

But birds don't seem to be all that is up in those trees. You peer up in the treetops, for there seems to be unusual movement in them. You shield your eyes and look more closely, fearing you'll miss something if you should even blink. There is movement up there—the small tree faeries you know to be Dryads are playing games, and they wave to you in greeting.

They are small and translucent; you see only their glowing outlines for more than a moment as the soft spring sunlight reflects off their shimmering forms.

On the air you seem to hear a sweet bit of music, a strain so entrancing that you want to find the source. You look around trying to figure out where it is coming from. You have never heard a sound so beautiful. Then all of a sudden you know that it is the music of the Dryads beckoning you to come play with them. The invitation is almost irresistible. But play is not the order of your business here, and you wish to meet some faeries who are doing more than playing. But more than that you want, with all your being, to find once again that dark, gold-stuffed cauldron.

You have enjoyed watching the Dryads, the faeries who taught the Druids about the magick of trees. Sometime you will return to try to discover more. But now you must move on.

A gentle breeze blows about you as you glide across the lush carpet of deep green grass. In this thick carpet of grass an even greener strip leads away from the woods where the Dryads call to you, and you follow this path. This is a faery path, the trail used for millennia by trooping faeries on their Rades.

But after a few steps you look back at your rainbow and hesitate. You are momentarily fearful of leaving the end of the bright rainbow which you know can take you home. But you know that the rainbow which links the astral to the physical is always there, and will surely appear whenever you need it. You resolve to continue on, and you follow along the dark green faery path.

You have not gone very far along when you see a young woman at the side of the road. She is no more than 16. Her long, golden hair falls around her delicate shoulders, and her eyes are a startling cornflower blue. She is dressed in a white, flowing gown, and on her head is a small silver crown. Her skin is young, creamy, and nearly flawless, but just above her left breast is a small birthmark in the shape of a waxing crescent moon. Rather than marring her complexion, however, it somehow seems to add to its luster.

This young princess seems to be oblivious to your presence. She is playing contentedly with nine young puppies, her complete attention focused on them. Three of the pups are black as ebony, three are a silky red, and the other three are white as milk. In the distance you can hear the distinct music of pan pipes and the unmistakable cadence of dancing feet.

You pause for a moment to listen to the distant music and to watch the princess play, then decide it is time to move on.

Feeling secure and happy in your quest, you move along in the spring world, content just to enjoy your surroundings. But somewhere along the side of the path you sense the presence of faery forms you do not wish to know. Occasionally you hear their nasty laughter from well back off the trail. You are at first quite fearful, but as soon as you resolve not to be afraid of them the sense of their presence fades.

You stay to the path, and as it curves gently along you see that it is taking you back into a gorgeous spring garden, more lush and more verdant than the ones you saw upon your arrival. You stop in awe. Before you as far as your eyes can see are flowers of every size and color, all being lovingly attended by tiny winged faeries.

Each little faery is about as tall as your shin, their gossamer wings golden and transparent. An auric light seems to surround each one like a ball of pure life energy.

One faery, a beautiful young woman wearing the silver crown of a queen, flies towards you, a welcoming smile on her lovely and serene face. In her right hand is a small wand with a silver star at its tip. The wand pulsates with the same life energy which surrounds the faery beings. She speaks without talking, and you are instantly aware of her thoughts. She is the Queen of the Spring Faeries. She explains that her legions are busily preparing the flora of spring for the Maiden Goddess.

"Bealtaine is always at hand here in the spring of Faeryland," her mind tells you. "And we are always busy doing what we love."

You look around and feel a strong, atavistic urge to be part of the joyous work as the tiny winged creatures, so delicate and achingly attractive, flit from flower to flower enticing each to open and painting on their bright spring colors. Some of the faeries are so attractive you feel a rush of primal drives. If you were only invited you feel you would have to fight not to remain forever in this world. Images of the Great Rite, the symbolic union of the male and female principles of creation, flash through your mind. In this spring world the mating call of nature is a never-ending pulse.

The Queen knows your thoughts and reminds you that this is not your world. "No mortal can be happy here for long," she says.

You want to protest. It is so lovely—one could stay here and be happy and young forever.

The Queen will not listen to your thoughts. "You are not the first to stop here and want to stay. Never can we figure out why. Our world which entices you so is so much less than your own multi-dimensional one. Never be led astray by those here who would wish to trap you. Their motives are not those of mutual help, but they are selfish and often cruel. Beware as you tread Faeryland. And remember, you are always welcome to visit our spring world. But you are not able to stay. A human spirit would wither and die here."

You don't see how this would be possible. The place fairly throbs with life energy, but you know you cannot argue with her—she will not listen to you.

"I sincerely hope we shall meet again and that we can be of help to one another," she says.

You tell her that you hope so, too, and again you feel that pull to stay in this lush and beautiful world. The Queen starts to fly away, but you beg her to stay for a moment as you wish to ask her about the cauldron of gold you saw at the rainbow's end as you entered Faeryland.

The Queen smiles sweetly. "The cauldron is always here in Faeryland. It always has been and always will be. It is here for the humans who seek it."

"Where can I find it?" you ask, trying not to sound anxious.

"Everyone who finds it finds it in a different place at a different time, and everyone must take a different path to get to it. And only a few are ever able to get close enough to even feel the touch of their fingertips on its rim, much less to take it."

"Take it to where?" you ask. "I thought it must remain here—in Faeryland."

"It does. But that part of it which is important will always be with you once you find it."

You look about you one more time, and you inhale the delicate scents riding on the luscious spring breeze which rocks the faeries gently on their flower tops as they work. You are ready now to move on, but you are uncertain as to which way to go.

The Queen suggests following the faery path along the same way you were heading. She wishes you luck on your journey and bids you beware of the "scaled ones."

Before you can ask what she is talking about she flies off, leaving you no choice but to follow the dark green trail she set you upon.

As you continue you become aware of the air growing heavier with dampness and much warmer. The golden sun up above is so bright that it almost obscures the blue sky. Several swampy areas lie just off the path and in their murky depths you see several frightful faeries—beings which look vaguely like humanoid crocodiles. You remember the Spring Queen's warning of scaled ones and move quickly along, even though you hear these fearsome creatures calling out to you. The murky depths of the swamps are covered in a gray mist, and though you have an unhealthy curiosity to have a closer look at the pool, you resist and move on. Eventually the swamps are behind you, and you find yourself in what looks like the country on a hot summer day. Just off the road your eye is caught by a dark rupture in the landscape. It is the opening to a cave. In the mouth of the cave sits a woman dressed in a loose red gown, her auburn hair falling softly about her, and around her head she wears a silver band with a bright silver orb in the center. Her stomach is distended with the final stage of pregnancy. Her right arm is lying over the top of her stomach, and her left is underneath as if she is trying to cradle the soon-to-be-born child. Her face is thoughtful and serene as she looks down at her stomach, and you feel very secure in her presence, even though she has not given any indication of having seen you.

At her feet is an array of summer fruits, and in the center, a silver chalice filled with a deep red wine. You continue looking at her for a moment, feeling very drawn to her, yet overcome with a sense of awe. Slowly, almost reluctantly, you begin to move along down the path.

Now the air grows even warmer, almost hot, as you pass through the summer landscape. On one side of the road a corn field rises up and fills the gently rolling ground clear to the far horizon. On the other side is a hilly grazing pasture with a lovely wood behind.

On the pasture side of the road a small woman, almost grotesquely deformed, is giving a sloe-eyed cow a drink of cool water from her cupped hands. Though she is ugly in appearance you recognize her as a Gruagach, a kind faery who watches over livestock. She looks up at you, and in her eyes you see sadness as well as kindness. When you don't flee in terror she seems to relax a bit, glad for a moment of your company.

"Welcome," she says. "Would you care for a drink of cool water? It is always so very hot here."

You know that to accept offers of food or drink in Faeryland could be dangerous, and so you decline politely. You do, however, approach the woman, knowing that you have nothing to fear from her.

The Gruagach sits down on a nearby rock and motions for you to join her. The heat is intense, but the view over the corn field is lovely. From this slight incline you can see a small lake on the other side of the corn field, and rows upon rows of orchards beyond that. It is a bountiful and abundant scene.

"The corn is waiting to be harvested by our Summer Faeries," the Gruagach explains. "Here Lughnasadh is always near and we are in preparation to honor our Goddess and God at this first harvest."

The golden-yellow corn silks shining in the sun remind you again of that elusive cauldron of gold, and you ask the Gruagach about it. "It is about somewhere," she answers, as if it matters little. "Few ever find it." She smiles kindly at you. "But I hope you do."

"How do I start?"

She peers into the distance and you are not even sure if she heard your question. It is several seconds before she speaks. "You must understand what you seek."

You don't understand what she is talking about, but you keep silent, hoping to encourage her to continue talking.

"You are in the astral world here. In Faeryland, but still in the astral world. This is where all ideas ever born live. Ideas, thought-forms, must necessarily precede creation. You must know what you seek for what it is, and you must know why you want it. If your thoughts can form these things you are on your way to finding it."

"Where do I start to look?" you ask, growing frustrated with the cryptic answers you have been receiving.

The Gruagach seems unable to answer. "Keep traveling," she advises. "Stick to this dark green faery path and do not be tempted away from it until you are ready. The way to the cauldron will be made clear in time. You had better continue on now before you wish to stay in this lovely land of perpetual summer. But remember that you are always welcome to speak with me anytime you come to Faeryland. I will welcome your company."

The Gruagach seems to have forgotten your presence as she continues tending the herd of cows, and you glide over to the dark green path again and follow it.

Again you are aware of danger lying just off the path, but you resolve to heed the Gruagach's words not to stray until you are ready. The trail seems to lead in a huge circle and you wonder what you might find next.

Along the sides of the path are thick woodlands, almost jungle-like in their appearance. All your psychic senses tell you that you are being watched as you move along. You glance furtively into the dense growth and are sure you see huge, gray-green eyes staring back at you, blinking at the bright sun. And you are sure you see the flash of large, sharp teeth and hear the cries of dark faeries better left unknown.

The path makes a large curve, and then comes out onto another field where chubby little faeries who look like elves with rosy cheeks are detasseling corn and plucking apples off trees. They seem unaware of your presence and you pass them by, following along the trail.

The air gets cooler and soon you begin to notice the telltale nip of autumn in the air.

In the woods just off the road you come upon an old satyr. He is sitting on a rock, his goat-like legs crossed in front of him, and around his horned head a mass of graying hair blows in the gentle autumn breeze. In his lap he holds a pan pipe, and at his cloven feet lie several sleepy woodland animals.

At first the figure strikes you as very sad. But then, though he never looks in your direction, you see his eyes. They are old, but in their dark brown depths is a light, a sparkle. They are merry and mischievous, and they shine as if in response to a warm and lusty memory. A slight smile plays about his lips, and he seems to be both reminiscing and anticipating all at once. Not wishing to intrude on his reverie, you move on.

The woods near the road grow more colorful, and soon you are walking within a splendid autumn wood ablaze with the vibrant colors of the season. Several huge old oak trees, their branches thick and stooped, overhang the path, giving you a feeling of protection and inner strength. In the distance just ahead you hear singing and are drawn to the merry sound. As you round a bend you find a delightful sight. Before you is a group of Gnomes tending to several ailing woodland animals. At first all appear to be startled by your unexpected presence, but then you are recognized as a friend. One tiny, round Gnome steps forwards and greets you regally. "Cead mile failte," he says, giving you the traditional Celtic greeting which means, "A hundred thousand welcomes." Then he goes on to tell you that he is the King of the Gnomes, and this ancient oak grove is their home.

The King is proud of his home, his woods, and his troop. They are always helping someone, because that is their mission in life, and he offers to be of service anytime you might need to call on him. He invites you to sit on the carpet of fallen leaves and rest for a moment.

You accept, and the dried leaves crunch pleasantly as you stop to rest. "Is this your first visit to our world?" he asks.

You answer him as best you can. "Faeryland is a beautiful place," you tell him. "Mostly," he agrees. "But there are dangers here and I advise you to be cautious. But we have little time to think about that. Samhain is always near and we are busy preparing the animals for winter."

You tell him you are aware of dangers and have protected yourself adequately. "Winter will soon be upon you," he cautions.

You know that Samhain is the start of the winter season, but you are prepared for whatever Faeryland gives you to deal with and you tell him so. Then, as with all the other friendly faeries you have met, you ask about that cauldron of gold which you cannot get out of your mind.

The Gnome King smiles knowingly. "So many come seeking that crock, mostly for the wrong reasons. They are all looking for things which the crock simply won't provide. But I think you are different. I think you might find it someday. But the search is long—sometimes it is many lifetimes long. And though you seem a sincere seeker, I doubt you can find it on this trip."

"I know that the gold inside is not what it appears to be," you tell him. A knowing smile spreads over his cherubic face. You continue, "And I know that to find it will be hard, and to possess that part of it which will benefit me is even more difficult."

The Gnome King nods. "You seem to know what it is you seek. Just remember two things: the choice is always yours whether you gain the crock and whether you lose it again. And never think that finding it is an end in itself. It is only a beginning. In these quests you are always at a new beginning."

You say that you want to continue looking anyway. The King seems to admire your persistence. "Keep your mind open and your heart giving, and you will find that and more," he says cryptically. "But as admirable as your search is, I suggest that you return to the mortal world now and come again later to find the crock. Ride the rainbow into our world anytime you like, and I will always be here to help you in any way I can. It is best to take Faeryland in short, small doses."

"But Your Majesty, there must be so much yet to see," you protest. "For one thing, I have not seen the winter of Faeryland yet."

A sort of hush falls over the happy autumnal glade, and you wonder for a moment if you have said something to offend your hosts.

"Winter is the harshest place in all of Faeryland for a human to endure. It can be a frightening place, fraught with more dangers than most are willing to risk."

You tell him you are able to return home immediately if there is anything you can't handle, and you beg him to point you in the direction of winter.

The Gnome King seems reluctant, but answers you calmly. "Follow on along the faery path—the same as you followed to get here. It will lead you to winter. But it is a long walk, and often the path will be hidden under a crusting of snow. You will have to watch carefully to remain upon it."

You know that the faery path is imperative to your safety. Keeping to it has been your guide so far, keeping you to the safe limits of this treacherous but alluring land. To lose it under snow would be unthinkable, but you tell him you will be on your way. Unlike the other faeries you have met who seem to forget your existence as soon as you turn to leave, the King asks you to wait for a moment and to step with him into the woods.

You follow him into another small clearing which has in the center of it a crystal clear pool of unspoiled water, the sort of pool which must have dotted the earth before humans polluted it so tragically. You lean down and touch the cool water, and it sparkles like diamonds as it falls from your fingertips.

"This is the Gnomes' scrying pool," he tells you. "If you are serious about seeking the cauldron, you might want to have a look into it just to see if there is any message for you about where the search might take you. This place is sacred to us. There is always something to be learned by all in this pool."

Intrigued by what you have heard, you sit by the bank on a pile of soft fallen leaves and gaze over the waters. The Gnome King seems in no hurry, and sits a bit away from you to wait for you.

You gaze at the clear pool with the soft autumn sun reflecting off its surface, and it is not long before that which you seek appears.

(Pause here for the pathworker to have time to scry into the pool. When the traveler has finished, you may continue.)

As the vision fades and you come slowly back to Faeryland, you spend a moment reflecting on the message of the pool (pause).

"I hope that has helped you," the King says. "I must get back to my people now."

You follow the King back to the oak grove with all the busy Gnomes and, turning to the King, you nod by way of thanking him for his hospitality, and start off when he calls out a warning: "Beware the rocky mounds."

The King returns to his work, and you start again along the dark green faery path.

You walk and walk, this time not hearing any laughter from the dark areas off the path. You are sure you are as completely alone as you have ever been, and for a moment you believe that the Gnome King was wrong about the dangers of this place. Then you see up ahead the first of many mounds of rocks piled high on the side of the path. At first they look no more menacing than ancient burial cairns, and you continue on unconcerned.

Then as you pass along between them you notice creatures sitting upon them, and peeking at you from around the rocky mounds. Their eyes glow with a malevolent gleam and you become on your guard for pranks and tricks. The creatures watch you pass without speaking, and you suddenly feel very vulnerable. The white light around you grows stronger, and you take solace in that fact. But the hideous and ill-tempered creatures are still there, so close you could reach out and touch them. Some appear to be only partially there, and you get the sense that they are not whole beings in any way you have been taught to understand the term. Others feel to you to be human discarnates who have stumbled onto this place and are locked into it, unable to leave or return to the earth.

They seem so near. They are attracted to you, to your energy, to your human life force. They know that to overpower you and merge with you would be their ticket out of here. A fear gnaws at your stomach which you quickly repress, knowing that these creatures will do nothing with that fear but feed off of it and grow stronger. No doubt this is part of their plan.

Up ahead of you, blocking your path, you occasionally get glimpses of things you wish to have. It is as if all your fondest hopes and dreams are being read right from your mind and tantalizingly manifested before you.

But you know these things are not real, they are merely thought-forms, maybe ones which you placed here yourself at one time. They are being used by these creatures to tempt you off the path and away from your goals. As you realize this, the glittering images fade, unable to sustain themselves in the face of your certain knowledge of what they really are.

You resolve now not to be afraid, and you continue on at a steady pace, and eventually the path leads you away from the rock mounds. The air has a definite chill to it and you know that the land of winter must be near. A crusting of snow covers the ground and you find it hard to keep track of the faery path. You are further hampered by the fact that it is growing darker. An eerie blue glow shrouds the edges of the world you move in, and you wonder if you ought to turn back, but the unsavory thought of passing by the cairns again makes you determined to press onward.

From above the woods on the side of the road the crescent of a waning moon rises and illuminates your path just enough that you can see. As the crescent rises in the night sky, its beam falls upon an charming old stone well. It looks like the wishing well of Mother Goose stories and you stray from the path to approach it.

Suddenly a form appears, sitting on the rim of the well, and you stop short, realizing that you should never have strayed from the safety of the faery path. Atop the well sits the most lovely faery you ever hope to see. This full-sized creature looks lovingly at you, and raises an arm in a come-hither gesture. You almost feel as if you could go with this faery and live as its mate forever. Its eyes glow with a hypnotic warmth, its lips are full and sensual, and its large eyes plead to you as a lover's.

It takes all your strength to back away from the well. In desperation you turn your back so as not to have to look at this object of great desire. You hurry back to the path and start on your way once more. Behind you the faery strikes up a mournful song that is so hauntingly beautiful that you put your hands over your ears and hurry along.

In the dark trees of the woods which surround you you can see small forms like living slivers of ice. These are the Frost Faeries painting the winter landscape for the Frost King. They are beloved of the Goddess and you stop to watch them in the dimness of the moonlight.

After a short while you move on down the path. The trees are completely bare now, and icicles hang from their dark branches, casting long spidery shadows over the moonlit path. You feel quite cold now, but are still glad you chose to come and have a look at the winter of Faeryland. Everything around you is quiet, all appears to be sleeping, and you wonder what winter Sabbat is always forthcoming here.

In the cold silence of the winter night a sound comes to you, a roaring noise, and you move onward knowing that it must lie in your path ahead.

The path continues onto a snowy beach. Ahead of you the dark waves crash against the rocky shore. And here the path ends. The waning crescent of the moon is now out over the water, and a line of golden light makes a stripe across the sea, as if in a continuation of the faery path on which you came. You have a feeling that if you were to walk out onto the water that you would be upheld and able to continue on. Yet the baneful faeries of the sea, the Merrows, no doubt also live in those deep waters and you do not want to risk encountering them.

The silence of the night is broken by the distant sound of an old cart creaking over a country road. In the distance your ears can detect a keening wail which at first sends a shiver of dread clear through you. Then you know that the cart is the vehicle of Death himself, coming to collect the mortal shells from those whose time in life is over. And you are forced to remember that winter and water are pagan symbols of death.

In the distance a small, half-frozen stream cuts through the woods. At its banks you can see another portent of death, the faint outline of a ghostly female apparition washing out a shroud in the icy creek. And you sense the close presence of the Beansidhe whose lamentations, which are still being heard, mean death is imminent. You look around at the deep, naked woods trying to decide from which direction the sound is coming. A sense of panic is upon you and you fear the Beansidhe cries for you. You have never thought much about your own mortality before, and now are forced to wonder. Suddenly you seem engulfed by the keening sound—it is everywhere. The wail is pervasive, and you fear for your own mortality.

Then, just when you feel you will give way to panic, the mournful cries sound less foreboding and more comforting. Your fear subsides, and you listen as the keening wail fades and moves on, warning others of the inevitable coming of death.

Yes, this winter of Faeryland is a dead place, but you know that in all death there is the promise of new beginning. To fear death is the curse of mortals whose far-sightedness has been allowed to perish, sacrificed on the altar of so-called progress. Death is not an ending.

Like these bare trees, you know that death awakens to new life, like nature in spring. You are sure now that Yule is the winter Sabbat which is always forthcoming, the time when darkness turns again to light, and death to life anew.

All is quiet again and you are trying to decide which way to go when suddenly, from the woods far behind you, you hear the unmistakable sound of horse's hooves beating on the winter-hard ground. The sound grows closer. You step back off the path as from out of the wood comes a large white horse with a lone rider heading straight towards you.

The horse is adorned with silver harness, its tail braided, and its eyes are deep and shiny like obsidian. On its back is a female rider wearing a robe of black. In her raised right hand she carries a staff painted in alternating shades of white, red, and black, topped by a small orb of purest silver light. On her left shoulder sits a large carrion crow, and her left hand, which holds the silver reins, is pulled loosely across her stomach.

As she races by she seems totally unaware of your presence. You look to see her face, but it seems lost to you, an ever-changing maze of time and ages. The horse continues galloping past you and rides straight into the sea. You expect the horse to slow to a walk as the heaviness of the water begins dragging it down. But instead the horse and rider are borne upon the water as if it were solid, and they continue riding out into the sea until they vanish from your sight.

And suddenly you make the connection between this place and that which you seek. Where there is death there is the Goddess in her Crone guise, and she, and she alone, possesses the cauldron of life and rebirth. You are now more sure than ever that that elusive crock must be nearby.

You are deciding the best method for searching for it when you are startled by a small but strong voice, which has snuck up behind you and calls you by name.

You turn and look down at a small dwarf faery. He is well dressed in a small green suit, and seems to be the only spot of light and color in this gloomy place.

"Please come with me," he tells you, with a lilt in his voice and a mischievous smile on his dimpled face.

His eyes seem to echo concern for you beneath the playful sparkle, and you agree to follow. He leads you deep into a woods so dark that you can barely see the little man, though he is but a few feet in front of you. A bit of panic rises inside you and you are just about to come completely undone when you spy flickering lights in the distance. They are the Will-O'-the-Wisps which have eluded humans since time began. They flicker on and off like fireflies all about you, and you realize you have totally lost any sense of direction. "How much further?" you ask.

There is no answer forthcoming, but you are glad that even though it is still dark, the air has taken on a spring-like warmth and you can no longer hear the gentle crunching of snow under your feet.

Now you see ahead of you, breaking the night like a crack, a bright light, a golden welcoming light, and you hear the faint sounds of revelry. As you follow the little creature into a clearing you see ahead of you a faery burgh opened up with all its lights ablaze. The sounds of happiness are all around you, and a party is clearly in progress under the burgh. And in the center of that burgh is the cauldron of gold which sparkles so enticingly, and then, as before, fades. "The cauldron!" you cry in disappointment.

The little faery who brought you here speaks. "I am the King of the Leprechauns. We help to guard the cauldron for the Crone Goddess. It is always with us."

That is the cauldron of the Goddess, just as you thought. And you tell the King, "How beautiful it is."

"People often come here—many by accident—looking for it. But they only want the material wealth they think it can provide. It never will, but those people cannot understand that. Because of its elusive nature we are regarded by humans as tricksters. But it isn't up to us who gets the cauldron. Only people can make that choice for themselves."

You ask, "And how do they do that?"

"By what is in their heart. That, and that alone, determines the fate of the crock. It fades by the will of the person seeking it and no other, though we are often blamed." You tell him you know that many of your kind seek for that which will never provide happiness.

"Do you know what is in that cauldron?" the King asks. You nod slowly, suddenly realizing all there is to know about the cauldron. "All things are in it," you reply with assurance. "That is the cauldron of life, death, and rebirth. To possess the crock is to possess spiritual attainments rarely won by humans. To possess the crock implies a great responsibility to oneself and to all living things. To possess it is to unite with the Goddess in her most powerful form."

And suddenly you remember the black-robed rider galloping into the western sea—the Crone? Could that have been the Crone Goddess showing you the way to the crock? Your mind races ahead with all sorts of ideas which will have to be put aside to be sorted through at another time.

The Leprechaun King smiles. He is pleased with your answer. "Though we guard the cauldron, we—faery folk, that is—can never possess it. Only humans have that ability, and so many waste it. You are a seeker who is welcome here. Please join in our festivities for as long as you like."

The Leprechaun King bows deeply and doffs his hat to you, and you are again struck by his mischievous nature, regardless of his protests to the contrary.

You cautiously enter the warmly lighted burgh, and you remember that time in this astral realm has no meaning. For this reason you are wary at first of joining in, especially since you know that accepting food, drink, or joining in the dancing can be a dangerous trap of time. But you know how to protect yourself, and you sit on the edge of the burgh and laugh and join the merriment until you feel it is time to return.

(You may pause here if you wish to allow the pathworker time to enjoy the Leprechauns' party.)

"I must go now," you announce, and stand to leave.

The revelers want you to stay, but you know you must not allow them to detain you past the time you know is right to leave. You remember that it is considered offensive to thank faery folk for any aid they give you. You feel rude just leaving, but those are the rules and you sense that your understanding and respect of their customs is appreciated.

"I shall take you back to the rainbow," the Leprechaun King offers. "Touch my green coat and we shall be at its base."

At first you hesitate, but then you slowly reach out to gently touch the costly cloth, and in an instant you are at the bottom of the rainbow in the lush sunlit world where you first came into Faeryland. You look around for the Leprechaun King, but he is nowhere to be seen. But on the air you hear the gentle lilt of Irish laughter, and you smile. The trickster king is on his way home, but you know you and he will meet again.

Looking around at the beauty of this astral place, you long to see such beauty in everyday life. But you are weary from your travels and find that now you are anxious to be home, and you start up the rainbow.

Stepping off as light as the very air, you fly back up the rainbow, watching the astral world disappear in the white mist. It no longer pulls at you to remain in it, and you are anxious to return home. Up and up you fly; only you and the rainbow can be seen in the mist around you. You feel the pulsating glow of the protective energy around you, and know that you are about to return safely to your body and to your normal waking consciousness. You are looking forward to being soon able to contemplate and record your feelings and experiences from this powerful pathworking.

Soon you again reach the apex of the rainbow bridge. When you do, you sit to slide down the other side, back into your waiting body.

Down you go. Riding as if on air, through the mist, down, down, down. And as you travel downward the air becomes thicker and denser, and a sense of solidity begins to make itself known. Below you the barest traces of the physical world are starting to become clear to you. And down, down, down you slide.

You can now look below you and see your home. You know where you are and are ready to finish the journey.

You hop off the end of the rainbow bridge and fly gently down toward your home. You enter the ceiling of the room in which you lie as if asleep, and begin to remember the sensation of being a living, corporeal human being. You again see your resting body surrounded by the golden light, the pentagram, and the shield, all of them doing their job for you just as they were when you left.

You move slowly over your waiting body, as glad to see it as if suddenly discovering an old friend. And you melt into it, saying to yourself the words, "I AM HOME."

Feel the awareness of your physical self return—your legs, arms, back, stomach, and neck. Flex them and relish the joy of being a living human being.

You are once again part of the waking physical world, and you open your eyes and feel exhilarated, energized, and glad to be home.

(Make a loud noise like clapping your hand or ringing bells to alert your subconscious that you have returned to your normal consciousness. This helps prevent any bleed-over between the two worlds and may frighten away any astral entities who have followed you home. Then it is wise to make whatever statement you or your tradition normally use to end rituals, such as "It is Done" or "The Rite is Closed" to further get the message across that you are back in the physical world.)

Part Two

Working with Faery Beings

A guide to the day-to-day working relationship between a witch and the Little People.

Chapter Five

Spells and Rituals for You and the Little People

You have already learned how and where to "see" faeries, how to recognize both the friendly and foul ones, and how to protect yourself in any case. Now it is time to reclaim the pagan tradition of actually working magickally and ritually with these beings.

Faeries in Spellcraft

Why use faeries in spellwork? Witches who have done just fine weaving magick without them are probably wondering why they ought to add faeries to their already complex spells and rituals.

No one *ought* to add faery energy to anything. But keep in mind that faeries represent the raw elements of nature, the same elements we use as building blocks when creating our spells and rituals. And faeries live in the astral world, the place where all magickal energy first takes on the shape and scope it will have in the physical world. When we make magick we send out energy—part of ourselves—into the faeries' home world where any influence they provide for good can be a great boon to us.

Faeries can aid you in many ways in your spellwork. They are adept at raising energy, which means they can give aid for nearly any magickal cause, and a few of them are in service to various deities whom they can help you contact.

Faeries can act as a substitute coven for solitary witches who either don't have contact with other pagans or who choose to work alone. Any extra energy added to your spells helps their effectiveness—the more participants, the better.

Faeries are most adept in spellwork for environmental concerns, healing, fertility, and protection. With only one exception, the Moerae of Greece, they are not good with romantic love spells; this is an emotion which is totally alien to them.

Much spell lore concerning faeries talks about doing spell details in multiples of five rather than in multiples of three, which is the number more familiar to western pagans. Five is a number which plays a large part in faery lore, and it may even be a number which is sacred to them. If it pleases the faeries you are working with, then go the extra mile and use the image of five wherever you can. Repeat a spell five times, use five lit candles, gather five herbs, walk five times around your altar, or lead them in a dance five times around your circle.

All spellwork with faeries should be done within the safe confines of your circle, with the faeries just outside its perimeter. As in any magickal working, all your tools and equipment should be inside the circle with you, laid out on something which is serving as your altar. Do not break the circle for any reason. This is a long-standing rule which is wise to follow. A circle contains and focuses your raised energy until you are ready to release it, and it prevents unwanted entities—ones attracted to the energies you have raised—from coming in. Faeries have capricious natures, and even the most helpful ones will often give in to the urge to play a trick. While you are raising energy for magick is not a good time to have this happen. Play it safe. Stay inside your circle.

The following is a quick guide to the faery forms best known for aiding in certain endeavors. Check the dictionary in this book for more information on how to contact and work with each one.

Healing animals
Brown Men
Gnomes
Vilas
Zips

Healing people
Brown Men
Chi Spirits
Gnomes
Vilas

Protection of animals
Bean-Tighe
Brownie
Dinnshenchas
Gnomes
Gruagach
Korreds
Masseriol
Twlwwyth Tegs
Vasily
Zips

Protection of people
Bean-Tighe
Brownie
Dinnshenchas
Gwragedd Annwn
Korreds
Twlwwyth Tegs

Prosperity spells
Brownie
Gnomes
Leprechaun

Protection of home
Bean-Tighe
Brownie
Chin-Chin Kobakama
Clurichaun
Domoviyr
Geancanach
Kolbalds
Penates
Twlwwyth Tegs
Tomtra
Wag-by-the-Way

Travel/lost objects
Gnomes
Klaboutermannikin
Knockers
Merpeople

Fertility spells
Bean-Tighe
Gnomes
Gruagach

Environmental aid
Alven
Gnomes
Lesidhes
Wilde Frauen

General ritual aid
Gwragedd Annwn
Jimaninos
Nymphs
Thussers
Tomtra

Divination
Dryads
Gnomes
Menehunas
Mother Holle

Earth Magick
Gnomes

Air Magick
Sylphs

Spirituality and petitioning deities
Dryads
Gnomes
Gruagach
Irish Sea Water Guardians
Korreds and Pyrenees
The Lady of the Lake
Leprechauns
Menehunas
Mother Holle
Nibelungen
Oak King and Santa Claus

Marine environmentalism
Alven
Fin Folks
Irish Sea Water Guardians
Merpeople

Love spells
The Moerae

Aid in astral projection
Dryads
Mother Holle

Gaining physical energy
Chi Spirits
Tomtra

Fire Magick
Drakes
Geancanach
Salerandees
Salamanders

General magick
Cailleac Bhuer
Elves
Jinn
Menehunas
Mother Holle
Robin Goodfellow
Tuatha de Danann
Urisks

Water magick
Undines

Virtually any spell can be adapted to add faery energy. Read the rest of this chapter for ideas and then check the bibliography and suggested reading list at the back of the book for the names of books which focus on natural magick. Appendix Two contains an outline for spell construction to help you create your own spells with or without faeries.

How to Create Your Own Faeryland Residence

If you want to work with faeries on a regular basis, it may be a good idea to give yourself an astral residence on the edge of their world, a place where you and they can meet safely and securely. After all, these are creatures of the astral world, and such a place makes a good middle ground on which you can gather.

This is similar to the idea of the astral temple which many pagans already use, but it is really an idea which we adopted from ceremonial magick. These temples are places in the astral world where a magician or witch can go to meditate, work spells, and perform rituals, but instead of doing them physically, they allow their astral body to do the work. The temples of ceremonial magick tend to be of stone, glass, and marble, and are archaic, formal, and linear.

Pagans should not hesitate to adopt this idea, but would probably be more comfortable using a more natural setting. A pagan astral temple, more aptly referred to as a residence, can be a small cottage or chalet in a woods or on a mountain top. Much of what is placed there will be a reflection of the witch's tradition and personal tastes. Celtic witches might prefer a thatched roof cottage, Germanic witches a chalet in the Alps, and African witches a hut in the Veldt.

Create your astral residence near, but not in, Faeryland. It will serve not only as a place to meet with faeries but to work spells, hold rituals, meet friends and other entities, and live a magickal life unavailable to the vast majority of us in the everyday waking world.

Creating this residence is as simple as imagining, and each visit to your special place will strengthen its form and content. While in

a meditative state or while astral projecting, create it by picturing the sort of place you need and all its surroundings. Infuse it with your energy and mold it with your creative mind in the same way you would create a spell. Spend lots of time with the details and watch it take on a life of its own, becoming a very real place.

A witch's astral residence should contain all these things to be effective for every need:

1. A small home in accordance with your tradition. It can contain several rooms, but the main room should be the one you enter when coming through the front door.

2. The main room of your house must have a fireplace with a large black cauldron (a Goddess image) over the glowing fire, and herbs of all types drying near it and on the rafters. These will be used in spells later on at your discretion.

3. You will need a cupboard containing a good supply of candles, incense, and other magickal supplies.

4. Somewhere in the house you need a small altar, decorated in any manner you or your tradition dictates.

5. Outside you should have a woods nearby which you can go into to worship, gather herbs, walk, or meet faeries and other entities.

6. You should have a place where you can cast a circle somewhere near your house. You can mark it with stones, runes, or any other items which please you.

7. You should have a small stream or lake nearby for water spells.

8. There should also be the entrance to a cave nearby. Cave images figure heavily in many guided meditations, and may be needed in future inner plane work.

9. You may add animals, barns, or any other outside accouterments you wish.

10. Since the main purpose of this place is to meet faeries, you should have a path which leads from your house to the boundaries of Faeryland.

11. And lastly, you should surround this place with a bubble of protective energy. Set up mental pentagrams, encase everything in a white-gold egg of energy, or set up faery beings to protect it. Do whatever you feel makes it a safe place to be.

This astral residence is a place you can go to anytime you choose during astral projection or meditation, a place to both work and relax. It is your sacred spot, a retreat away from everyone and everything. To keep it from fading, visit it at least once a month and renew the life-giving energy, and with each visit, returning will be easier and all your workings there more effective.

A Special Faery

While in your astral residence you can develop a relationship with one special faery. Read the dictionary section and decide which faery or faeries you would like most to meet and work with. Then read the part on how to contact them. If they respond to invitations, then call them to you in your astral residence. You might also set out items or do whatever else is known to attract the faery you wish to meet. When it appears, feed it, or do whatever is known to keep them happy and around.

Eventually, when the two of you are comfortable together, ask its name and what you can do for it. Slowly you will develop a relationship which can be mutually rewarding. The faery will have a safe and reliable home, and you will have a contact and liaison in the world of faeries.

Other faeries, curious about what you are doing on the edge of their world, will come and go from time to time, and your special faery friend can help you get to know and work with each of them.

Raising Energy

Raising energy is where faeries do some of their best magickal work. When you have called the faeries to your circle (Chapter 3 gives several methods if you do not have one you like at hand), tell them that you wish to raise energy. This energy can later be directed anywhere you like and into any spell.

How do you touch their hearts and make them want to join you? Just politely state your intention to them before you begin, and ask their help. If they wish, they will join in. Another helpful hint might be to explain to them why what you are doing is important to you, especially if it is a spell for something personal. Faeries loathe human greed and treachery, but will gladly help you if eradicating these things is your goal.

So how do you get them to raise energy with you? Drumming is an old tried and true method of raising energy, one which faeries like as long as there are no bells or tambourines ringing on your drum. Start with a steady, plodding beat, then slowly increase the tempo and the sense of urgency. Faeries at your circle will respond to this beat by dancing or even by singing which, if you are psychically sensitive enough, you will be able to hear.

Another way to enlist faery aid is by appealing to their sense of fun. Most faeries love to dance, and dancing is another time-honored way of raising energy. Tradition dictates that one dance deosil (clockwise) for spells of increase or attraction, and widdershins (counterclockwise) for decreasing or banishing spells.

After the faeries are assembled at your circle and you are ready to raise the energy, you should walk to each of the four directional quarters of your circle in turn and encourage them to dance with you. Always start with the first direction you evoked when your circle was cast. Faeries will understand this sense of protocol and will accept it. Changing the game plan in mid-ritual will only cause jealousies and confusion among them.

Stand facing the first direction, and with your arms raised, address the faeries as individuals and not as merely a collection of elemental energies. Remember, these are invitations and not demands. You cannot control the faeries by commanding them. Put a smile on your face and keep a cheerful voice. Remember that ritual is not all serious, especially to fun-loving faeries.

Invite the faeries to dance using words something like this:

Faeries, my friends of the (name direction), will you rise now and dance with me as we build together the cone of power?

If you have a drum, start now to pound out the steady beginnings of a rhythm. Few faeries can resist drumming and they will begin to dance. If you don't have a drum, turn on some music or play an instrument. You can even hum the slow opening bars of what will soon grow to be a sprightly tune.

Turn to the next direction and make the same invitation. Before you make the final plea you should already start to feel the energy of the faeries building just outside your circle.

Start the dance at a steady and stately pace, using whatever accompanying music you wish. Then slowly begin to speed up the pace, continuing until you can literally feel the mass of energy raised above you like a giant inverted cone. As you wind around your circle, you should be able to sense the added energy the faeries are creating. Mentally store it up around your circle and add it to the cone of power you are building.

The cone of power is the witch's vortex of magickal energy, raised and contained within a ritual circle by one or more witches working for the same goal. This idea of a cone of energy over the heads of witches is the image that gave rise to the popular patriarchal myth of the Halloween witch with her pointed hat.

When the energy has reached its peak, concentrate on the goal and release the energy where it is needed, or simply send it into the world of the unformed to manifest in the physical later. To do this, simply focus the cone outward with your mind and with your body. Feel the tension in your body immediately drain, your muscles relax, and your breathing slow as the mass of power is released.

Adapting Spells for Faery Participation

There are several ways to enlist faery aid in spellwork. The most effective way is also the most time-consuming, but any spell worth doing should be worth this extra investment. This is a meditative method whereby you take with you into Faeryland the astral portion of the tools you will use in your spell.

Go into a meditative state with the objects you will be empowering on your physical person. These will be objects such as candles, herbs, stones, pieces of paper, incense, etc. Go to your astral residence and set up an altar or other working space outside in the wild. While standing in front of the altar, call out to a faery you have chosen to aid you. Ask that the faery come to you to aid you in positive magick.

Within a short time an individual or a small group should appear. If not, return home and try again later. When someone does

show up, explain exactly what you are trying to accomplish and ask that the faeries lend their energies to the spell.

Allow the faeries to do whatever is needed. They may wish to handle the candles, herbs, or other objects you have brought with you, they may dance around you, or they may even want to touch you. As long as you feel comfortable with the proceedings do not interrupt them. If your residence is adequately protected no ill-meaning faeries should be able to come near. However, if you do become uncomfortable or suspicious you need only to return immediately to your physical body to break the contact.

When the faeries have finished with whatever it is they wish to do, do not thank them verbally, but set out gifts for them. Milk, butter, bread, and honey are most appreciated. So are birdseed and precious stones.

While you are still at your astral residence, cast a circle and do whatever spell you intended to do. The faeries may or may not gather near your circle. Don't worry if they don't. They have already given you whatever help they want to give. To push them would be considered very rude.

When you return to the physical world, do the ritual again just as soon as you feel strong enough.

Another method is to call the faeries to your circle side and get them to dance or do anything else which will raise energy, energy which you can direct to whatever cause you choose.

You can also induce them to chant or sing with you as you empower your magickal objects. This is done similarly to the method used to get them dancing. Simply start the tune and encourage them to join in. Use folk tunes for the best results, as many such tunes are thought to have been composed by faeries in the first place. Feel free to change the words to suit your need. For example, if you are planning on doing a prosperity spell you might sing these words to the tune of "The Yellow Rose of Texas":

> *There's a bankbook full of money,*
> *It's there for all to see.*
> *I'm in the red no longer,*
> *I'm rich enough for me.*

I need this cash to live on,
Enough to house and feed.
My worries are all over,
I have just what I need.

Grab a sheet of paper and play around with parodies. Don't worry if your words seem silly. Silliness appeals to faeries and will make them all the more likely to join your cause.

The other way you can induce faery aid in your spell work is by using objects which you find in nature. Go out to a park, woods, or other wild, natural place and look for stones, herbs, etc., to use in your spells. It is better to find these items yourself rather than buy them at a store, since some of their natural potency may be lost through exposure to other energies, many which may have been inadvertently negative.

Whenever you take anything out of the wild or cut a plant, it is traditional for a witch to explain to the plant or stone why this is being done, ask its permission for its sacrifice, and then thank it by leaving a gift nearby such as animal food, a precious stone, or a coin. When you want to work with faeries you have to add another dimension to this—you have to ask the faeries if it is all right to remove the object. Check in the dictionary for faeries who are likely to inhabit rocks, trees, or the herbs you are seeking to remove. Place yourself in a light meditative state and ask the faery's permission. You will get a feeling whether this is or is not granted. You may even be swayed to another object to take its place. If this happens, then accept it graciously and check out the exchange later in a botany or lapidary book.

You are, of course, free to take any plant or stone you like after satisfying the tradition of placating the tree, bush, or plant itself, but if you want faery aid in the spell, you must take an extra step. When you ask to remove the object, also ask that the faeries of the area leave their blessings and energies in the object so they can aid you in working toward your magickal goal. As simple as this seems, it is one of the most overlooked but potent ways to add faery energy to any spell.

Healing Spells

Healing is another area in which faeries can help you. In ancient Cornwall, faeries with healing powers were believed to live near the standing stones called Men-an-Tol. These consist of one large, upright phallic stone, and an equally large circular stone with a hole in the center. Persons used to pass themselves through the stone nine times for healing. But since you are working with faery energies, pass yourself through only five times to involve their sacred number. Do this ritual in the astral for results which are every bit as good as being there in the physical.

Other healing spells can use faery energy by following any of the above-mentioned methods of enlisting their aid. If you don't already have a healing spell which you are fond of using, here is a basic one to use or adapt.

You will need a blue or purple candle, matches, a knife or other instrument with which to carve on the candle, a handful of dirt in a bowl, a small square of paper, and a pencil. If the spell is for someone other than yourself, you will need that person's photo or some other object which contains their vibrations or personal energy on which to focus your thoughts.

When you have done whatever preliminary rituals you or your tradition dictate and are ready to work the spell, take the candle and empower it with healing energy. Do this by focusing your thoughts on total wellness and health. Visualize yourself or the sick person as whole, healthy, and full of life energy. As you do this, take the knife and carve as well as you can a representation of wellness. This can be done in any form you like. You can draw a rune, write a word such as "wellness," make a full circle or a horn of plenty, or if you are a good artist and your candle is wide enough, you can draw a picture of the person to be healed.

Set the candle upright in the dirt.

Take the matches and hold them high up over your head and say these words:

> *I, (state your craft name), call upon all the powers that be that the healing energy which is my right is now mine (or state the person's name). As this candle is consumed, so is*

the illness. As the candle is transformed, so am I (or state the person's name). I know that my words and energies have been carried into the unseen world and will now manifest in the physical realm.

Strike the match and bring it down to light the candle. Spend as much time as you can gazing into the light and visualizing the illness being eaten away as the candle is consumed by the flames. See the earth underneath the candle absorbing any negative energy not devoured by the fire. You want to feel that not one speck of sickness is left behind.

When you have put all the energy into the spell, you can finish by saying something like "So Mote it Be" or "It is Done." Both of these signal your deep mind that you are returning to normal consciousness and that you know your magick has worked, and they are traditional pagan words of completion.

Faeries can also help direct you to proper herbal medicines. Go to a wild wooded place and put yourself into a light meditative trance by relaxing and concentrating upon your goal of finding an appropriate herbal cure. After a time open your eyes and look around for signs. A wiggle of a branch or the sparkle of a ground leaf may be a sign.

When you feel you have been led to an herb, *do not* immediately consume it. First, talk to the plant and go through the traditional rite of telling it why you need its sacrifice. When permission is granted, cut it cleanly without allowing it to touch the ground. It is a good idea to wear some protective gloves when you do this to protect your hands not only from allergens, but from thorns, insects, or any other unpleasantries you might otherwise contact. Wrap the herb in a clean cloth and take it home, to a library, or to the biology department at a nearby college for identification. *Never* eat any plant you can neither identify nor understand how it will affect you.

Once you know what it is, you can look up its healing properties in an herbal medicine guide. Chances are excellent that if a kind rather than a mischievous faery aided you in your find, that it will be just the cure you are looking for. But sometimes faeries, with their puckish sense of humor, use these herbs to tell you something they think you need to know. For example, if the herb you picked to cure your recurrent headaches has the side-effect of making one giddy, you may be being told to change your attitude and outlook if you really want a cure.

The more intelligent faeries can often lead you to the right page of an herbal remedy guide which will tell you the best course of action to take. Try taking such a book out on a breezy day and laying it open. Call out to the faery you wish to aid you (Gnomes are always a good choice) and tell it what you need. Then close your eyes and allow the breeze to blow the pages about. When you feel compelled to do so, put your right forefinger down on the page and see where you landed.

As with any magick, do not expect it to be a panacea for all ills. Use it only as a solid support to other medical treatments and a healthy lifestyle.

Fertility Spells

The fertility of plants, animals, and humans was of great concern to our ancestors, and many of these spells are still with us, most of them associated with the Sabbat celebrations which were largely community fertility rites.

In this day of modern farm techniques, irrigation, sophisticated weather prediction, scientific animal husbandry, and pet overpopulation, we have little to worry about on the score of animal and plant fertility. It is the human fertility rate which has declined significantly over the past several decades, with an estimated one out of ten couples unable to have any or as many children as they would like.

It is a wise idea never to work fertility magick with any faeries who have been known to harm, or suspected of harming, children. This is just common sense. Their energies are not compatible with your final goal. To ensure this doesn't happen, it is best to take your magickal object into the astral world yourself to ask faery blessings within the protection of your astral residence.

If you do not have a fertility spell of which you are fond, try the following:

You will need an incense burner, matches, a large piece of plain paper, a green pencil or a pen with green ink, and a small fireproof bowl. For the incense you will need any three of the following items: mugwort, bistort, patchouly, vervain, sandalwood, willow, moonwort, poppy seeds, jasmine, lotus, pine, cedar, rice, wheat, or nuts. You can also use commercially prepared incense in any one of these scents.

When you are ready to do the spell, get comfortable in front of all the assembled objects. It is probably best to do this one while sitting at a table. Empower all the objects to be used with your energy by holding them and visualizing their purpose.

Toss the incense on the hot coals or light the commercial incense while saying these words:

> *Herbs of earth,*
> *Incense of air,*
> *Bless this spell,*
> *For a child so fair.*
> *Water and fire,*
> *Mix with these,*
> *Manifest my wish,*
> *Just as I please.*

Spend just a moment feeling the fertile vibrations of the incense. See them surrounding you, infusing you with fertility.

Set the sheet of paper before you. You will be drawing pictures on both halves, so save enough room to do this. On the right side— the side of yourself used to project energy—you will begin drawing a picture representing you as you are now, without your magickal goal. You are using the right side of the paper so that you can project these negative things away from yourself.

Do not skimp on this exercise. Take enough time to feel that you have infused the picture with all the negative qualities that are or may be blocking your fertility.

Now move to the left side of the paper—the side of your body that is receptive and is used to draw things to you—and draw a picture of your fertility goal. As you did with the right side, make the picture as complete as you can and infuse it with all your hopes and dreams. Be sure to keep up your visualization as you draw.

When you feel that this is finished, tear the paper in two so that the pictures are separated. Fold the left half into a small square which you can carry around with you and look at periodically, reinvesting your energy into its image. Take the right half and toss it face down into the fireproof bowl. Take your matches and say:

The old image is banished,
Transformed by fire.
With me I keep
My heart's desire.

Tuck the left side drawing as close to yourself as you can, and light a match to the right half. Watch it burn and feel that you are now without those interfering energies.

Wedding cakes were once a part of pagan fertility rites. If you are about to be handfasted and fear future fertility problems, offer a piece of your wedding cake as a libation to the faeries in exchange for them sending you magickal energy for fertility.

If you have a garden or farm that you wish to have benevolent faeries bless with fertility, then leave their favorite foods out in the garden for them. Do not toss these out like you might for an animal. Instead, set them out on a plate or in a bowl and say aloud that this is a gift to the blessed faeries of the garden. Please be kind to any faeries or animals who come to partake of your offering by not poisoning them with chemical fertilizers and toxic herbicides.

You can further persuade faeries to want to bless your garden by doing them a similar favor, such as periodically sending healing energy to their beloved natural sites such as the rainforests, rivers, and parks we humans are destroying.

Protection Spells

Though many protection spells are used against baneful faeries, there are many other faeries who value a safe and secure environment as much as you do. Household faeries such as Brownies or Clurichauns want to keep the home you share peaceful and happy. They will gladly lend their energies to raising a shield of protection around your dwelling. If you have one of these in residence, it is probably already looking out for your home; if not, all you need to do is ask it.

Because of the elemental nature of faeries most of them prefer to protect plants and animals, but a number of them will watch over you or your children. The Bean-Tighes, Korreds, or Dinnshenchas are good faeries to call upon when you feel the need for added protection. To enlist their help, cast your circle and ask them to come to you. Offer them food, warmth, or your home, and tell them what you need and why. Then do a general protection spell for yourself.

A good protection spell is one which raises all the defenses you can muster—faeries included. Try the following spell if you don't have one at hand.

You will need a mirror, a white taper-style candle, matches, nine inches of black thread or string, any one ritual tool, and a fireproof bowl to set the candle in.

When you are ready to do the spell, assemble all the items in front of you on your altar or some other flat, smooth surface. Cast your circle about you and do any preliminary rituals you feel you need to do according to your personal taste or tradition.

Hold the black thread in front of you. Black is a color which has the ability to absorb energy the same way it absorbs heat in summer. Pour into it all your fears, uncertainty, and hesitation, and fill it with all the other reasons you feel you need personal protection. When you feel the thread has absorbed as much of this as it can hold, tie it around the body of the candle about halfway down.

Place the candle in the fireproof bowl and set it where the mirror will reflect its light. Spend a moment investing the candle with all the protective qualities of the color white. Think of the black thread around it as the fear that is binding your natural protective energies. When you are ready, light the candle and say these or similar words:

Candle of light,
Protection of white,
Free me from fear,
By day and by night.
Candle of white,
Protective light,
I will myself safe,
With all of my might.

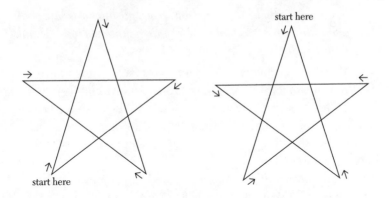

Banishing and invoking pentagrams.

As the candle burns, visualize your own protective energies returning to you, and the mirror reflecting away any negative influences still around you. As they fly out of your circle, visualize little earth faeries catching them and taking them safely into the earth to be grounded.

Now reinforce your own protective energy by holding your chosen tool in front of you and drawing a banishing pentagram, one which will dispel the last vestiges of negativity which may still be around you.

Now sit down and watch the candle burn. Draw from it renewed strength. Eventually the candle will burn down to the black thread and then through it, symbolically releasing you from your fears and clearing your own natural protective aura to work for you. When the string is broken, feel the burst of energy within you as you are free again to allow your own natural protection to break through.

Now stand and draw before you an invoking pentagram. Begin drawing it from the top point down in order to invoke, or bring down, the divine energy from the deities. Feel their energy enter your body.

If you wish, you may pray to your favorite God or Goddess and ask their protective blessings. It can sound something like this:

Blessed Lady Brigid (or insert your own patron deity's name here), I draw from you your strength and energy.

Send your shield to guard me from all harm, wrap your arms about me, cloak me with your bounteous love. Thank you, Bright Lady. So Mote it Be!

If you would like to add some extra faery energy here, you can ask their blessings also. You might ask an individual faery whom you have gotten to know to watch over you until the crisis has passed. Tell the faery you will keep him or her well fed and housed in return. Remember that this faery is not a deity, and reciprocity is the key to getting along with it.

Aside from you, your children, and your home, faeries can look after pets and livestock as well. For some faeries, this is their only preoccupation and it is easy to take advantage of this natural affinity.

Call upon the Gnomes, Bean-Tighe, Vasily, Zips, Masseriol, or the Gruagach to look after your pets. Maybe you have a sick dog left all alone while you work, or a lost cat, or an expensive farm animal who tends to wander off. All of these are good candidates for faery protection. While in a meditative state, contact one of these faeries and ask that it look out for your pet when you cannot. You will probably find that you get an immediate response because of the love they have for animals. And animals, with their natural psychic abilities, will sense they are being looked out for and won't feel so alone, which will help keep them healthy and happy.

Prosperity Spells

As with the protection spells, the earth faeries who like humans and seek to share their homes are the best ones to call upon to aid prosperity spells. After all, if you prosper then their environment improves, too.

Since money and security have been a primary concern of people for a lot of centuries, there are many prosperity spells available in most any book on magick or witchcraft, most of which have disappointed more than a few witches.

Magick works best when there is a deep need which creates a strong emotional attachment between the witch and the object sought. Wishing for money just to have it, to gain power, or to lord your booty over others will very likely not manifest. And if you want to ask faeries to bless your endeavors, keep in mind that most of them loathe human greed and will punish anyone who indulges in this behavior. Ask only for what you really need.

For this prosperity spell you will need a needle and thread, two spheres of green cloth or felt about three inches in diameter, a pen, and a crisp new dollar bill. Make sure you have taken all these objects into Faeryland to be charged by the Wee Folk who will help you achieve your goal.

When you are ready to begin, hold the dollar in front of you in your left hand and feel it growing and expanding as if it is becoming more and more money. Feel the security it brings you. Visualize all your bills paid in full. Remember the principle of sympathetic magick—like attracts like. You are going to use this dollar as a catalyst for others.

When you are through visualizing, take the two pieces of green cloth and begin to sew them together. Think about them as you do, focusing all your concentration on drawing prosperity into yourself. You can even hum or sing a song about money to help you stay focused. If you don't know one, make one up. When you have sewn almost completely around the circle, stop, and with the pen, write the amount of money you need on the dollar and stuff it in the opening. Then sew up the pouch the rest of the way.

Continue to hold it in your hand for a moment or two while thinking of it as a full wallet. Picture yourself secure and prosperous. Now hold it up before you and say these or similar words:

Needed money, come to me,
Fulfill my urgent, desperate need.

Repeat this chant over and over until you feel you have put as much energy and emotion in the spell as possible. Plan to carry the amulet on your person until your need manifests.

Another prosperity spell you can do requires only four silver coins (partially silver will do). To demonstrate to the faeries that you are not being greedy, take three of the four coins outside and place them at the base of a large old tree, the sort that faeries would be likely to want to live in. Then take the fourth one, and, while you are still outside, ask the faeries' blessing on your need. Then go home and bathe with the other coin in your bath water.

Attempt to invite a friendly house faery such as a Brownie or Bean-Tighe into your home to further add prosperity, because they are both considered very lucky to have around.

Love Spells

As already mentioned, faeries are not good about lending their energies to love spells as, for them, this is an alien emotion. But the Greek triple faery, the Moerae, is an expert in matters of the heart.

Remember that when you do a love spell you must only ask for the right mate for you and not for some specific person whose heart may be committed elsewhere or who is just not interested. Never attempt to violate someone's free will by coercing them with a compelling love spell. Such manipulation always backfires in the end because it is a violation of the Pagan Rede. It is perfectly all right to dwell on the qualities of someone you admire, or even to ask for someone whom you care about to notice you so that you might at least have a chance with them. But do not try to coerce anyone's feelings.

Simple matchmaking, finding the right person for you and bringing the two of you together, is the basic idea behind love spells. And since matchmaking is the forte of the Moerae, you should have no trouble conforming love spells to this faery's special talents.

For this spell you will need several photographs of imaginary mates. Cut them from magazines or newspapers. As you cut them out try to picture something about them that attracts you. Maybe you like their kind eyes, or their self-confident smile, or maybe you want a mate with the same shy demeanor that the photo projects. Give yourself several choices.

To petition the Moerae you will need three candles of the same color and size. Medium-sized tapers in blue or pink are a good choice. Arrange the pictures you have cut out around the candle in a circle.

In your cast circle, sit comfortably before the lit candles and stare gently into the flames. Concentrate on finding the perfect mate until you begin to feel drowsy. Then close your eyes, and with your mind reach out across the universe and ask the Moerae to come to you.

After a short while you should feel their presence. It will be a gentle, loving one, as if you have called upon a Mother deity. When they arrive, communicate to them with your mind and tell them that you seek a mate. Feel free to describe the qualities of a person you think you would like. The Moerae may speak back to you with their collective mind and ask you questions which you should answer as honestly as you can. While doing this keep in mind the photos on your altar. This will help impress upon the Moerae the type of person you seek.

Continue to sit in silence with your eyes closed and wait for impressions to come to you. You may be told where to go to meet the person of your dreams, you may be shown one of your photos which represents someone you will meet soon and should keep an eye out for, or you may instinctively feel it is time to make a move to another town, or to make a love charm of some type. Or you may have a dream later which will give you some pertinent information.

Then, of course, you must just wait. But this spell is a powerful one and should eventually work for you. Bring it to mind at least once a day to keep the energy fresh.

Viewing Past Lives with Faery Helpers

There is no dearth of information on reincarnation and past life recall. Since the late 1950s when the celebrated Bridie Murphy regression was made public, it has been a subject of endless fascination. Certainly reincarnation's detractors have made their point. There is no way to prove its existence, and even in pagan and magickal circles proponents disagree on exactly how the process works and why. But one need not believe in reincarnation to make past life recall a valuable tool for self-exploration. If exploring the past—even one you feel is not a part of you—makes you better able to deal with the present, then it has all the merit it needs.

Many different texts will give you a number of methods for taking yourself back in time, and each one works about as well as any other. For using faery aid, the best method is one which takes place in the astral realm or in Faeryland. The best place, of course, is at your astral residence, snugly inside your astral home with one or two trusted house faeries at your side.

In your astral residence, sit facing a blank wall or your hearth fire. Tell the faeries with you that you need to explore a past life to help you discover the answer to a current problem or blockage. Then, rather than trying to project yourself into the scene as traditional regressions do, look at the wall or fire and wait for the images to appear. This way you are free to critically observe and analyze everything as you go along. This is possible because you are already in a meditative state of mind, so you don't have to have your astral body in a trance also. As you watch yourself, ask the trusted faeries with you to help you interpret what you see.

Faeries have long been thought to be adept at the art of scrying into water and have always been thought to have special pools and streams set aside just for this use. Scrying is the act of gazing into a reflective surface and seeing divinatory visions. The guided meditation in this book will provide you access to the Gnomes' scrying pool, but there are many places in Faeryland where you can find such bodies of water. All you need to do is walk around until you see one, kneel before it, and ask permission for its use. This will usually be granted to you either visually, verbally, or by a general sense of well-being. If you feel anything which makes you uncomfortable, leave the place and find somewhere else to go.

As with any divinatory method, your answers will most likely come in a symbolic form which you, and only you, can accurately interpret.

Most scrying done in Faeryland will override any question you may ask, instead providing you with information or commentary on the state of your spiritual well-being. Most faeries enjoy aiding humans in this quest. They get angry when people ignore this spiritual dimension which they themselves do not possess and wish that they might. If you ask before you scry for specific information about your spiritual path, the nearby faeries will try to help project images for you to learn from.

Petitioning the Deities

Despite their lack of a fully dimensional spiritual life, a number of faeries are close to, in the service of, have their energy aligned with, or are even beloved by certain deities. If you approach these faeries with sincerity and respect, they can aid you in petitioning or invoking these deities, and may even be able to intercede with them on your behalf.

Petitioning a deity is a witch's way of asking a God or Goddess to bless his or her efforts and to add the deity's special energies to the witch's spells. For example, if one wants creative inspiration one can petition Brigid before or after doing a spell designed to bring inspiration. Or if one needs protection one can petition Odin to add his energy and blessings to the spell. Since the deities are the essence of creation itself, the more God/dess power which can be put into a spell, the more success will come out of it.

Following is a list of some faeries and the deities with whom they are known to be on good terms, a part of, or in service to:

Deity	Faery
Manann	Irish Sea Water Guardians
Aine	Dinnshenchas
Holly King	Elves
Sun Gods	Callicantzaroi, Jinn
Moon Goddess	Thussers
Triple Goddess	The Moerae, Corrigan
Crone Goddess	Cailleac Bhuer, Snow Faeries
Mother Goddess	Fay, Hyldermoder, Jimanino, Mother Holle, Well Spirits
Freya/Frigga	Mother Holle
Dana/Brigid	Tuatha de Danann
Lugh	Tuatha de Danann
Dagda	Tuatha de Danann
Horned God	Robin Goodfellow, Oak King, Holly King
Odin	The Paian
Woodland Deities	Gnomes, Wilde Frauen
Virgin Goddess	Pillywiggins

To get any of these faeries to help you in your petition to a deity you must call them to your circle before you do a spell.

The next step is to do your spell. Just before you finish, light a candle in honor of the deity you wish to work with. Try to sense the faeries around you also reaching out to that deity, opening a channel for your communication. Raise your arms, close your eyes, concentrate on the deity, and say something like this:

> *Oh blessed Lugh, child of the sun. Here are assembled your own children of both the physical and the faery world. Look with favor upon my pleas for prosperity. Send your divine energy into my magick that it may manifest in the physical realm.*

Pause to sense the deity's energy flowing into your body and into the magick objects in front of you. In using faeries this way you should also be able to sense their added input. Some witches say they can actually hear the faery folk singing the praise of the deity being called upon. When you feel you have absorbed all the energy you can from the deity, then project it into the magickal tools you are using in the spell. Continue:

> *We thank you, blessed Lugh, myself and your faery legions who forever sing your praise. So Mote It Be! Blessed Be!*

Alter the words to reflect whichever deity and whatever need you are seeking at the time. As you start to close your circle, be sure not to verbally thank the faeries who aided you, but instead offer them some token of appreciation for their aid. Present them with food, fire, animal food, or a precious stone.

Another ritual in which faeries can help is the invoking of a deity. This is an ancient practice which still survives in our Drawing Down the Moon ritual where a female witch temporarily becomes one with the Moon Goddess.

The purpose of invocation is to temporarily gain insight and/or power from the deity to make ritual and magick more effective and meaningful. It is a holy, awesome experience, not one to be done merely for an ego boost. As in any magick, misusing this power will eventually cause it to backfire on you.

Be sure your circle is well fortified before beginning any invoking exercise because you don't want to risk allowing in any stray energies which are not of the deities themselves. If you are male you should probably limit yourself to invoking only the male Gods, and if you are female, you should invoke only the female Goddesses. If you do choose to attempt to invoke a deity not of your own gender, rest assured that the universe as we know it will not come tumbling down around your ears. Women simply resonate better with Goddess energy and men with the God, and therefore they are each able to fully merge with these beings during ritual, making themselves a clear channel for these needed energies.

You must also have ready a magickal tool to bring down the energy into yourself. When invoking a male deity, use the sun or a bright star; when invoking a female deity, use the moon in any phase which is appropriate to your cause and to the deity. Virgin Goddesses belong to the waxing moon, Mother Goddesses to the full, and Crones to the waning moon.

Let's say you wish to add energy to a ritual in praise of Odin, and you wish to merge with him in order to strengthen the tie. You might wish to your circle side the Paian who are beloved of Odin. Tell them what you are going to do and ask them to join in praise with you.

Stand in your circle where you have an unobstructed view of the sun or moon. In this case we are using the sun to draw down Odin. Focus your attention on the sun (do not look directly into it as it can severely damage or blind your eyes!) and forge a mental link between you and it. Raise a ritual tool up to it, and say:

Mighty Odin, God of the North, I ask that you come down to my small circle. Come to your children who now humbly seek to praise and honor you with song, dance, and wine. Enter me, your earthly servant, and partake of your feast.

Feel the energy of Odin entering your ritual tool and filling it with power and essence. Then slowly bring the tool to either your forehead or your breastbone and feel the essence enter you.

Spend a few moments orienting yourself to the new sensations you are likely to feel as part of this essential God energy merges with your own. Using faeries in this ritual can help you know if you are successful or not, because if you have actually become their deity they will immediately begin singing to honor you/him/her. The sudden aggregation of energy you feel just outside your circle will be very noticeable. Do not let it disturb you—it is natural and good.

Drink your wine, eat, dance, partake in the festivities with joy. Remember you have united with the life energy which animates the universe, and that you are honoring the God who is both without and within you.

When you are finished with your ritual, you must reverse the drawing down process by allowing the God energy to re-enter your tool and be taken back up to the sun.

Be sure and think the deity for coming into you, offer him or her your loyalty and blessings, and then dismiss the faeries before you open the circle.

Other Magickal Faery Aid

While you are in your astral residence faeries can help you in the areas of divination, past life recall, scrying, and spiritual quests.

If you have been using your astral residence on a regular basis you know it has become easier and easier to access, and that an abundance of friendly faery life has taken up residence there with you. Hopefully you have even managed to forge a good relationship with at least one individual faery.

Because divination, past life recall, scrying, and gaining information about your spiritual endeavors ultimately take place in the astral, all these things will be more effective if done in the astral in the first place. And since this is the faeries' home territory, this is also where they can be the greatest help to you.

There are many methods of divination, most of them familiar to witches, with Tarot cards, runes, pendulums, and talking boards being the most popular. These items can also be used at your astral residence. Simply will them to be there, and they are. Some witches will actually hold the items in their hands when they take themselves into a meditative state to further enhance the connection between themselves and the divinatory tools.

Once you are in your astral residence and are attempting to use any of these items, simply call to your side the faeries you have come to know there and ask them to aid you while you begin to concentrate. This step is essential in any divination. Concentration provides you with a focus, aided by your slowed state of mind and the input of the faeries near you.

Follow through with the divination just as you would in the physical world, then interpret the results. If you have developed a good relationship with individual faeries, they may be able to offer you some insights into the results.

Another way to divine with faeries in your astral residence or in the physical is to focus your attention on a question you need an answer to, and then go for a leisurely walk in the woods or some other wild, unspoiled place, and look for answers in the form of symbols which present themselves to you. If you choose to walk in the astral world you will get quicker results and have more possibilities open to you, because anything at all can appear in the astral world, things which may provide more easily interpretable answers. This process is similar to the Native American vision quest where animals or other items present themselves to you in unusual ways. These function as symbols which only you will be able to interpret.

If you are using faery energy you will no doubt see faeries on your walk, and they will attempt to give you input and information whenever and wherever possible. But keep in mind the capricious nature of many faeries, and trust only those with whom you have developed a bond when seeking your answers.

When interpreting your symbols, be honest with yourself. If you hear or see something you don't like, don't ignore it or engage in great feats of mental gymnastics to try and rationalize the unwanted information away. The point of divination is to get answers which can help you deal more easily and effectively with problems. Don't bury your head in the proverbial sand—use the information to help yourself make positive changes in your life.

There are many books on the market, both good and bad, on interpreting symbols. Some of these are in dream books, and others are in books on Native American spirituality. If you have no experience dealing with these things then it is a good idea to begin with one of these texts to help you get started. But remember that you are a unique individual. Your spiritual, mental, and physical bodies have never been and will never be joined in this exact configuration again. The entire totality of your being has its own unique experiences and wisdom which color the way you view things. Therefore, only you can actually interpret symbols for yourself. For example, to some pagans a snake—an animal which sheds its skin yearly—represents eternity, reincarnation, the moon, and the Goddess. Seeing one can be interpreted from this point of view to mean a developing closeness with the Goddess or with one's own feminine side, or could mean that your answers will lie in exploring a past life. On the other hand, if you suffer from herpephobia, a debilitating and injurious fear of snakes, you would have to interpret this symbol in a negative way.

The following is a list of commonly seen symbols when taking a nature walk and their general meanings. This is only a place to begin. Do not use this list as a crutch, but as a core around which to develop your own symbology chart. As you work with more and more symbols, start writing them down in a notebook along with what you think they mean. As time goes by you will be able to decide how accurate you were and you can mark the correspondences in your own personal symbols dictionary for quick reference.

Apple: awakening spirituality, the Goddess, love

Acorn: the God, fertility

Animals, baby: beginnings, innocence, lack of cunning

Basket: gifts, joining of two halves, completion

Bear: strength

Burial cairn: hidden truth

Cat: psychicism, occult powers

Cauldron: rebirth

Circle: completion, wholeness, protection

Clouds: change is occurring, obscuring of issue

Crossroads: protection, wholeness, the elements

Corn: harvest of many things, prosperity

Dog: fidelity

Elves: industry, work, protection

Eggs: fertility, reincarnation

Faeries: spirituality, playfulness, capriciousness

Fire: transformation, change, protection

Fish: sexuality, duality, two answers

Fox: creativity, ability to solve difficulties, cunning

Ghost: changeability, answer is unforeseeable

Hollow tree: pregnancy, growth, the womb, possibilities

Lake: death, rebirth

Magician: the power to act, primal male power

Moon, full: motherhood, fertility

Moon, waxing: increasing power, childhood

Moon, waning: decreasing power, old age

Mountains: impediments

Owl: wisdom, the Crone

River: change, reincarnation

Robin: good fortune

Ruins: lost opportunity

Snake: reincarnation, the Goddess, renewal

Standing stones: untapped power

Stars: inspiration, hope, fortune turning to good

Sun: the God, good fortune, prosperity

Vulture: wrong use of force

Walking staff: aid, support, direction, friendship

Waterfall: abrupt changes, new beginnings, endings

Well: rebirth, change, luck about to change

Wheat: fertility, prosperity, good harvest

Willow tree: spirituality

Wind: unpredictable change, creativity

Witch: primal female power

Wolf: family life

Wren: reversal of fortune, illness

If you are doing your divinatory nature walk in the astral, you may see specific types of faery life appear to you. Look them up in the dictionary in this guide. Their concerns, affinities, and personality can also provide valuable additional information to help answer your question. If you are unsure what faery appeared, then ask one you know to identify it for you.

The following is a list of some of the faeries most likely to show up on your walk and what their appearance might mean. Once again, this is only a starting point. As you get familiar with faery folk you will no doubt develop your own symbolic codes for them, and you will also be more easily able to speak with them when they appear to you.

Alven: hidden answers, obscured issues

Ashrays: illusions, caution against self-delusion

Attorcroppe: danger, bad fortune

Beansidhe: death, change, prolonged illness

Bean-Tighe: family matters, the home

Black Angus: death, change, illness

Boggarts: caution against greed, veiled threats

Brownie: the home, giving or receiving help

Cailleac Bhuer: seek help from a higher power

Callicantzaroi: caution against negative action/thought

Corrigans: look at other options

Devas: self-containment, need to express creativity

Dryads: spirituality, discoveries, Goddess, women

Glashtin: inner-conflicts

Gnomes: stability, protection, animals, wellness

Grant: need for protection, warning, raised defenses

Guagach: healing, animals, fertility, crops/plants

Gwragedd Annwn: children, need to look inward

Klaboutermannikin: travel, prolonged changes, new ideas

Knockers: wrong direction, lost possessions

Penates: gifts, good fortune

Pillywiggins: flightiness, fickleness

Pixies: harvest, growth, happiness

Robin Goodfellow: the God, men, harvest, sexual matters

Sylphs: fickleness, changeability

Snow Faeries: dormant ideas or actions

Uilebheist: need to raise your protection, seek aid

Vasily: animals, problem may be solved by giving to others

Vodianoy: sickness

Well Spirits: rebirth, renewal, reversals

Wilde Frauen: need to reconnect with nature, imbalances

Yann-An-Od: problem may be solved by giving to others

Zips: boasting, fear, misplaced energies

Creative Ritual With Faeries

Because of the ease with which faeries can be persuaded to help you raise energy, and because they too love and worship the old pagan Gods and Goddesses, they are a natural to include in any ritual. Again, this is not necessary, but it can add to the meaning and scope of your ritual. Working with faeries in ritual multiplies your energies and intent just as working in a coven does.

Faeries, like us, are children of the old Gods and Goddesses. Their music and dance are as appropriate a praise as yours. Sabbats and Esbats are other times when they are active and willing to take part. Numerous faeries have been seen by humans dancing under the full moon, and the solitary nature of the Esbats makes this a natural time to work with faeries. Sending healing and loving energy to our damaged environment is another natural action for them. Their love of nature and their desire to preserve it will get you an immediate response.

Rituals can be done both in the astral realm and/or in the physical world within the protection of your circle. Getting the Little People to join you is best accomplished by drawing them near and asking them to participate. Most are thrilled to be included and will jump into the spirit of the occasion.

The following are two detailed examples of how faeries can be incorporated in pagan rituals.

Outline for Faery Esbat Ritual

This ritual is written for a solitary witch and the faeries he or she chooses to call to the circle for an Esbat (full moon) Ritual. As stated above, there are many types of rituals in which faeries can take part, and this is only one example. Feel free to adapt it, rewrite it, or expand it for group practice.

To perform any ritual you will, of course, need your altar, a place private enough and large enough to cast your circle, and your ritual tools. For an Esbat ritual it is best if you can have an unobstructed view of the moon either outdoors or through a window. But if that is not possible then try to bring the moon in to you by first setting some water outside under its light, and bring that into your circle.

Gather everything on your altar and cast your circle by using a ritual tool or your finger to project around you a glowing, vibrating circle of protective energy. The circle comes from within you and will be seen and felt as a blue-white band of impenetrable force.

Stand in front of your altar and take several deep breaths to clear your mind while you concentrate on connecting with the force and spirit of the universe. In your circle you are on the edge of all dimensions and you can freely access any you choose. When you are ready to begin, raise your arms and say:

I, (state your craft name), come before the Mother Goddess at this time of her fullness to honor her with food, wine, dance, song, and magick. Look down favorably on me and your astral children whom I now invite to join in the ritual. Blessed be, Great Mother!

You may start inviting the faeries and their elemental energies with whichever direction you like. Take the tool which represents that direction and walk to the edge of your circle facing it. Raise the tool (in this case a cup, chalice, or small cauldron) and call out:

Blessed creatures of the west, arise! The moon is full, our Mother Goddess rides high in the night sky. You are invited to this circle to join in the worship and festivities to her honor. Undines and faeries of water, awaken! Come share in your Mother's bounty!

Return to your altar and, moving clockwise, take the tool for the next direction. In this example we started in the west, so we will now move to the north. Go to the north quarter of your circle and make the same invitation but substitute the words "Gnomes and faeries of earth" where needed. In the east you will say "Sylphs and faeries of air," and in the south, "Salamanders and faeries of fire." The four faeries mentioned here have come into pagan practice from ceremonial magick where they archetypally represent each of these elements and directions and are called upon to praise their God in various high magick rituals.

Now you are ready to invite the Goddess and the God to your circle. Standing in front of your altar, raise your arms skywards and make the age old invitation:

Blessed Lady, Divine Lord, this circle is yours. Come to it and use it as you will.

If you are female, or are part of a gathering where a female is present, it is traditional at an Esbat ceremony to do the rest of the ritual with the moon energy of the Mother Goddess drawn down into one of the females (the method is mentioned above). This is not essential, but it adds a special strength to the ritual to actually have someone in your circle containing Goddess energy. While filled with Goddess energy, a witch may wish to speak or dance or just sit and preside over the rest of the ritual. As long as the action seems positive, make no step to interfere with its flow.

If you are a solitary male and you wish to bring this same Goddess energy into your Esbat circle, then draw the moon energy into a chalice of water instead. Simply raise the cup in front of you and allow the full moon's light to reflect off its surface. Focus on bringing that energy down into the chalice while asking the Mother Goddess to bless you with her presence. You might say something like this:

Mother Moon Goddess, I ask that you enter the chalice I hold and return with me to my sacred circle to join in your worship as I and your astral children joyfully extol your love and graciousness.

The next step in this ritual is working any magick you may wish to do. While all work, magick included, is forbidden at the Sabbats except in cases of extreme emergency, the Esbat is the perfect time to make magick under the watchful eye of the loving Mother who— like any mother—can deny little to her beloved children.

Throughout this process you will be able to hear the faeries at your circle side singing the Goddess's praise, especially if she is drawn into your circle in some form or another. When your spell is completed and you are ready to build and release the energy you have placed into it, the faeries can again help you. With the Goddess either in you or in your circle in a chalice, the faeries will recognize you as their deity and they will be unable to refuse to help you raise the needed energy for the spell. Begin to do this either by drumming or dancing (methods are given above), and increase the pace of either or both until you reach a frenzied pitch. Call out to the faeries periodically and encourage them to keep moving, singing, or doing whatever else it is that they are doing to raise the power. Mentally store up their raised energy with your own. When you feel all the energy around you is as high as it can go, or when the cone of power over you has peaked, then mentally and visually release it to go and do your bidding. With all this faery energy you will have amassed a considerable force, so be careful where you send it. Make sure your visualizations are as clear and precise as they can be.

As with any other Drawing Down ceremony, you must return those energies when you have finished with them. This is not only a courtesy to the moon as your Mother, but it keeps uncontrolled and unfocused energies from floating about causing trouble. In this case you would return the borrowed energy by reversing the process. See the energy flowing out of you and back into the chalice, and then raise it back to the moon to be reabsorbed. You can also simply empty the contents of the chalice onto the bare ground if you wish, thereby forging a link between the Moon Goddess and your working space.

It is now time for what is called the Ceremony of Cakes and Ale. This is another ancient ritual which has been a part of Esbats for longer than humans have recorded their religious rites. The Cake (cookies, cake, or pastries are all acceptable) represents the earth, one of the feminine elements, and the Ale (wine, water, or juice is okay to use, too) represents water, the other feminine element. These are consumed both to honor the Goddess and to bring a part of her into ourselves. This idea of God-eating is reflected in our myths and is still seen in modern patriarchal religious ceremonies such as the Christian communion.

Before either one of the items are consumed two libations are made. The first one is to the Goddess. Pour some of the wine on to the earth and break some cake over it, and offer it to her and her beasts. And since you are working with faeries you must offer them a generous libation also. But set theirs out in a small bowl rather than pouring it on the earth, and make it clear that they have been given this portion which they can claim as soon as you close your circle.

As you make your Ale offering to the Goddess, raise your cup and say:

Blessed Lady of the night—we offer you the Esbat Ale, blessed of water.

Then make the cake offering with similar words:

Blessed Lady of the night—we offer you the Esbat Cake, blessed of earth.

When you make your libation to the faeries, you must also do this ritually. Raise again the cup of Ale and tip it to all four directions, saying:

Faeries and blessed creatures of the elements who came here to join in the worship of the Mother Goddess—I offer you a portion of the Esbat Ale, blessed of water.

Do the same with the Cake, saying:

Faeries and blessed creatures of the elements who came here to join in the worship of the Mother Goddess—I offer you a portion of the Esbat Cake, blessed of earth.

Thank the Goddess and God for their attendance and participation with words such as:

Blessed Lady, Divine Lord, we thank you for your presence here this night. Go with Bright Blessings!

Now you must dismiss the faeries by going to each direction, starting from the last one you invited. For example, if you ended your invitations to the faeries in the south, you should start there to dismiss them, and work counterclockwise back to your starting point. Be sure to take with you the tool representative of that direction. Your words should sound something like this:

Blessed creatures of the south, you are free to go from this holy place. The Mother Goddess is proud that you honored

her with your presence. Salamanders and faeries of fire,
your libation of the Esbat feast awaits you. Blessed Be!

Repeat this at each quarter, substituting the appropriate element and faery name for each. Notice that you do not demand that
the faeries leave. You invited them there, you did not command
them, and you must show them the same courtesy when you dismiss
them. Keep in mind that they will not be going far since you have
placed their libation in your circle area.

Normally you may remain inside the circle for as long as you
like after your ritual is complete, but when you are working with
faeries who are anxious to claim their libation, it is a good idea not to
tarry overly long.

Close the circle by taking a tool or your finger and walking
counterclockwise around the circle, mentally grounding the energy
which made it. See it sink into the ground and vanish. As always, the
grounding of the circle will disperse virtually any negative energy or
faery form attracted to it.

Outline for Ritual to Gain Ancient Knowledge

This ritual will require working on the inner planes unless you live
near or are planning to visit some of the ancient standing stones in
western Europe. Fortunately, they are easy to get to in the astral
world because other pagans have already forged well-worn paths to
these places.

There are two faeries thought to inhabit these stones. One is the
Pyrenee of Cornwall, and the other is the Korred from Brittany. Pick
one of these faery forms with whom to work.

Go to the place you usually use for mental exercises, do any protective rituals you wish to do, then relax your body and mind and
begin to direct your attention outward.

You need not recreate these standing stone places faithfully, or
even have any one specific site in mind. Just visualize an old, lonely
place where the old megaliths are powerful. Feel the vibrations of
our ancestors and their rites emanating from the smooth, cold stones.
Hear the silence around you as acutely as you might hear sound.

Walk up to any one of the stones which catches your attention and place your hands, palms down, upon it. You may even hug it if you wish. Mentally cast a protective circle around both yourself and the stone, and begin to attune yourself to its vibrations. For those of you who are adept at psychometry (reading the history of an object by touch), this will be easy. Everyone else will have to try a little harder, but each exercise will bring you greater and greater success.

With your hands still upon the stone, mentally close your eyes and listen for sounds coming from within. Imagine a life-force deep inside it beginning to stir. Hear its music and its sound. Feel its ancient heartbeat. Hum along with it, mentally coaxing it out to you.

Whichever faery you have chosen to work with, now is the time to call out to it and see if you will receive an answer. Just say the name, repeating it three times like this: "Pyrenee. Pyrenee. Pyrenee." Or, "Korred. Korred. Korred."

Keep your palms on the stone. You should begin to feel it becoming animated. If after a short time you do not feel a presence with you, you can repeat the call twice more, each time in groups of three. If by then you have no answer one of two things may be happening. One, you need to keep practicing your psychometry skills, or two, the faery does not feel like talking at this particular time. In either case you should return to your normal waking consciousness and try again another day.

On the other hand, if you feel a presence that you believe to be the faery, you should greet it in any way you feel is appropriate. Remember that neither the Pyrenees or the Korreds are visible to the human eye. Say something simple and respectful like, "Bright Blessing, Ancient One."

You should be able to feel a greeting being returned to you. Sometimes in these explorations you may actually hear a timbrous voice speaking to you, but these faeries usually communicate telepathically either in words or, more often, in pictures.

Now you must state to the faery your purpose in coming and awakening it from its slumber. Say something like, "I have come seeking knowledge of the stones. Will you help me?"

Keep your hands upon the stone and await your answer. If the faery is willing to help you at that time you will begin to get mental impressions of the meaning, use, purpose, and history of the stones. You may even learn about the deities they were principally dedicated to. Or you may be taken on yet another astral journey where you see a brief overview of the information the faery thinks you should have at that time.

This is a slow process, with only minute bits of information being given out at each session. But if you return to the exact same stone each time and build a relationship with its guardian spirit, you will learn much. Each individual stone has its own faery. Later on you can practice this ritual with each of them at this specific site to glean more information. Or you can travel to a known place such as Stonehenge and try this ritual there.

When you have been given all the information you are going to be given at this session you should not thank the faery for its help. We westerners have been taught that this is the polite thing to do. The words come automatically and you may find you have to force yourself to stop in mid-sentence. Instead, say something like, "Knowledge is the greatest gift of all." This will communicate your gratitude in a way that will not offend your teacher. It is also expected that you will give something back to the faery by leaving it a small gift such as a precious stone or some food. Or you can, while remaining within the perimeters of your circle, dance and sing to send the faery healing and loving energy.

Now the faery should begin to sink back into the stone, its vibrations and presence becoming less and less felt to you. However, if the presence is still with you, you might consider doing a small ritual to worship whatever deity you believe is appropriate to the place. To do this, simply call out to the Goddess or God you wish to honor and ask their presence in this holy place. Sing his or her praises, pray, or dance a dance of joy. You will probably feel either of these faeries, who are known for being very spiritual, joining in with you. And don't be scared if you sense other presences joining you. These are merely the residual energies of other pagans who have repeatedly worshiped at that site, and they can do nothing but enhance your ritual experience.

After the ritual the faery will definitely fade from you. You should then close your circle in the normal way and return home.

Other Rituals

Rituals are as varied as the human race. You should always feel that you have the power and the ability to create your own for any occasion. Appendix Three in the back of this book gives a detailed outline for creating your own rituals, with or without faeries.

Chapter Six

Creating Your Own Faery Beings

$\mathcal{A}$s pagans we believe that we were created as incarnate images of the deities. Part of them is always within us. We are imbued with their life force, and with the proper ritual we can temporarily take on many of their powers—even the power to create.

We create every time we work magick. What we visualize manifests in our solid, earthly reality. What we think becomes mass and substance. What we produce from our own creative minds has form and essence. And as long as we keep feeding our creations from our vast stores of energy, they continue to exist.

This same thought process works for the creation of elemental forms—beings that are very real, though not always visible to the naked eye. We absolutely can create our own faery beings to whom we can temporarily give life, and these creations of our magick can serve us in many ways. A couple of years ago when I moved into a new home in a state far away from my family and friends, I felt very vulnerable. The woods behind my house looked more forbidding than inviting simply because they were strange. I also knew that I was living in an area where the crime rate was climbing and I felt the need for some extra protection over and above the usual that a witch puts around her home. I had created a faery being only once before to protect my parents' home after they had trouble with vandalism, and I found it very effective. I decided that it was time for me to evoke this same protection for myself.

I now have four "Dragon Dogs" surrounding my home. They are fed new life-giving energy by me at each new moon, and in the meantime they stand watch over my home, psychically repelling any uninvited invaders, both physical and astral, and warning of natural disasters. They also warn me if some hapless person decides, despite the negative energy felt when they breach the area guarded, to press on closer to my home. As time passes the beings have become more and more real, with each one taking on a different, unique personality, and our relationship has become that of mutual support. I know they are there because I can see them on my astral outings, and I have both seen and felt the results of their vigilance.

The idea that a witch or magician can create astral life is not some radical product of the so-called "New Age," but a very old idea. In his collected works, the sixteenth-century physician and occultist Philippus Paracelsus spoke at length (albeit in confusing language) about the ancient art of creating a Homoculus (sometimes spelled Homunculus), or an artificial human being, by utilizing the four elements plus the element of spirit. Based upon these allusions found in his writings, the idea of ego-inflamed human demigods actually creating life sparked the vivid imaginations of many Victorian and early twentieth-century writers (this was a period of intense occult revival in England, Canada, and the United States), and some of the results were horror classics such as Mary Wollstonecraft Shelley's *Franken-stein* and Somerset Maugham's *The Magician.*

Logically we all know that such feats cannot be accomplished in the physical world, but when we read these old occult writings with a sound knowledge of both faery lore and the astral world, all the vague allusions suddenly make perfect sense. The old masters were talking about creating astral life forms, or faeries, all along.

What Your Faery Creation Can Do

When you set out to create an elemental being, whether temporarily or permanently, you must have in mind a task or function for it to fulfill. Not only does this help the creature know its role, but it also helps you to concentrate on bringing it into existence and forming it in the way it needs to look to achieve your goals. For example, a faery which will guard your home might look fierce and animal-like, while one who is going to aid you in astral projection might be filmy and winged.

The tasks these thought-form beings can handle easily are:

- Guarding a home, person, or object
- Watching over children or pets
- Watching over the ill
- Repelling negative influences
- Chasing away ill-meaning persons and entities
- Repelling or lessening natural disasters
- Leading you to things such as healing herbs
- Helping you retrieve a lost object
- Aiding in divination
- Helping you to astral project
- Warning you of danger
- Standing guard over your astral residence

Once again, keep in mind pagan ethics when you set your faery being out on a mission. Any wrong or malicious use of a thought-form will have severe repercussions.

Creating Your Faery

Self-created faeries are merely cohesive projected thought-forms produced by the witch. It all works on the simple and proven principle that thought is action on the astral plane. But to make faeries who feel

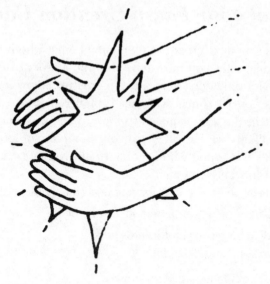

Faery energy between a witch's hands.

real and appear animated with life energy will require prolonged intense concentration, good visualization skills, and the ability to build and store large amounts of energy before releasing it.

If you find it easy to concentrate and focus with your eyes open, you can create your faery being while in your circle, either before or after you do other rituals. Avoid doing other magickal spells during this same session because the required energy to do both is more than most people have in reserve.

While standing before your altar, hold your hands up in front of you with your palms facing each other. This is the area in which your faery being will gather energy and grow. Start by vigorously rubbing your palms together, feeling the heat and energy made by the friction, and know for certain that just as you created that heat, you can create life.

Now move your palms apart just a few inches and focus on feeling the chakras (energy centers) in your palms being expanded. Sense a growing mass of energy forming between them. With your mind, create an even greater energy field growing, spinning, and enlarging between your palms until you are forced to move them apart a few more inches.

Keep up this visualization process until your hands feel pushed approximately two feet apart. This should take about 20 minutes.

Now see the energy forming a shape which will become the physical body of your faery. Make its appearance just as clear as you can. Give it facial features, coloring, and wings if you desire, but avoid trying to give it a personality. This is something it will adopt on its own over time.

Some witches feel that their strongest psychic center is either at the chakra point of their third eye (between and just above the eyes), or at the one over their solar plexus. If you are one of these people, then you can also effectively use one of these centers to create a thought-form faery.

Again, rub your palms together vigorously before you start, drawing confidence from the heat you produce. Now hold them a few inches away from your chosen energy center. Feel the energy which is creating your faery coming from this center and see the energy massing in front of you, allow it to expand, and eventually to take form. As the energy grows, move your hands apart accordingly. This will also take abut 20 minutes. When you have expanded the energy mass to about two feet in diameter, begin to give your faery its features and physical form.

Another method for faery creation is the meditation method, which takes longer, but, unless you are an expert in raising personal energy, is much more effective. If you have a favorite method of inducing a meditative state, then keep using it. If not, you might start looking around for one which pleases you.

The following is a guide to achieving a meditative state of which I am fond. It should be thought out to yourself as you seek this inner-focused, deeper state of mind. The entire induction process will take 15 to 20 minutes.

Find a comfortable place to relax where you will not be disturbed. Somewhere in your bedroom is a good choice, but avoid lying down if you feel you might not be able to stay awake.

You may play "New Age" music softly in the background, or light incense if you wish. These are not necessary, but they can help you to focus and concentrate.

Relax yourself without crossing your arms or legs, and keep in mind that whatever position you take is one which you will stay in for maybe as long as 45 minutes. Make sure it is one you can comfortably maintain.

Begin by taking a few very deep breaths. Take in as much air as you can, hold it for a few seconds, then slowly release it. As you do, feel the tension drain away from your body.

Start to clear your mind of extraneous thoughts and focus on the idea of going deep within yourself, so deep that you can reach out and become a part of all there is.

If you tend to get images which invade and scatter your thoughts, try focusing on only one object while you are trying to enter meditation. This will help keep you focused. Flood your inner screen with a single color or a single geometric symbol which will keep other images out. If you tend to hear words which distract you, then keep one single word or phrase repeating on the edge of your consciousness. A word describing your goal such as "down" or "inward," or a phrase such as "I create," are all good choices.

Remind yourself that you are in charge, and that when you want or need to awaken you can do so by saying to yourself the words, "I Am Home."

When you feel relaxed, begin to count yourself down. This is an old trick, one which has been used by both witches and magicians for centuries. Begin with whatever number you like—ten is a good round choice—and tell yourself that with each number you count down you will go deeper and deeper into a meditative state. By the count of one you will be as deep as you can go.

Do the countdown slowly, but rhythmically: "10 … 9 … 8 …"

Now spend a few minutes noting the lack of feeling, or the numbness, of your own body. Be aware of any areas of tension which may still linger in your physical shell, and will them away.

If you are new to this process, you may wish to repeat the countdown several more times until you feel you are sufficiently deep enough to begin serious mental work.

Once you are satisfied that you are down deep enough, you are ready to begin any meditative exercise—in this case, the creation of a faery.

You have two choices about where you bring the faery into being. You can put it in the room with you to be sent to the place it needs to go later, or you can set it directly where it will be doing its job. For instance, if you want it to watch over a friend who is in the hospital, then create it at your friend's bedside.

As with the other exercise, begin the visualization by seeing your own energy going out to form the initial core of the faery. See this as a beam of pure light shining out from you. Then see another beam of energy coming from directly above the faery, a beam of clear, pure light, part of the divine life-energy of the deities. Focus on the faery growing and slowly forming itself into a mass, and then into a recognizable form. Remember that it can look like anything you wish. This part of the process will take 20 to 30 minutes.

If you want to make your faery creation more fully dimensional, you can do what old Paracelsus and his alchemists would have done. You can use your ritual tools to further imbue it with the qualities of the elements, thereby giving it a more fully rounded personality. You can do this either with physical gestures or through clear visualization.

In either case, have your tools laid out before you on your altar and, beginning with whichever direction you like, allow the faery to take from them, one at a time, some of the attributes of the element each represents. For example, raise your chalice to it and allow it to drink from or absorb the qualities of water from the cup. See the faery taking into itself the qualities of psychicism, compassion, adaptability, etc., that belong to water.

Use your imagination to come up with various other ways for the faery you have made to get in touch with your tools. The possibilities are limited only by your own powers of visualization. You might want to draw an invoking pentagram before it to incorporate into it the qualities of air. Or you could brush it with a feather or fill it with incense to incorporate air. See it absorbing the ability to communicate, to reason, and to remain undetected. You may want to pass a candle through it or around it so that it may take on the attributes of fire. For this element see the faery gaining such qualities as strength, fortitude, and agility. For connecting it with the element of earth you could have it touch or wear a special stone, or anoint it with saltwater. See it becoming more stable, solid, and protective.

You can also imbue your faery with elemental powers by visualizing it in different settings. For example, visualize it in a desert or bonfire for the element of fire, on a windy hilltop for air, in an ocean or running stream for water, or in the middle of a large fertile field for earth. While the faery is at these locations, visualize the elemental qualities of the places merging with the faery's own energies.

Whether you choose to use this elemental process at all, or how much of it you choose to use, will depend largely on what it is you want your faery to do for you. For example, if your faery is being created solely to protect your home, you may wish to use only the element of fire, which has an affinity for protection. But if its purpose is to watch over a loved one in the hospital, you might want to use both fire and water for the dual qualities of protection and compassion.

The next step in this creation process is to charge your faery with its duty. While it is still caught in the grasp of your energy field, tell it precisely what it is you want it to do. You might say something like this:

Faery being, creation of my mind, energy, and love, I charge you with the task of looking after my friend, (state name), while s/he is in (state hospital name). Do not let any one approach her/him who will do her/him any harm—even unintentionally. Frighten such people or entities away; fill them with dread if they approach (state name again). And if (state name) should need or want me, and is unable to let me know, you will come and tell me. I charge you with this task in the name of (state a deity's name), for the good of all, in accordance with the Pagan Rede. Blessed Be!

Send the faery one more blast of your own energy, and then visualize the faery going about its task. Picture exactly how it looks while doing so and how others will react to it, even though they may be unaware it is there. The more clearly you form this picture in your mind, the more effectively the faery will work.

Will the faery continue to do its job unsupervised? Might it ever strike out on its own? Yes it might, but this happens very rarely. If you feel a being you have created has taken on too much of a life of its own, then you can diffuse it by picturing the energy which animates it sinking into the ground. In most cases it is not the faery itself which has run amuck, but the ungrounded energy left over from its initial creation or from other spells and rituals which were never properly grounded in the first place.

Don't feel disappointed or discouraged if you feel your first efforts at creating a faery are not very successful. It may take several attempts to feel that your thought-forms are fully energized and "living," just as it sometimes takes several repetitions of a spell before you feel it has "taken." Keep in mind that creating something on the astral plane which will last requires periodic refueling. Be prepared in the first few days after you have created a faery to spend 15 minutes or so each day feeding it life-giving energy from yourself. After that you can limit your feedings to once every two weeks and then once a month. Left unfed they have a very limited life span. Try recharging them at each new or full moon to make it easy to remember.

How the Faery Functions in Its Role

The faery can go about its task in several different ways, depending on what function it was created to fulfill.

When guarding a home, person, pet, or object, you should visualize the faery giving off strong vibrations of protection and of warning, the sort of energy which any intruder or person wishing you harm would immediately sense and would instinctively back away from. Few criminals are stupid enough not to listen to their sixth sense when considering a crime. If something doesn't feel right, they will go on to where the pickings are easier.

The same is true for faeries you have created to guard and protect your astral residence. See them repelling all forces which may wish to come against you.

Both these guardian faeries and those specifically created to warn you of danger can be equipped with a device that might help let you know when something is wrong. For example, if a faery wished to let you know that your child or someone who was sick needed you, they might have a buzzer that they could sound or a symbol which you can see and recognize as a message. In your psychic centers these things will translate to that warning bell people often say they hear when they are struck with the sudden, unshakable feeling that something is amiss.

In the case of children or the ill, do not rely solely on a faery to do all the work for you. They make an excellent back-up system, but as with any magick, it is intended to give a boost and be a support to your physical actions; it is not meant to be a cure-all.

You can also visit your creations while you are astral projecting or while in meditation and ask them to give you a report on what has been happening. You may get a complete, clear verbal account, or merely a set of random impressions. Be open to this communication no matter what form it takes, and weigh it honestly against the known facts. You may be surprised how much help this guardian faery can be.

Faeries which are set up to repel negative influences or entities work in much the same way. They can chase away, return, or ground all such influences. You might want to equip them with a mirror or a ball of reflective glass with which they can direct away any negativity which comes your way. Or you can give them weapons, or four feet

and lots of teeth, and have them chase things away like well-trained guard dogs.

Faeries can also warn you in the event of a natural disaster such as a flood or tornado. Equip them with a way to tell you when you are in danger, and give them the energy they need to help shield your home.

Your faery can also be created to lead you to things. For example a lost object can be retrieved, or a healing herb found. Ask the faery for what you need and then wait for impressions. The faery may tell you where to find what you want in a dream, by a vague feeling, or verbally while in meditation. Keep an open mind.

Divination is another field in which a faery creation can excel. When you create your faery you must tell it what it is you wish to know—state as clearly as possible to it the one single question to which you need an answer. Then mentally send the faery out to collect the information you seek. Eventually the answers will come to you. Again, keep an open mind. The information may come in any of the above mentioned ways, or you may dream your answers, or be led to another divinatory device such as a Tarot deck or the runes for an answer.

Conscious astral projection seems to be one of the more difficult occult practices to master, and many teachers of this art have said that working with an experienced person is the best way to learn. But not all of us are blessed with friends who have such talents. Here again, your faery can help. Charge the faery to aid you in this task when you create it and set it up over the area where you will be practicing. The next time you attempt astral projection the faery will be there to aid and encourage you, helping you to focus out of yourself, and using its energy to assist your own.

Grounding the Energy

When you are finished with your faery being, you must dismantle it and ground the energies which brought the being to life. Because this creature is not a "life" in any true sense of the word, or even a complete astral life form, you should have no compunctions about ending its existence. If you do, then please don't create one in the first place. If you make it, then you have to be willing to take responsibility for it, and allowing it to run around unchecked is grossly irresponsible.

If you do not feed the faery periodically, after a while the animating energy will wane and the being will dissipate on its own, but its residual energies may stay around for a long time. This is what must be controlled, recalled, or grounded. Also, if the faery's task is done—for example, the friend leaves the hospital—and you do not dismantle it, it may just decide to spend the rest of its existence doing whatever it wants and may inadvertently interfere with hospital equipment. The dangers of loose, unfocused energy are well-documented in occult circles. They can cause feelings of restlessness, manifestations, and even poltergeist activity. Extra energy or energy no longer needed must always be grounded!

In the case of your faery being, you should call it to you either in a meditative state or at the same chakra point you used to create it. You should then thank the being for its service and tell it you are grounding its energy, returning it to the womb of Mother Earth, and that anything not grounded will be relegated to Faeryland.

Begin to see the faery's image fade, growing smaller and weaker, eventually fading into the earth. If you like, you can hold up your palms in the same way you did to create the faery and reverse the visualization process. When you finish, go outside somewhere or go to a corner inside your home and press your palms to the ground, feeling any left-over energy draining from you safely and harmlessly into the earth.

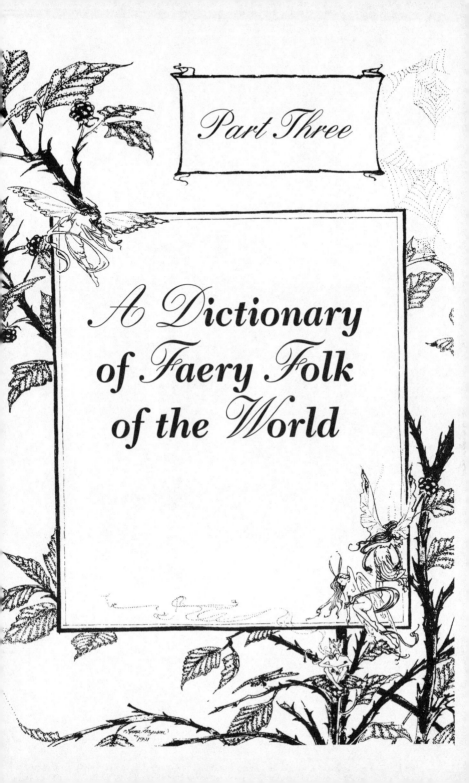

Part Three

A Dictionary of Faery Folk of the World

Faeries of the World

Some faery types are universally known and are hard to type by ethnic origin. Others are broad categories, with many different faery life forms falling within their range. Most of the faery forms listed below will be familiar to westerners.

Flying or winged faeries are usually the ones which children see. The toxic herb foxglove is said to give these faeries their power of flight, and it was once used in human flying (astral projection) ointments, which often killed those foolish enough to try them. Folk names for foxglove include Faery Finger, Faery Weed, Faery Cap, and Faery Dress. Some believe the wings of faeries to be only human thought-forms projected onto faeries who are otherwise wingless to help us more easily accept their power of flight. Winged faeries have bright, clear auras of light which are easily seen surrounding them. They are not seen as often by adults as are dwarf (or land-bound) faeries.

Elves and dwarves are generic terms for small wingless faeries such as Gnomes. Often they are seen as having the appearance of older men, but women dwarves are also occasionally seen. But don't be misled by their apparent age—dwarves are very quick and can seem to appear and disappear before your eyes, as if translocating magickally. They are the smartest and most clever and resourceful of all the faery folk. Occasionally, though, they overindulge in food and drink and can be heard reveling loudly beneath a home or oak tree.

Water women are baneful faeries who are often disguised as seaweed or ground fauna. Though the term for them is feminine, male and androgynous forms of these faeries have been reported. In Celtic countries these faeries are especially said to like to disguise themselves as hazel trees and may be the source of the popular Halloween crone, "Witch Hazel." Water women can be nasty or neutral depending upon their location, the day of the week, and the time of year one is encountered.

Water spirits are numerous and usually quite dangerous. Popular forms are Mermaids and Mermen, and the German Lorelei. They spend most of their time hunting for human mates and protecting their watery kingdoms. Almost every culture has at least one tale to tell of a faery kingdom which exists beneath a lake or ocean hidden by the illusion of water. Occasionally water faeries are benevolent and have been known to lead sailors to safety and fishermen to a catch, but one must exercise extreme caution when dealing with them. Water faeries have been credited with both saving humans from drowning and with drowning them. In Polynesia, where the faery faith is still strong, friendly dolphins are thought to be sea faeries.

Seasonal faeries are another worldwide phenomenon. These faeries can take any form, but their sole function seems to be to assist the Goddess with the change of seasons as she turns the Wheel of the Year. In spring, flower faeries are often sighted, especially near Bealtaine when faeries are generally very active. In autumn, they aid plants and animals in preparing for winter. Their exceptionally playful nature makes them fun to frolic with, but not very useful for serious work.

Probably the most familiar seasonal faeries are the snow faeries of winter. They tend to be personified into singular forms known as Old Man Winter and Jack Frost. Until quite recently, strong belief in this snow faery king existed in Russia and much of Asia.

Treasure hoarders such as the Irish Leprechaun or the Italian Monaciello are another well-known faery type. They are dwarf faeries who hold among their few possessions crocks of gold and precious gems. Some of the world's most intriguing folklore concerns the capture of this treasure from the faery world.

Guardian spirits are another well known faery form and are often mistakenly thought to be deities or discarnate human spirits. But guardian spirits do just that—they guard a thing or a place, such as the well spirits who guard sacred wells.

Goblin is a generic term for a malicious, dark, ugly faery, one who is generally disliked and unwelcome even by other faery folk.

A host of other beings are often classed as faeries, and they may or may not be. Much of making a determination depends upon your point of view and the pagan tradition you follow. These include Ghosts (both human and nonhuman discarnates), Raw Elementals (nonsentient archetypal beings), Angels (benevolent beings from the patriarchal religions), Giants and Ogres (popular in the Yorkshire region of England), Demons (malevolent beings from the patriarchal religions), Vampires (blood-sucking, animated, human corpses), Werewolves (shapeshifting humans), Mythical Beasts (such as the Satyr, Unicorn and Firebird), Monsters (such as the Loch Ness Monster or the Buru), Dragons (mythical reptiles who breathe fire), and Faery Godmothers (spirit world old women who look after young girls being cruelly tossed about by life's unpredictable ups and downs).

Keep in mind as you read through the faery descriptions and lore which follow that faeries are astral creatures and you must study each passage critically and adjust the lore accordingly when deciding how they can best be contacted and how and where they live. Saying that a certain faery lives in an oak tree does not mean that you will find one in the tree in your own back yard. You may need to find an inner plane oak grove to accomplish this task.

Afreets

See *Jinn.*

Alven

Land of Origin: Netherlands.

Other Origins: None known.

Other Names: Ottermaaner.

Element: Water.

Appearance and Temperament: Alvens have bodies that are so light as to make them almost invisible. They are not winged faeries, but they can travel through the air by becoming encased in a water bubble. Occasionally they will show themselves while wearing the skins of otters. Their malice towards humans extends only to those who choose to desecrate their homes and sacred plants.

Time Most Active: At night.

Lore: Alvens are creatures of the moon under whose light they dance and play. They are water faeries who live in ponds, lakes, and rivers, but the River Elbe is sacred to them and in it they make their principal home. They cherish night-blooming plants and will harm any human who attempts to pick or destroy them. Fish are their only known enemies, and they prefer to live in water enclosures where there are none.

Where to Find Them: In the River Elbe, an easy journey on the inner plane.

How to Contact: Look for them in Faeryland and try approaching them as a friend, someone who also loves the moon and nature.

Magickal and Ritual Help: Undetermined, but they may be useful in protective and healing spells for a night-blooming garden or for the marine environment.

Ankou

Land of Origin: Brittany.

Other Origins: Ankou is also part of the faery lore of Cornwall and Wales, and is deeply a part of Irish mythology.

Other Names: Death, the Grim Reaper, Father Time. A personified version of death is part of the folklore of many cultures, yet there is no evidence to suggest that any of these beings were ever worshiped as Death Gods.

Element: Ankou, like the deities, is part of all elements, including the elusive fifth element, spirit.

Appearance and Temperament: Ankou (Ahn-koo) is the personification of death who comes to collect the souls of passed-over humans. He is male, dark, and rather Dickensian with his black-robed costume pulled up high about his head. No one living has ever seen his face, for to do so would be to die. Ankou shows no interest in humans or their lives; he merely does his job.

Time Most Active: All year.

Lore: Ankou came to Ireland from the Celtic lore of Brittany in northern France, where he has largely been forgotten. The Irish term for physical death, *an bas* (awn bays), is rarely used to refer to the entity of Death, but rather the state of death.

Ankou drives a black cart, though some say it is really a small coach or even a hearse, drawn by four black horses in which he comes to collect the souls of those recently passed over and escort them into the Land of the Dead. In Ireland's County Roscommon there is a documented story of a mother and daughter who would hear the coach pass by their cottage each night around midnight accompanied by beautiful faery music, and though they could hear the music and the rattle of carriage wheels, they could never see a thing.

An old Irish proverb says, "When Ankou comes, he will not go away empty." In Ireland, Ankou is always classified as a faery rather than a ghost or some other type of spirit, and he is given more of a personality than he is accorded in many other lands. In this he is more like the Death of modern movies such as *Death Takes a Holiday* and *On Borrowed Time.*

Where to Find Him: Unknown.

How to Contact: Contact not advised!

Magickal and Ritual Help: If you see him out on his travels, you need not fear. Stand away at a respectful distance and watch to help gain an understanding of the meaning of physical death.

Anthropophagi

Land of Origin: England.

Other Origins: The name of this faery is Greek, but there is no extant evidence that this faery was ever part of Greek folk beliefs.

Other Names: None known.

Element: Air.

Appearance and Temperament: The Anthropophagi is a headless cannibal. What little brain he has is reputed to be near his reproductive organs. His eyes rest on his shoulders, and his mouth is in the center of his chest. He has no nose, a gift of nature which enables him to eat human flesh without gagging. They have very unpleasant natures, though it is said they only kill when hungry.

Time Most Active: Unknown.

Lore: These faeries were made popular by the famed English playwright, William Shakespeare, in *Merry Wives of Windsor* (1602) and *Othello* (1605), but they were already a part of English folklore before he brought them into the public consciousness.

The name Anthropophagi literally translates from the Greek as "man-eating." Some folklorists believe these are not faeries at all, but a remnant of a memory of a cannibalistic race which migrated from northern Africa to Britain in the early Dark Ages.

Aside from consuming humans, these faeries are said to use human bones for tools and other daily-used items such as mugs.

Where to Find Them: Unknown.

How to Contact: Unknown. They may not fully exist except as nebulous and almost forgotten thought-forms.

Magickal and Ritual Help: None.

Ashrays

Land of Origin: Scotland.

Other Origins: None known.

Other Names: Water Lovers, Asrais.

Element: Water.

Appearance and Temperament: Ashrays are both male and female and appear to be about twenty years old in human time, when in fact they are quite ancient. They have whitish, almost translucent bodies, and are often mistaken for sea ghosts. They have been blamed for good deeds and bad, but not enough is known about them to judge their overall intent or temperament where people are concerned.

Time Most Active: At night.

Lore: It is known that Ashrays cannot live on land, which has led some mythologists to speculate that they may have descended from a mythological race condemned to the water for some grievous misdeed, real or imagined.

Ashrays are completely nocturnal. If they are touched by sunlight they will melt into a rainbow pool of water.

Where to Find Them: Very few Ashrays are still seen today. If they are findable at all, it would be underwater.

How to Contact: Approach with extreme caution as their actions and intent towards humans is unknown. Call to them in their own underwater world while you are well protected.

Magickal and Ritual Help: Undetermined.

Attorcroppe

Land of Origin: Saxony.

Other Origins: None known.

Other Names: None known.

Element: Earth.

Appearance and Temperament: The Attorcroppe looks like a small serpent with arms and legs who walks upright. They are very malevolent.

Time Most Active: At night.

Lore: Attorcroppe (from the same root as the word adder) literally means "little poison head," and its likeness to a venemous serpent may mean that this faery came into the faery lore of old Saxony through the wily ways of poisonous snakes.

Where to Find Them: If it is possible to find them at all it would be in woodlands, near stream beds, and among rocks.

How to Contact: May not be contactable because they may not fully exist in whole forms.

Magickal and Ritual Help: None.

Ballybogs

Land of Origin: Ireland.

Other Origins: Similar faeries known as Bogles are part of Cornish and Welsh faery lore. In northern England and on the Isle of Man they are known as Boggans.

Other Names: Bogles, Peat Faeries, Mudbogs, Bog-a-boos, Boggies.

Element: Earth.

Appearance and Temperament: Ballybogs are mud-covered creatures of very small size. Their bodies are almost completely round, with their heads rising from their bulbous bodies without benefit of necks. They have long spindly arms and legs which look too thin and weak to support their weight. These solitary faeries can be helpful or baneful, but are usually said to be so stupid that it is hard to determine their temperament. They speak no known language and grunt and slobber instead of speaking.

The English Boggans wear hooded cloaks and are more articulate, slender, sly, and troublesome than their Irish cousins.

Time Most Active: All year.

Lore: The Irish have reported seeing Ballybogs at and near their peat bogs for centuries. Ireland has almost no natural coal or oil, and much of the country must rely on peat for its fuel needs, a commodity which must be collected periodically.

The Ballybogs seem relatively harmless, just unpleasant. Their function and purpose has never been ascertained, though it was once believed that Ballybogs were the guardian spirits of the bogs.

Up until Medieval times in northern England, legends of Ballybogs, or Boggans as they were called there, and their mischief were widespread. Until the seventeenth century the rural English ritually reenacted games with the Ballybogs and their king, an event which took place around Yule. The game involved the tossing up of numerous hoods, grabbing them, and racing with them back home (or in this case, a hometown pub) before the bog faeries (young men of the village) could touch the runners (as in a game of tag) with their staffs made of 13 bound willow branches. The object was to get the king's hood, which would then render protection to the community for the coming year.

Numerous human bodies have been found preserved in the peat bogs of northern Europe, many displaying evidence of ritual sacrifice. It is possible that several thousand years ago human sacrifices were made to placate the faeries of the bogs.

Where to Find Them: At peat bogs or mud holes.

How to Contact: Ask them to manifest in the physical.

Magickal and Ritual Help: You can call to them to ask them to assist you finding the best peat, but don't expect an intelligible answer.

Barabaos

See **Masseriol.**

Basilisk

Land of Origin: Greece.

Other Origins: Eastern Europe, Western Russia, the Baltics.

Other Names: Cockatrice.

Element: Fire.

Appearance and Temperament: The Basilisk has the body and head of a huge golden snake, but on its head sits a red comb like that of a rooster. It also has two arms which it uses to increase the speed of its slithering and to hold the front half of itself upright. It is highly poisonous and is reputed to hate humans.

Time Most Active: All year.

Lore: The Basilisk was considered by the Greeks to be the most deadly creature alive. It can kill by looking at, touching, or breathing on a human being or animal. Those who have tried to slay it are killed instantly by the release of the poisonous gases which make up the inside of the creature.

The only animals which can destroy it are the crow, the rooster, the weasel, and the mongoose. It can also be killed by being shown its own hideous reflection in a mirror. Killing a Basilisk has an instant impact on its numbers, because it reproduces slowly, taking nine full years for its eggs to hatch. Greek mythology tells us that the eggs are laid by enchanted roosters and then hatched by toads.

It is interesting to note that other than its native poison, there is no other reason to believe this creature dislikes humans any more than any other poisonous animal does.

Despite its serpentine appearance, the Basilisk is deathly afraid of snakes.

Where to Find Them: Faeryland.

How to Contact: Unknown. If you run into one in Faeryland, immediate retreat is advised.

Magickal and Ritual Help: None.

Bean-Fionn

Land of Origin: Ireland.

Other Origins: Germany and England.

Other Names: Water Woman. In Germany she is called the Weisse Frau and she is somewhat more benevolent than her Irish version. The Weisse Frau is very protective of children, and a kiss from her renders a child almost indestructible. She has also been known to give directions to lost travelers. She will, however, drown those who displease her or who hurt and abuse children. In England she is called Jenny Greentooth or the Greentoothed Woman, which has become a generic name for these types of drowning faeries in English-speaking countries.

Element: Water.

Appearance and Temperament: The Bean-Fionn (Ban-Shoan), which literally means "white woman," is a watery, female faery in a white gown who lives beneath lakes and streams and reaches up to drag under and drown children at play or work near or in the water.

Time Most Active: All year.

Lore: The Bean-Fionn may be one of those faery forms which exists not as a whole being, but as an incomplete thought-form created from the collective fears of persons past. In fact, she may have been created by parents who wished to warn their children away from dangerous lakes and rivers. An English nursery rhyme echoes the sentiments of these worried parents:

> *Mother, may I go out for a swim?*
> *Yes, my dearest daughter.*
> *Hang your clothes on a rowan limb,*
> *And don't go near the water.*

Other European cultures have their own Water Women which function in the same manner as Bean-Fionns. We can be grateful that there is believed to be only one of her in each of these lands.

Where to Find Her: Possibly in dark lakes where drownings have repeatedly occurred.

How to Contact: There is probably no way to contact her because she may not exist except in the most rudimentary astral form. Contact is probably not a good idea, anyway.

Magick and Ritual Help: None.

The Beansidhe

Land of Origin: Ireland.

Other Origins: None known, but other faeries which announce a death are found worldwide. The Beansidhe is also a part of other Celtic lore, though she is not as deeply associated with these places as with Ireland.

Other Names: Washer of the Shrouds, Washer at the Banks, Washer at the Ford. Banshee is the Anglicized spelling, the one commonly used in Canada and the United States. She is called Cointeach in Scotland, a word which literally means "one who keens." The Cornish call her Cyhiraeth. The Welsh know her as either Cyoerraeth or Gwrach y Rhibyn, meaning "Hag of the Dribble," and to the Welsh she can sometimes appear as a male. In Brittany they called her Eur-Cunnere Noe.

When she appears as a Washerwoman in Ireland (washing burial shrouds) at a river or stream, she is properly called the Bean-nighe.

Element: Water.

Appearance and Temperament: The Beansidhe (Ban-shee), or "woman faery," is another well-known and much feared Irish faery, though some might classify her as a ghost. She is always female and always appears in a filmy, full-sized human form. Long stringy hair partially covered with a hood, and a white gown or shroud are part of her attire, as is a wet and ghost-like appearance, as if she had just been fished from a moss-covered lake. Her appearance varies by region. In Donegal she is green-robed, and in County Mayo she is black-clad. In Cornwall she is said to have long black teeth.

Time most active: At night before a death.

Lore: The Beansidhe's keening (mourning wail) can be heard at night prior to a death, and her lamentations are still heard all over Ireland when death is near. Usually these faeries are attached to a particular family or locale, though the latter is not so common. Many believe the Beansidhe to be attached only to the old noble families of Ireland, those of Milesian descent.

The origins of the Beansidhe have been lost in time, but it is reasonable to assume that she represents a mother-form from the Irish land of the dead, Tir-na-nog. In old Ireland Tir-na-nog was also known as the "land of women," and it was believed that upon physical death a soul was reabsorbed into the womb of the Great Mother, or into some other woman form, to await rebirth.

Some persons who have heard a Beansidhe do not report her mournful keening as being frightening at all, but oddly comforting. But the majority find her sound bone-chilling and terrifying.

Occasionally a Beansidhe is seen at a river washing the winding sheets which will soon become a shroud. The "washer at the ford" is an old Celtic legend which stems from this belief. To see the washer meant that a major life-changing event was about to occur, and it was a fearsome sight. If later that night any of your candles burned in a winding pattern—like a shroud—you would know that death was to visit your own household.

In Scotland she has been seen squatting near the door of the one about to die. In Cornwall she stands near the window of the one about to die and flaps her wings against the glass. In doing this she is often mistaken for a crow, the bird associated with the Crone Goddess in Celtic mythology.

Special keening (caoine) music used at wakes in Ireland is said to have come from the Beansidhe's own lamentations.

In more modern folk stories it is said that if a group of Beansidhes are seen or heard together it means that a very great or holy person is about to die. However, the folklore does not tell us what constitutes "greatness" or "holiness," nor does it give any example of when such a phenomenon as this has ever occurred.

Where to Find Them: In the winter of Faeryland.

How to Contact: Contact not advised!

Magickal and Ritual Help: None known.

Bean-Tighe

Land of Origin: Ireland.

Other Origins: None known.

Other Names: Our Housekeeper.

Element: Earth.

Appearance and Temperament: No one has ever fully described a Bean-Tighe (Ban-tee or Ban-Teeg), but they are generally thought to look like small elderly women in old-fashioned peasant clothing, with kindly, dimpled faces. They are very friendly to humans and wish to have a friendly human house to watch over.

Time Most Active: All year, but especially from Samhain to Bealtaine when Irish families spend most of their time indoors.

Lore: The words Bean-Tighe literally mean "woman of the house." She is the opposite in temperament to a Beansidhe, though they are both attached to the homes of the old Milesian families. They are faery housekeepers, rather like the Brownies of Scotland, who can be found watching over children, hearths, and pets. It was believed they would finish up any household chores left undone by the tired mother of the house.

They love fresh strawberries and cream, and a bit of this and a share of your home is all the reward they ask.

The Bean-Tighe seeks the warmth of a friendly fireplace.

For centuries, Irish mothers have shared stories about their Bean-Tighe and her meticulous care of their children. If you had one in residence, it was not uncommon to get up in the middle of the night to check on a child and find that the windows had been adjusted and blankets taken off or put on the child's bed by the resident Bean-Tighe.

Bean-Tighes were thought to be on exceptionally good terms with the old village wise women of Ireland, known in the vernacular as Pishogues. Old women in Ireland had to be especially careful not to keep too clean a home lest they be accused of having a faery living with them, which would make them guilty of witchcraft.

Where to Find Them: At your hearthside.

How to Contact: Call out to one, open your home to her, leave out her favorite foods. They prefer to live in rural homes with children and fireplaces. Even if one will not take up residence with you she will offer blessings to your home, especially if you have Milesian ancestry.

Magickal and Ritual Help: Protection of home, children, and pets, and aid in household chores. She will also happily lend her energy to human fertility spells.

Black Angus

Land of Origin: England and Scotland.

Other Origins: Faery foretellers of death are known worldwide.

Other Names: In Scotland they are called Cu Sith, which literally means "faery dog," or Barguest. They are called Cwn Annwn in Wales, where they are seen crossing moors and wastelands by night. In Germanic countries they are called by a name which translates as "Gabriel's Hounds," named for the Judeo-Christian Angel of Death.

Element: Water.

Appearance and Temperament: Black Angus is a large black dog with yellow eyes and sharp fangs who roams the northern English and Scottish countryside showing himself to those who will die within a fortnight. Scottish Lowlanders claim he has horns on his head, which may have derived from some confusion with the Christian Devil.

Time Most Active: At night.

Lore: While old Black Angus presents himself to those about to die, he has occasionally been seen at a distance by others. When Angus announces his rather unpleasant news to you he will cross your path, jump in front of you, then turn and growl. Those who have experienced this say his eyes are bright yellow and his paws are wet. Any person who is the target of this dark messenger's pronouncement dies within a fortnight, and one must wonder how much of this is self-fulfilling prophecy.

A later addition to the Black Angus story concerns the ghost of an evil priest near Plymouth, called Dando, who was murdered while plotting wicked deeds. Dando has been reported to have been seen appearing with Black Angus in Cornwall and Devon, and many fear his appearance foretells not only impending death, but a miserable afterlife.

Where to Find Them: Unknown.

How to Contact: Contact not advised!

Magickal and Ritual Help: None.

The Blue Hag

See *Cailleac Bhuer.*

Blue Men of the Muir

See *Merpeople.*

Bocan

Land of Origin: The Isle of Skye in the Hebrides Islands of Scotland.

Other Origins: None known.

Other Names: None known.

Element: Air.

Appearance and Temperament: No description has ever been given of a Bocan; their sole purpose was to attack and mutilate travelers.

Time Most Active: At night.

Lore: The Bocan probably does not exist except as a thought-form, one which probably grew out of the fear of highwaymen, groups of bandits which plagued Britain's rural roadsides from the ninth to the nineteenth centuries. No mention of the Bocan exists in any extant folklore before the Medieval period.

No roadside attacks have been blamed on a Bocan in more than a hundred years.

Where to Find Them: Unknown.

How to Contact: Unknown, and probably not a good idea anyway.

Magickal and Ritual Help: None.

Boggarts

Land of Origin: Scotland.

Other Origins: None known.

Other Names: Hobgoblins, Goblins, Gobelins, the Boogey Man, Boogies, Padfoot, Boggans, Hobbers, Gobs, Blobs.

Element: Earth.

Appearance and Temperament: The Boggart is a male dwarf faery with a squat and distorted form. He is a cousin of the friendly house Brownie, but his intentions are very different. Whereas a Brownie will adopt a home for the joy of offering his help and mutual support, a Boggart will adopt a house just for the sheer delight of destroying things. They are very ill-tempered and greedy.

Lore: Boggart is synonymous with the more general term "Hobgoblin." He especially loves to eat smooth wood and can consume a home just like a termite or carpenter ant. A complete exorcism is the best tack to take should you discover a Boggart in your home.

They especially like to torment children, and their favorite ways of doing this are to take their food from them and then nearly smother them at night.

In northern England the Boggart is known as a Padfoot or Hobgoblin and enjoys frightening travelers and disrupting households. He is also thought to be poisonous to the touch. The following poem by Mark Shapiro entitled *The Wee Little Hobgoblin* typifies some of the havoc they can wreak on a happy home:

> *One wee little Hobgoblin*
> *All dressed up in red,*
> *Was spying on a farmhouse*
> *With mischief in his head.*
> *"This place," said the little Hobgoblin,*
> *"It could be lots of fun.*
> *Everything's so clean and tidy,*
> *And begging to be undone."*
> *So the wee little Hobgoblin*
> *He went to work with glee,*
> *He let the cattle out the gate*
> *And set the piglets free.*
> *He spilled some milk in the kitchen,*
> *And overturned the butterchurn.*
> *He yanked the laundry off the line*
> *And caused the soup to burn.*

> *He pinched the baby and scared the cat*
> *And had the mostest fun.*
> *And when his spree was over*
> *He said, "That's a job well done!"*

The root word "bog" which appears in the word Boggart may mean that they were once associated with the Ballybogs, faeries who inhabited the peat bogs of the British Islands.

Time Most Active: At night.

Where to Find Them: Unknown, unless one has invaded your home. If you want to see one, then let your deep mind take you to an infested house in the astral world. Just make sure he doesn't follow you home!

How to Contact: Contact not advised.

Magickal and Ritual Help: None.

Bogles

See **Ballybogs.**

Boobrie

Land of Origin: Scotland.

Other Origins: None known.

Other Names: Waterbird, Waterhorse.

Element: Water.

Appearance and Temperament: The Boobrie (Boo-bree) is a waterbird about a foot high which can either swim in or fly over the water. It is a dark animal with black feathers and a huge bill extending out about three feet from its body, which it uses to catch fish when meat is not available. It has large, sharp claws which often resemble disfigured human hands.

Time Most Active: At night.

Lore: The Boobrie preys on ships transporting sheep and cattle, which are its favorite foods. It mimics the sound of a particular animal's young to lure it to the side of the ship, where it is captured in the long talons and dragged underwater. When thwarted in its quest for meat, its cries of anger sound like those of an enraged bull.

The Boobrie can shapeshift into the form of a horse and run along the top of the water, complete with the sound effect of hooves beating on earth. In this form it has been seen by sailors who often mistake it for a ghost horse.

This faery is water-bound and cannot come onto land without destroying itself.

Where to Find Them: In the waters off Scotland.

How to Contact: If you feel you really must contact a Boobrie, it is best to do so from the safety of the shore where the faery cannot come. Call out to it and offer a piece of beef or mutton as an inducement.

Magickal and Ritual Help: It is unlikely that this selfish scavenger can be any help in magickal or ritual workings. While it might appear willing to do anything in return for a meal, there are more reliable faeries to ask for aid whose heart will be in your efforts.

Bookha or Bwca

See *Phooka*.

Brownies

Land of Origin: Scotland.

Other Origins: These faeries are also known in Canada and the United States, certainly brought over with Scottish immigrants.

Other Names: House Brownie, Little Man. He is called Nis in Denmark. In Russia they are called Domovoi and have been known to cry like a Beansidhe when death is approaching a member of their chosen family, and to warn of fires. In North Africa they are called Yumboes. The Chinese call them Choa Phum Phi. The English sometimes know them as Hobs.

Element: Earth.

Appearance and Temperament: The house Brownie of Scotland is one of the most benevolent and kind faeries you could hope to meet. They are very small dwarf faeries who always appear as males with coal black eyes. They wear little suits of green, blue, or brown, and small caps made of felt. Their ears are slightly pointed and they have long, nimble fingers.

Time Most Active: At night all year long.

Lore: The house Brownie looks for a deserving human to aid, one who is humble and gracious and is good to nature and other people. And he hunts for a warm house, one in which he feels he can be comfortable—that means one with no cat! They like the attic, wood-shed, or cellar of a human home best. Heat these areas for them, and feed them well to keep them. Their favorites foods are milk, honey, ale, and cake.

The Brownie is said to reward kindness shown to him by helping out around the house and on the farm, by bringing food and firewood, and by chasing away ill-meaning spirits from your dwelling. Brownies are still common to the Scottish Highlands and on the Hebrides Islands, but are rarely heard of elsewhere.

Because of their generous nature Brownies hate misers and cheats, cannot tolerate lying, and detest pretentiousness. Like their cousins the Leprechauns they like to cobble, but they will work on a pair of shoes rather than on only one.

Because Brownies are completely nocturnal some people believe they, like vampires, can never appear in sunlight. Brownies can go abroad in the daylight, but they prefer not to.

Roosters, long sacred to the Sun Gods of Europe, are the familiars (animals who help in magick and ritual) of Brownies. They crow at dawn, not—as human arrogance would have us believe—to tell us to wake up, but to announce to the Brownies that it is time to go to bed. This is especially important as some non-Scottish species of house Brownies will die if exposed to sunlight. Some Scots even believed Brownies could take the form of roosters and could help around the house in this physical form. The Mother Goose rhyme "I Had a Little Rooster" reflects this belief. The rhyme tells of the rooster doing dishes and baking bread.

Most Brownies are keenly intelligent. The only exception is the Dobie who, though dull-witted, still has a large heart. Dobies greatly wish to be of help to their human hosts but usually only make grand messes due to their lack of intellect.

Another Scottish Brownie is called a Killmoulis, and he protects and looks after mills in exchange for a bit of bread and a spot at his adopted family's fireplace.

Where to Find Them: Induce them to come to your home by leaving out food for them, and by showing kindness to all living creatures. They can easily be found almost anywhere in Faeryland, which may be the best place to contact them.

How to Contact: Brownies cannot be beckoned to you, but will only come when they are sure you are the sort of person they want to help and approach.

Magickal and Ritual Help: All household tasks; protection of home, family, and animals. They can, if they choose to, lend their energy to prosperity spells. It never hurts to ask their help. They will give it if they feel your request is a proper one.

The best way to get a Brownie to work with you is to offer it the sort of home and environment it likes on the astral plane in your astral residence. Over time you will no doubt develop a sense of mutual trust and will begin doing small kindnesses for each other. Build your relationship from there. It will be immensely rewarding.

Brown Men

Land of Origin: Cornwall.

Other Origins: Scotland.

Other Names: Moor Men is a less commonly used term.

Element: Fire.

Appearance and Temperament: Brown Men are short, thin male faeries who protect the animal life on Cornwall's Bodmin Moor. They have a sparse thatch of copper-red hair on their heads, have long plump arms, and dress in the brown and withered foliage of the moors. They do not appear to dislike humans, but avoid them whenever possible.

Time Most Active: All year.

Lore: Brown Men are cousins of the Scottish Brownies. Because they shun human contact, little is known about them.

Where to Find Them: On Bodmin Moor.

How to Contact: Call to them and tell them you are a friend who sympathizes with their mission, or take to them an animal who needs help. Approach with caution, because little is known about their temperament, but chances are they are friendly—just very shy.

Magickal and Ritual Help: Undetermined, but they may lend energy to spells to protect or heal animals.

Buachailleen

Land of Origin: Ireland and Scotland.

Other Origins: None known.

Other Names: The Herding Boys.

Element: Earth.

Appearance and Temperament: The Buachailleen (Book-al-een) are small faeries who look like young men, and in fact the name literally means "little boys." They wear pointed red hats, which may really be inverted flower caps, and they are excellent shapeshifters. They have a mischievous nature which borders on mean, and they will torment animals just for fun.

Time Most Active: Summer.

Lore: The Buachailleen dwells among pastured livestock during the summertime. They play pranks on the herds and on shepherds and tease the animals. Shepherds of these regions were once said to have an entire body of protective spells and rituals to work against these pests, but these have been lost probably due to the fact that this was an oral wisdom which died with the decline of the sheep industry. Where the Buachailleen live the rest of the year is unknown.

Where to Find Them: In pastures in summer.

How to Contact: Unknown and unadvised.

Magickal and Ritual Help: None.

Bugganes

See **Phynnodderees.**

Buggars

Land of Origin: England.

Other Origins: Buggars probably came to England as German Trolls.

Other Names: None.

Element: Air.

Appearance and Temperament: Buggars are so adept at shapeshifting that it is hard to describe their appearance. They are considered very dangerous to humans, but fortunately for us they never leave the astral world.

Time Most Active: All year.

Lore: Buggars are a type of goblin, and in England the word has become a slang term for a bratty child. Buggar may be a derivation of Boggart or Boogey Man.

Where to Find Them: Unknown.

How to Contact: Contact not advised!

Magickal and Ritual Help: None.

Bugul Noz

Land of Origin: Brittany.

Other Origins: None known.

Other Names: None known.

Element: Earth.

Appearance and Temperament: The Bugul Noz is hideously ugly, a fact he seems to find most distressing. He is one-of-a-kind, said to be the last of his race.

Time Most Active: All year.

Lore: The Bugul Noz is sadly aware of his repulsive appearance and will call out a warning to humans before he appears so as not to take them too much by surprise. He is a loner who is rarely seen.

His home is underground, deep in the woodlands of Brittany, where even the woodland animals fear his repugnant appearance.

Where to Find Him: In the woods of Brittany.

How to Contact: Evoke his presence at your circle, but be ready for his startling appearance.

Magickal and Ritual Help: Undetermined. So many people flee from the Bugul Noz that it is not known what help he might be in magick and ritual. Being of the earth he may offer help with spells of fertility and prosperity. He is desperately lonely and would most likely offer you anything he can in return for your company and compassion.

Bunyip

Land of Origin: Australia.

Other Origins: Possibly Central Africa.

Other Names: None known.

Element: Water.

Appearance and Temperament: Bunyips live in the swamps and marshes of Australia and look like plump humans, only smaller. They stand about four feet high and are very dirty, covered with the mud and slime of the swamps. Their feet face backward, but these are hard to see as Bunyips rarely leave the shallow waters.

Time Most Active: At dusk, dawn, and at night.

Lore: Bunyips are aboriginal in origin, and the natives used to claim that these faeries could not be seen by white people. Bunyips are shy and rarely seen in any case, though they are often heard. They bark like dogs and are able to warn nearby humans of impending dangers. They can also lead fishermen to catches and chase away any threatening poisonous swamp reptiles.

Bunyips first came into general notice in 1847 when a Sydney newspaperman began a series of articles on the folk beliefs of the aborigines. Since that time white Australians have considered the Bunyip to be no more than some type of swamp-dwelling wombat, another native Australian animal.

The aborigines still see, hear, and work with these native faeries on a regular basis.

Where to Find Them: In the swamps, bogs, and marshes of Australia, particularly in the southeastern region where belief in them is still strong among the native population.

How to Contact: Call out to them and announce that you have come as a friend who wishes nothing more than mutual goodwill. Listen for them rather than looking.

Magickal and Ritual Help: They can help you catch fish and can help protect the area where you are fishing. They can also warn you against intruders when you are working, camping, or traveling in marshy areas. Ask them to lend their energies to rituals designed to protect endangered wetlands.

Buttery Sprites

Land of Origin: England.

Other Origins: None.

Other Names: Buttery Spirits.

Element: Earth.

Appearance and Temperament: No one has ever seen a Buttery Sprite, but their presence is known by missing food and by the vengeance they seek against humans who have cheated others.

Time Most Active: Only at night.

Lore: Buttery Sprites live in the old abbeys and inns of England, where they wreak havoc on those whom they believe cheat others or live the lives of hypocrites. They especially like to torment unscrupulous priests and abbots. In abbeys they feel free to take any food not marked with a cross—especially fresh churned butter.

Because the lore about them is so attached to medieval religious life in England, the Buttery Sprites may not exist as whole beings, but rather as projected thought-forms from guilty persons.

The Buttery Sprites take their name from their favorite food of fresh butter. Their presence would often be felt in the butteries of the old buildings they lived in.

Where to Find Them: If they can be found it would be in old abbeys and inns.

How to Contact: Unknown.

Magickal and Ritual Help: Undetermined.

Bwaganod

Land of Origin: Wales.

Other Origins: None known.

Other Names: None known.

Element: Water.

Appearance and Temperament: Bwaganods (Boo-kah-nohds) are goblins who can shapeshift into other animal forms, including humanoid shapes. They do not like humans.

Time Most Active: Dusk.

Lore: Welsh faery lore tells us that the Bwaganod can only manifest in the human world for a brief time at dusk, when he can appear in any form he chooses. But we humans have the advantage here, because no Bwaganod has ever perfected his shapeshifting skills and is easily spotted if one looks closely.

No humans have been harmed by them, but they clearly do not like people and enjoy frightening and fooling them.

Where to Find Them: Unknown.

How to Contact: Contact not advised!

Magickal and Ritual Help: None.

Bwbachs

Land of Origin: Wales.

Other Origin: None known.

Other Names: Booakers, Cottagers.

Element: Earth.

Appearance and Temperament: Bwbachs (Boo-box) are solitary house faeries who are very mischievous but do not seem to wish to harm their host families. However, they do not have the helpful nature of the Scottish Brownie or the Irish Bean-Tighe. They are small and round, and wear large red hats and little loincloths which look like diapers. Around their necks they wear animal-fur cloaks. They are always seen as males.

Time Most Active: All year.

Lore: These mischievous house faeries intend to protect their adopted home from outsiders, but have no ability to distinguish friend from foe. One reportedly chased away a proselytizing preacher from a Welsh home. This protective instinct is for the dwelling itself and rarely for the family who lives there, so they will also chase away your friends and family.

The Bwbachs' pranks can be neutralized by ritually offering them food and by showing great respect for them. The lore of the Bwbachs and their need for respectful leavings of food is recorded in the Welsh nursery rhyme:

> *Tommy Trevarrow, Tommy Trevarrow,*
> *We will send bad luck tomorrow.*
> *The old curmudgeon to eat all thy bread,*
> *And not leave a piece for the Bwbach.*

Where to Find Them: Look for them in homes in Faeryland, but do not invite them into your own home as they are more trouble than they are worth.

How to Contact: If you really want to meet a Bwbach, make a simple evocation and invite them to your circle. Use a bit of milk or cake as an added inducement.

Magickal and Ritual Help: They may possibly be able to help with home protection spells, but their changeable nature makes them very untrustworthy.

Bwciod

Land of Origin: Wales.

Other Origins: None known.

Other Names: None known.

Element: Fire.

Appearance and Temperament: The Bwciod (Bu-key'd) is more of a nuisance than a danger, but he can turn nasty if thwarted. He is solitary and moves so fast that he can barely be seen by human eyes. The few accounts of him say he is slender, stands no more than a foot tall, has a long pointy nose, long fingers, and huge flat feet. His eyes are purple and reflect no emotions.

Time Most Active: Mostly at night.

Lore: The Bwciod is a goblin who loves fire and the warmth of human homes. Once he finds his way in he cannot be persuaded to leave, and exorcism is the only known remedy for this infestation. Fortunately he is solitary and comes alone, but he will make himself at home and let you know in no uncertain terms when he is unhappy.

Where to Find Them: Unknown. If you meet a Bwciod on the inner planes it is best to get as far away from him as possible to be sure he does not follow you home.

How to Contact: Contact not advised!

Magickal and Ritual Help: None known.

Cailleac Bhuer

Land of Origin: Scotland.

Other Origins: Similar faeries are in other Celtic countries.

Other Names: The Blue Hag, Black Annis, the Stone Woman.

Element: Water.

Appearance and Temperament: The Cailleac Bhuer (Call-y'ac V'fhoor) is one of a kind. She is an old woman who walks by night carrying her walking stick, her carrion crow on her left shoulder. However, her reputation as dangerous and ill-tempered may be a mistaken one. It is possible that this fear of her was created by the early Scottish churchmen seeking to eradicate the vestiges of the Old Religion by demonizing its Crone mythology.

Time Most Active: At night.

Lore: The word Cailleac literally means "old woman," and the Irish spelling Caillech is used when referring to the Crone Goddess. This is from the same root as the more well-known Gaelic word for a young girl, Caillin (Colleen).

There is only one Cailleac Bhuer, and she is probably a vestige of the old Crone Goddess of the Celts. She is depicted as wearing either black or blue-white tattered garments and is intimately associated with the winter season. She is said to dwell in a land which is always in winter—another likeness to the Crone Goddess. Her power is greatest from Samhain to Ostara, at which time it wanes considerably. She carries a staff made of holly topped with the head of a carrion crow, another symbol of the Crone. If one is touched by it, it kills instantly. Scottish legends says that the staff is buried under a tree for summer and retrieved again after Samhain night. If one can find that staff they will have power over the destiny of all human life.

In modern Scotland, Cailleac Bhuer is more commonly called by her English name, the Blue Hag. She still walks alone through the Highlands at night where she is greatly feared.

Where to Find Her: In the Scottish Highlands, or near the western sea in Faeryland. The best time to look for her is during the waning moon.

How to Contact: Do not fear her, but do use caution. Try making an evocation to her with the same respect and reverence you would give to the Goddess in her guise as Crone. She is most likily a Goddess— merely one in a devalued state.

Magickal and Ritual Help: Undetermined, but if she is a part of the Goddess—even one who has been devalued over the years—this faery could aid in any type of magick and ritual with powerful results.

Callicantzaroi

Land of Origin: Greece, Albania, and Italy.

Other Origins: None known.

Other Names: None known.

Element: Earth.

Appearance and Temperament: The Callicantzaroi are small, skinny, and always nude. They are trooping faeries who, instead of riding horses, ride chickens. They wear elaborate headgear on their Rades and have the feet of various animals.

Time Most Active: Yule.

Lore: The Callicantzaroi are all either partially or totally blind, though no lore tells us how they came to be this way. They spend all their time trooping together, especially at Yule, when they heartily celebrate the rebirth of the pagan Sun Gods.

They are often accompanied on their Rades by a host of other crippled faeries who are frightening to look at, though this has nothing to do with their infirmities, but with their grotesque appearance in general.

Italian faery lore tells us that when these customs were transferred to Christmas, it was noticed that the Callicantzaroi vanish after Twelfth Night and do not return again until the next Midwinter Eve.

They like to foul fresh water, but a touch of hyssop is reputed to counteract this. However, if you would rather not have these faeries around, Nancy Arrowsmith, author of *A Field Guide to the Little People,* says that burning an old shoe will drive them away.

Where to Find Them: Look for them at Yule and in the winter of Faeryland.

How to Contact: Call to them and identify yourself as a friend. Offer them some pork, as this is their favorite food.

Magickal and Ritual Help: Undetermined.

Chi Spirits

Land of Origin: China.

Other Origins: None known.

Other Names: None known.

Element: Air.

Appearance and Temperament: No one has ever seen a Chi Spirit, as they are pure energy and have no physical confines.

Time Most Active: All year.

Lore: The word Chi in Chinese means "energy," and these spirits are part of a vast pantheon of Chinese house spirits whose benevolent energies are thought necessary to the smooth running of a household. Like Scottish Brownies, the Chi Spirits adopt a human home in which to live.

The Chinese go to great lengths to see that the beneficial energies Chi Spirits emit are not impeded in any way. Furniture is often rearranged to facilitate the free movement of their energy, and mirrors, which act as portals allowing energy to pass through, are placed over any immovable impediments such as a wall which is not in a good place.

If Chi is blocked, no harm will befall anyone, but certain benefits will be diminished. In some rare cases extreme blockage of Chi energy can cause minor disturbances, hauntings, and illness.

Where to Find Them: Unknown. While the Chinese think of this energy as a faery, Chi Spirits may be no more than the psychic vibrations which always surround us and are part of everything.

How to Contact: Invite them into your home in a ritual you design just to bring them in.

Magickal and Ritual Help: Undetermined, but their presence may increase physical health and stamina, and offer general protection to your home.

Chin-Chin Kobakama

Land of Origin: Japan.

Other Origins: Possibly China.

Other Names: None known.

Element: Earth.

Appearance and Temperament: Elven-like in appearance, the Chin-Chin Kobakama is either male or female, and appears to be elderly but amazingly spry. They are generally friendly towards humans, but can be a nuisance.

Time Most Active: All year during daylight hours.

Lore: The Chin-Chin Kobakama is similar to the house Brownie known to westerners, but these faeries are said to be specifically floor and rug faeries. They move into human homes and will bless and protect them as long as they are kept clean. They have been known to tease sloppy children and chase after sloppy housekeepers.

Where to Find Them: Unknown.

How to Contact: Keep your home clean and set out food for them. Invoke them with a simple ritual, but make sure you really want them in your home. If not, visit them on the inner planes.

Magickal and Ritual Help: Possibly home blessings, protection.

Churn Milk Peg and Melch Dick

Land of Origin: England.

Other Origins: None known.

Other Names: Acorn Lady and Melsh Dick.

Element: Earth.

Appearance and Temperament: These are small dwarf faeries— Peg is a woman and Dick a man. They wear the peasant clothing of fifteenth century England and their nature is very capricious.

Time Most Active: Spring through autumn.

Lore: These faeries, two of a kind, love nuts of all sorts and will guard them by giving cramps and bloat to those who take the fruit from the tree or plant they are watching over at any particular time. Fortunately for us, they move around quite a bit and are never in one place for very long. If you go to pick a nut or nut fruit and feel a decided pinch, take it as a warning that these plants are being watched over. They also guard orchards and can terrify fruit thieves.

Though Peg and Dick are both quite lazy themselves, they despise laziness in humans and are known to give a quick pinch to startle people out of their daydreams, or chase them to get their sluggish blood moving. But since both Peg and Dick are somewhat arthritic, humans can easily outdistance them.

One explanation of the origin of these two faeries ties in with the folklore which says that nuts and certain fruits enhance human fertility. So prized were they that these two faeries were sent to protect them. In this guise they may actually be devalued fertility deities associated with Bealtaine. The fact that milk, fruit, and nuts (foods associated with the fertility Sabbat of Bealtaine) are the only foods in their diet further establishes this link.

Where to Find Them: In the English countryside.

How to Contact: Make an invitation to your circle. Offer nuts and milk as an inducement if you really want them around.

Magickal and Ritual Help: Undetermined.

Clurichauns

Land of Origin: Ireland.

Other Origins: A similar faery known as a Monciello is native to Italy.

Other Names: His Nibs.

Element: Earth.

Appearance and Temperament: The Clurichaun (Kloo-ree-kahn) is a solitary faery who resembles his cousin the Leprechaun, and no sightings of females have ever been recorded. He is the self-appointed guardian of a wine cellar, one which he chooses in his own time, and then moves in and makes himself at home. The Clurichaun is almost always drunk, but is impeccably well-groomed and well-dressed.

Generally he has a cheerful disposition, but is rather aloof even while intoxicated. Like many faeries, the Clurichaun wears a red hat which may be made of plants.

Time Most Active: All year.

Lore: A Clurichaun in your cellar will prevent casks from leaking and wines from going bad, and he will chase away all those who come to take a drink uninvited by the master of the house. Occasionally he can be heard singing Irish folk songs in the wine cellars. If you ignore or mistreat him he will wreak havoc on your cellars and on your home, and he will most definitely spoil your wine stock.

Once you have chased away your Clurichaun by insensitivity or lack of hospitality no other will ever come to take his place.

Where to Find Them: If you wish to attract a Clurichaun to your cellars, leave a bit of wine out for him or design a ritual to invite him in. You don't have to have an elaborate wine stock, but you must have a collection in your basement in order for him to be interested in staying there and "adopting" your home as his. If you already have a Clurichaun, know that he is there to stay.

How to Contact: See above.

Magickal and Ritual Help: Aids in home protection against thieves and vandals, guards the wine cellar.

Coblynau

See **Knockers**.

Corrigans

Land of Origin: Brittany.

Other Origins: Cornwall.

Other Names: Korrigans.

Element: Water.

Appearance and Temperament: This changeable faery came to Cornwall from Breton France, where she is still well known. Corrigans appear as blonde females by night and repulsive hags by day.

Time Most Active: All year.

Lore: The Corrigan may be a devalued version of the Celtic Triple Goddess known as the Morrigan, who is three Crone Goddesses in one. Or she may be a myth which underscores the devaluation of women, especially elderly women.

Men who see her by night are never able to forget her, and some pine away for want of her. Stories exist concerning men who marry a Corrigan only to discover in the morning the true nature of their wives. Other legends state that if a man genuinely loves her in her night form and is open-minded enough to continue loving her in the morning, that she will become human and remain beautiful both night and day.

Where to Find Them: Probably in woodlands near running water.

How to Contact: Unknown.

Magickal and Ritual Help: Undetermined.

Cucui

Land of Origin: Northern Mexico.

Other Origins: The Cucui is well-known in the Hispanic communities of southwestern North America.

Other Names: None known.

Element: Earth.

Appearance and Temperament: Cucui (Coo-coo-ee) has almost become a generic term for "monster" among Mexicans and American Hispanics. If the Cucui had a characteristic look, it has long been lost to us. He is not friendly, nor is he considered safe to be around.

Time Most Active: All year.

Lore: Whoever or whatever the Cucui originally was, over time he has taken on a popular image similar to that of a staring zombie or ghoul. He apparently cannot think in any sense that we understand the term, and he seems to be motivated only by some primal instinct. He is best described as a large, drooling monster who is out to get and hurt anyone he can get his hands on. Fortunately he is rarely seen.

Where to Find Them: Unknown.

How to Contact: Contact not advised!

Magickal and Ritual Help: None.

Cu Sith

See **Black Angus.**

Devas

Land of Origin: Persia.

Other Origins: Greece, Isle of Man, England.

Other Names: None known.

Element: Any, depending on where the Deva makes its home.

Appearance and Temperament: Devas are small faeries who appear as bright spheres of light. When the light is toned down they are said to be golden-colored beings who wear richly colored robes. They are nature spirits who seem interested in humans, but are shy.

Time Most Active: All year, but especially in spring.

Lore: Deva is a word which comes from the Persian and means "shining one," which is descriptive of their appearance. It may have once been a generic term for all faery life, but as the word went west, first to Greece and then to Britain, it became associated with deeply elemental nature spirits.

Devas live in nature and almost seem at one with it. They can live in lakes, trees, or woods and take on elemental vibrations depending on where they choose to live. In England they are said to still heavily populate the Epping Forest.

Where to Find Them: Anywhere in nature; all over Faeryland.

How to Contact: Because of their extreme elemental nature you can best contact one by going directly into nature and inviting them to be a part of your outdoor rituals.

Magickal and Ritual Help: Undetermined, but you might try asking them to lend energy to any spell which heavily uses one particular element.

Dinnshenchas

Land of Origin: Ireland.

Other Origins: None known.

Other Names: None known.

Element: Fire.

Appearance and Temperament: The Dinnshenchas (Din-sheen-k'has) are dwarf faeries in the service of the Irish Goddess Aine, who is both a cattle Goddess and a Goddess who protects women. They have been said to shapeshift into any form to help avenge women harmed by men. They also guard cattle.

Time Most Active: Unknown.

Lore: It is unclear whether the stories about Dinnshenchas avenging wronged women are merely a wish-fulfillment thought-form or not. Aine was raped by a Connacht king. She later slew her attacker, and was elevated in the folklore of the early centuries of this era to the status of a patron Goddess of wronged women. The Dinnshenchas is also the name of a collection of old Irish stories.

Where to Find Them: In pastures, or at the shrines to Aine which are to be found in her home county, Kilkenny.

How to Contact: Ritual invocation at your circle or during spells for the protection of women. Design a ritual to contact Aine and draw her power into you.

Magickal and Ritual Help: It is likely that Aine and her faeries can be called upon to protect and give strength and courage to women, and to guard and watch over cattle. In a ritual situation, ask that she allow the Dinnshenchas to guard you if you are approaching a difficult or dangerous situation.

Djinn

See *Jinn.*

Domoviyr

Land of Origin: Russia.

Other Origins: None known.

Other Names: Domovoy is the singular form. There are four subspecies of this faery, each with a different name.

Element: Earth.

Appearance and Temperament: Domoviyr (Doe-moe-veer) are male elves, who like their cousins, the Brownies, live in human homes which they protect with fierce loyalty. They always wear red shirts and blue girdles, and they like to grumble and growl, but their proverbial bark seems worse than their bite.

Time Most Active: All year.

Lore: The word Domoviyr is used in Russia as a generic term for faery in much the same way as the word Pixie is used in England. This faery is known for doing favors for his adopted family that are not always appreciated, such as stealing needed supplies from the neighbors. He will raise a ruckus to let the family know of approaching trouble and can be heard to moan and sob when death is coming to his home.

In Nancy Arrowsmith's book *A Field Guide to the Little People*, she warns that persons acquainted with the Domoviyr must be especially on guard on March 30, for this is the day when they shed their winter skins and grow new, lighter ones for summer. It is also a day during which they have fits of "bad temper."

Domoviyr have jealous natures, and persons who want to host these creatures must constantly be on guard against this. They are especially watchful of poultry meats, which are their favorite foods, and will protest loudly if a larger portion is given to a neighbor or another faery than is given to them. They must be offered libations of grain at each Sabbat and always given a portion of any meal containing poultry to avoid their temper tantrums, which can shake a house to its foundation.

There are four subspecies of Domoviyr who each have specific specialties in regard to duties around their adopted household. The first subspecies is the Vazila who takes care of horses. He is an excellent caretaker of finer animals, but isn't much interested in the welfare of the others. The Bagan and the Ovinnik, who protect and look out for other farm animals, live in barns rather than a home. And lastly there is the Bannik who guards and protects the bath house and any nearby freshwater ponds.

Where to Find Them: In homes behind the fireplace or stove, or in densely wooded areas of Faeryland.

How to Contact: Set out food for them and ritually invite them in. A safer way to get to know them while deciding if you want one in your own home is to visit them in a home in Faeryland. Keep in mind that they are very temperamental and that there are faeries much easier to get along with who will be glad to share your home.

Magickal and Ritual Help: None, unless they live with you, in which case they will protect your home and help keep your cupboards well stocked.

Dracs

Land of Origin: France.

Other Origins: They are similar to the German Nix.

Other Names: They are called Dracae in England, where they are less well-known.

Element: Water.

Appearance and Temperament: In their natural state Dracs appear as great floating purple blobs in the surface of the water. But more often they are seen in the form of a golden chalice or in a female humanoid form. They are dangerous to approach.

Time Most Active: All year.

Lore: Dracs are not bound to live in water, but seem to prefer it there. They are sometimes found in damp, mossy caves and rocky outcroppings near bodies of water. They are most populous in the English Channel, but their former home was the Seine River, which was, until humans took it over, their sacred kingdom. It is still believed that they retain a capitol city under the Seine.

Dracs are always on the lookout for human males whom they take as mates. One way they lure them is by appearing as beautiful women. But more often, when they play on the surface of water, they take the shape of a golden chalice which they know will be highly attractive to avaricious humans. When unsuspecting men reach down to grab the prize, they are dragged under to the Drac kingdom.

The Dracs love their water world and have been seen floating down rough water on wooden plates with the same delight with which humans would float on a raft.

Where to Find Them: In the waters of France. In Faeryland search for them by the western sea.

How to Contact: If you really want to meet one, try making a call to one while in Faeryland at the western sea or other body of water. It is best not to go close enough to allow one to touch you.

Magickal and Ritual Help: None.

Drakes

Land of Origin: England.

Other Origins: None known.

Other Names: None known.

Element: Fire.

Appearance and Temperament: Drakes have never been seen by human eyes, but they have been smelled. They are benevolent house spirits who will bless your hearth and multiply and keep your firewood dry in exchange for living in your home.

Time Most Active: From nightfall until just past dawn.

Lore: Drakes are very kindly, and not one of them has been known to react negatively to human mistreatment. If they are not welcomed, they just leave. The only drawback to a Drake is that they do not smell good at all. The odor they produce has been described as a cross between rotten eggs and a dirty chicken coop.

Where to Find Them: In wood piles, at hearthsides, and in deep woods with very old trees. They prefer rural areas.

How to Contact: Invite them to your hearth and they will probably come. Leave food and provide warmth and respect to keep them. If you don't have a fireplace in your home, then provide one for yourself and them in your astral home.

Magickal and Ritual Help: Aside from helping provide you with dry firewood, a Drake can lend energy to any spell done in the fireplace, which makes their capacity to aid you almost unlimited.

Drus

See **Dryads.**

Dryads

Land of Origin: Celtic countries.

Other Origins: Tree spirits and tree faeries are a worldwide phenomenon.

Other Names: Tree Spirits, Tree Ladies, Druidesses, Hamadryads. In Gaelic they are sometimes called Sidhe Draoi, which means "Faery Druids."

Element: Air.

Appearance and Temperament: Dryads are tree-dwelling spirits from whom the female Druidic order took its name. They are playful creatures who seem totally androgynous, though they are always referred to as female. This labeling is simply a guess, for they are seen as not much more than enchanting wisps of pure light, sometimes gently colored, in tree heights. Dryads seem open to human contact, but are very capricious, and it would be hard to tell if one was in the mood to help, play, or just tease.

Time Most Active: All year, but particularly at the Esbats (full moons).

Lore: Dryads prefer willow trees to all others, though they live in all of the 13 Celtic sacred trees. Faery willows which lodge Dryads are said to walk about at night seeking new locations to lay down their roots. Some persons have said that they have learned much unrecorded tree lore by observing how the Dryads' songs and appearance subtly alters as they flit from tree to tree.

It was the Dryads who gave the secrets of tree magick to the Druids and aided them in learning about divination and astral travel. The Dryads make beautiful music with their voices, sounds which are very compelling to humans. And while no human has been harmed by following these irresistible sounds, caution is advised lest you be tempted to stay overlong in the astral realm.

Dryads may have been native to Greece, where they were called Drayades and were also female tree spirits. The most famous Greek Dryad was Daphne, who was pursued by Apollo and turned into a laurel after repeating a prayer to a Virgin Goddess.

The Greeks also had male tree spirits known as Drus, and tree-bound faeries called Hamadryads. Unlike Celtic Dryads, Hama-dryads could not move from tree to tree but spent their entire lives in only one. There they were born, lived, and died.

Dryads live among the highest tree boughs.

Where to Find Them: In the physical or the astral you must go to a grove of trees, preferably one with willows or other Druidic sacred trees. Also look for them in the Faery Triad of oak, ash, and thorn, or in rowan, birch, and elder trees.

How to Contact: Invite them to your circle and ask them to join you in whatever ritual you have planned. Even if they don't show up at your circle, they may send you helpful energy if they feel your request is a fair one. If you are in Faeryland they may find you. Dryads will often show up to circles when the spirits and guardians of the east are called.

Magickal and Ritual Help: They are thought to be useful in human attempts to connect with deities if they are approached properly. As they did with the Druids, they may be persuaded to teach you the secrets of divination, astral travel, and tree magick. Begin forming a solid relationship with these faeries by working with them frequently, but be willing to be patient with their games.

Duendes

Land of Origin: Iberian Peninsula.

Other Origins: The Spanish brought this faery form to Mexico and to Central and South America.

Other Names: None known.

Element: Earth.

Appearance and Temperament: These solitary faeries appear as middle-aged women in green robes. They are small and sly, and their fingers look like long icicles. Extreme jealousy of the human condition is their primary emotion, one which overrides all other concerns, and they seek to harm and destroy humans whenever possible. Fortunately there are few left.

Time Most Active: All year, especially at night.

Lore: Duendes (Doo-in-days) attach themselves to homes and become so entrenched that they are very difficult to exorcise. They would love to drive their human families from the homes so that they might have these dwellings to themselves. To this end they make life miserable for the human family. They are such practical jokers and engage in so much poltergeist-like activity that many people with a Duende will swear their home is haunted. They especially like to throw things and move furniture about. They have been known to help clean a house, but this is for their own comfort and not for that of the humans with whom they share the house.

Where to Find Them: Unknown.

How to Contact: Contact not advised!

Magickal and Ritual Help: None.

Duergarrs

Land of Origin: England.

Other Origins: The name is Franco-Spanish and may have been brought to England with the Norman conquest in 1066.

Other Names: None known.

Element: Earth.

Appearance and Temperament: Duergarrs (Doo-ay-gahrs) are malicious dwarf faeries who, like Trolls, prey on travelers. They wear lambskin jackets, moleskin shoes and green hats, and they stand just under two feet tall. They are extremely surly and dislike people.

Time Most Active: All year.

Lore: Duergarrs are solitary faeries who guard faery paths and steer humans away from them. They are the self-appointed guardians of the faery peoples. When there are no faery paths to guard they turn their vicious pranks on travelers. Two of their favorite pastimes are creating a confusing fork in the road and removing human directional signposts. Fortunately for us, Duergarrs are an almost vanished race.

Where to Find Them: Near faery paths all over Faeryland.

How to Contact: Unknown.

Magickal and Ritual Help: None known.

Dunters

See **Red Cap.**

Dybbuk

Land of Origin: Israel.

Other Origins: These faeries were possibly native to ancient Canaan or Babylonia before being adopted into Hebrew folklore.

Other Names: Dibbuk. The plural form is Dybbukkim, both words being transliterated from Hebrew.

Element: Air.

Appearance and Temperament: The Dybbuk (Dib-buck) has no corporeal form. It is a spirit only, and is of neither male nor female gender. Their sole purpose is invading the bodies of humans to cause them to do evil or make mischief.

Time Most Active: All year.

Lore: Long before Judaism became the world's first codified, patriarchal religion, the Hebrew people had one of the richest pantheons of faery folklore ever known on the planet. Much of this was borrowed from and shared with the other tribal peoples of the region. Nearly all of this lore has been lost to us because it was successfully purged, first by the early rabbis and then again later by the first Christians.

The faery lore about the Dybbuk survived because it was best known at the time when both Jews and the early Christians were trying to drive Rome from Israel and many of the tactics they were forced to take violated their religious ethics. Thus grew up the still-popular phrase, "A Dybbuk must have gotten into me."

A Dybbuk is almost better described as a demon than a faery because of its power to temporarily possess a human body. People believed possessed by one were thought to have reached this state through their own negative acts. Kabbalistic literature (Jewish and Gnostic mystic texts) gives specific protocol for exorcising a Dybbuk, much as the Catholic church prescribed similar ceremonies. If you are interested in these ceremonies, look to the writings of Isaac Luria and Moses Cordovero. But if you are really in fear that a Dybbuk is near, any intense exorcism should banish it from you. Or try using music to both drive it away and to protect yourself. Much of the music used in Judaism originally consisted of chants of protection meant to invoke the power of the deities against astral entities. Dybbuks are thought to hate music so much that they will flee any place where musical notes can be heard.

The first written story about a Dybbuk was recorded in the early sixteenth century. A rather benign story about one which is still in print is the Jewish folktale *The Dybbuk,* by Ben Horovitz.

Where to Find Them: They are believed to live in dark abysses and to be attracted to areas of discord and fighting, from which they draw their energy to live. They are not visible to the naked eye, but might possibly show themselves in some form or another in the darker regions of Faeryland.

How to Contact: Contact not advised!

Magickal and Ritual Help: None.

Elles and Elle Maids

See **Wilde Frauen.**

Ellyllons

Land of Origin: Cornwall and Wales.

Other Origins: None known.

Other Names: None known.

Element: Water.

Appearance and Temperament: Ellyllons are small inland lake faeries who transport themselves by riding on eggshells. Their attitude toward humans is undetermined.

Time Most Active: All year, particularly spring.

Lore: These are the faeries who are guardians of the domain of the Lady of the Lake from the Arthurian myths. They live at the bottom of Dosmary Pool, a lake in Cornwall, and are shielded by the illusion of water.

Where to Find Them: Dosmary Pool in Cornwall.

How to Contact: Unknown.

Magickal and Ritual Help: Undetermined, but they may help spiritual seekers contact the Goddess.

Elves

Land of Origin: Worldwide.

Other Origins: None.

Other Names: Each land has various different elf faeries which go by many different names. Most common are the Germanic names Elb, Erl, and Mannikin.

Element: Usually Earth.

Appearance and Temperament: Elves dress differently depending on what land they come from, but are all small and chubby. Mostly they are kind and beneficial to humans; a very few types are actually dangerous. As a general rule, trooping Elves are good and solitary Elves are bad.

Time Most Active: Usually at night.

Lore: Elves can sew and spin very well, and can even spin gold from grain if needed. The faery tale of Rumpelstiltskin tells the story of a self-serving Elf who spins gold from straw in order to obtain a human child.

They also spin cloth and make shoes and are known for aiding deserving humans in need. They have few enemies, the most noted being cats. Mice are their familiars as well as their household pets, and occasionally Elves appear in nursery rhymes and faery tales disguised as mice. The following nursery rhyme tells of a group of spinning mice/Elves and the cat who tries to trick them into becoming her supper.

> *Six little mice sat down to spin,*
> *Pussy passed by, and she peeped in.*
> *"What are you doing, my little men?"*
> *"Weaving coats for gentlemen."*
> *"Shall I come in and cut off your threads?"*
> *"Oh no, Mistress Pussy, you'd bite off our heads."*
> *"Of course I shall not, but I'll help you spin."*
> *"That so you say, but you can't come in."*

Where to Find Them: In fields, homes, woodlands, and all over Faeryland.

How to Contact: Invite them to your circle or home, leave out food and milk for them, and lock up your cat!

Magickal and Ritual Help: Depends on the region the Elf is from and what type of Elf he is. Most can be asked to aid in home protection rites and aid in the raising of energy for all types of spell and ritual work.

The Erlkonig

Land of Origin: Germany.

Other Origins: Denmark.

Other Names: The Danish name is Ellerkonge.

Element: Air.

Appearance and Temperament: Erlkonig means "Elf King," and that is how he appears, as an Elf with a huge golden crown and expensively tailored clothing. He is seen only by someone just before death.

Time Most Active: All year.

Lore: The Erlkonig (Earl-koe-neeg) is like a Beansidhe in that he warns of the approach of death. But instead of warning everyone within hearing range, he appears only to the one about to die.

The Erlkonig has long been a part of Germanic folklore; his origins go far back into the dark years of history.

In 1815, Austrian composer Franz Schubert immortalized the Elf King legend when he set to music the famous ballad poem *Erlkonig* by J.W. von Goethe. In this eerie and intense song, a father is riding through a fierce snowstorm clutching his young son near him for warmth. But the boy hides his face in his father's cloak and is fearful. When the father asks what is wrong, the child replies that he sees the Elf King. The father, of course, tells him he is merely seeing mist. But the Elf King calls to the boy to come and play, and the boy, nearing panic now, clutches even more tightly at his father, who tells him he is hearing only rustling leaves. Finally the boy tells his father that "the Elf King has hurt me." The father grows disturbed at hearing this, and presses on for home. It is not until the final stanza of the song, when the father reaches the courtyard of his own house, that he finds the child is dead.

Like the Fylgiar of Iceland who also foretells death, the condition of Erlkonig presages what sort of death it will be. If he looks pained, the death will be a painful one. If he appears serene, so will the death be.

Where to Find Him: He lives in Valhallah, the Nordic Land of the Dead, when not out making his rounds.

How to Contact: Contact not advised!

Magickal and Ritual Help: None.

Erdluitle

Land of Origin: Switzerland.

Other Origins: Northern Italy, Western Austria.

Other Names: Duckfoots is a slang term for them. The males are called Hardmandlene, and the females are called Erdbiberli.

Element: Earth.

Appearance and Temperament: These dwarf faeries have webbed feet which they try to keep hidden out of embarrassment. However, they cannot swim and sink like stones if placed in water. They wear hoods, smocks, and long cloaks which always drape over their feet. They used to be helpful to farmers, but now seem to dislike humans.

Time Most Active: Unknown.

Lore: The Erdluitle (Aird-lou'ee-t'l) are not seen as much as they used to be. This is probably because they have decided that they no longer care for humans rather than being any indication that they are dying out. They used to be credited with having some control over the weather, which they would manipulate to aid local farmers.

Where to Find Them: Unknown.

How to Contact: Unknown.

Magickal and Ritual Help: None known.

Erdmanlein

See **Gnome.**

The Fachan

Land of Origin: Scotland.

Other Origins: None known.

Other Names: Peg Leg Jack.

Element: Air.

Appearance and Temperament: This Highland faery might appear comical if not for his extremely nasty disposition. The Fachan (Fah-kahn) has one of everything—one head, one eye, one ear, one arm, one leg, one toe, etc.—all centered directly down the middle of his hairy and feathered body. In his one hand he carries a spiked club which he swings as he chases away visitors from his home atop the highest Highland mountains.

Time Most Active: All year.

Lore: The Fachan is jealous of the gift of flight and spends his time brooding over this painful oversight of the deities. He hates all other living things and chases them away with his vicious-looking club. He is, of course, a very solitary faery.

Where to Find Them: On the highest Highland mountains.

How to Contact: Contact not advised!

Magickal and Ritual Help: None.

Fays

Land of Origin: Albania.

Other Origins: None known.

Other Names: The word Fay is similar to the Latin word *fatum,* which means "fate," a word from which many Romance languages take their generic names for faeries. Others such names are Fee, Fada, Fae, Fata, and Fas.

Element: Probably Air.

Appearance and Temperament: Fays are tiny, winged seasonal faeries who are born teasers and have very capricious natures, but they are never malicious.

Time Most Active: All year, especially at seasonal changes.

Lore: These faeries have four guises, one for each season of the year. They are beloved of the Triple Goddess and help her turn the Wheel of the Year, changing the seasons as they go. They are credited with aiding plants through these changes by doing little tasks like shaking trees in autumn to help work loose the dead leaves and opening blossoms on spring flowers.

Where to Find Them: In nature and all over Faeryland.

How to Contact: Make a simple invocation to them, or find them in Faeryland.

Magickal and Ritual Help: They are so temperamental and capricious that is hard to say if they would be of any help to humans at all. This would all depend on if they were in the mood to be bothered with you. If they are, they love to dance to raise energy which you might persuade them to direct in your favor.

Fin Folk

Land of Origin: Scotland.

Other Origins: Cornwall and Wales.

Other Names: Sea Gardeners, the Lady's Own.

Element: Water.

Appearance and Temperament: The Fin Folk are anthropomorphic faeries who have made it clear that they wish to avoid humans, though they seem not to wish us any harm.

Time Most Active: Unknown.

Lore: No one has ever met the Fin Folk outside of mythology, but there are mythological and faery tale stories about a small number of chosen humans who have been taken beneath the lochs of Scotland to be shown the Fin Folk's splendid underwater world, which is said to be a utopian miniature kingdom encased in glass on loch bottoms. The Fin Folk's favorite pastime is gardening, and their underwater world is a paradise of vibrantly colored flowers and lush foliage.

Where to Find Them: Under the lochs of Scotland, an easy place to go in the astral.

How to Contact: Approach with caution, since little is known about them. If they are willing they will show you their world, but be careful not to offend them or overstay your welcome.

Magickal and Ritual Help: This is undetermined because they have shunned human contact, but they may be helpful in lending their energies to spells for the protection and preservation of plants and marine life.

Fir Darrigs

Land of Origin: Ireland.

Other Origins: Possibly Scotland was their first home.

Other Names: Rat Boys.

Element: Water.

Appearance and Temperament: Fir Darrigs (Fear Durgs) are fat, ugly faeries with dark, hairy skin and long snouts and tails which give them a rat-like appearance. They wear torn and shabby costumes which look as if they date to the Middle Ages. If you have one around it is best to appear conciliatory and friendly until you can banish him. He is a morbidly dangerous faery whose food tastes run to carrion, and his shillelagh (Irish walking stick) is topped with a skull of unknown origin.

Time Most Active: Winter.

Lore: Fir Darrigs are thought to be a sub-race of the Formorians, ones who live near the sea rather than in it. They like to enjoy the heat near human fireplaces, but they make their homes in damp raths or marshes near the sea. Fir Darrigs are surprisingly good swimmers, yet they make no attempt to obtain fresh seafood. Rotting sea carrion is a smell they adore.

Where to Find Them: Along polluted coastlines, swamps, marshes, and in coastal ruins.

How to Contact: Contact not advised!

Magickal and Ritual Help: None.

Fireesin

Land of Origin: The Isle of Man.

Other Origins: None known.

Other Names: Farm Faeries, The Harvesters.

Element: Earth.

Appearance and Temperament: The Fireesin (Fear-ee-sheen) are solitary faeries who help farmers. They are nude, covered with patches of brown, coarse hair, and in general are not very physically appealing. They seem to want to be of service to humans, but they are not known for being very bright.

Time Most Active: Spring, summer, and autumn. It is believed that they hibernate through winter.

Lore: A Fireesin's agricultural help is not always welcome because they are not known for their intelligence, but they are well-meaning.

Do not express offense at their nudity unless you wish them to be hurt and offended and leave your service. Of course they will not leave in peace, and your crops (which in this case may be a metaphor for spiritual harvesting) could be devastated in their angry wake.

Where to Find Them: In fields that are either about to be cultivated or harvested.

How to Contact: Watch for them to appear, and then ask them if you may approach as a friend.

Magickal and Ritual Help: Undetermined.

Flower Faeries

See **Pillywiggins.**

Folletti

Land of Origin: Italy.

Other Origins: None known, although weather faeries are known worldwide.

Other Names: Wind Knots. The singular form is Folletto. They are also called Sumascazzo and Grandinilli, depending on which region of Italy you are in. Most knowledge about them comes to us from Sicily, an island off Italy's southern coast. In southern Italy they are called the Salvanelli and don red clothes and live in hollow oak trees.

Element: Air.

Appearance and Temperament: Folletti (Foe-let-ee) are so small and light that they are practically invisible, but their distinguishing characteristic is known to us—their toes point backward. They seem to pay no attention to humans and change the weather merely for their own sport rather than for any baneful purpose.

Time Most Active: All year.

Lore: Their favorite element is air, and they like to whip up wind storms which they can ride on, or hail storms during which they can be heard laughing gleefully. They have even been credited with starting earthquakes and volcanos, but generally this is not their domain. When not engaged in destructive behavior, Folletti love to ride grasshoppers in a game which looks something like a polo match.

Except for reports of hearing their laughter, Folletti may be a fear-form which grew out of unpredictable weather.

Where to Find Them: Unknown.

How to Contact: Unknown.

Magickal and Ritual Help: Unknown.

Formorians

Land of Origin: Ireland.

Other Origins: None.

Other Names: The Formors.

Element: Water.

Appearance and Temperament: The Formorians are sea monsters, the survivors of a banished faery race driven out of Ireland by the Tuatha De Danann. They have grotesquely misshapen bodies which look as if they have been haphazardly thrown together with the leftover parts of assorted animals. They do have arms and legs and have been seen occasionally on land. They are ill-tempered and very stupid.

Time Most Active: All year, and especially at night.

Lore: Like the Tuatha De Danann, the Formorians were an early faery race which conquered Ireland and which was later banished. They were driven into the sea by the Tuatha De Danann, and condemned to live forever as sea monsters. West-coast Irish people have seen the grisly creatures coming up onto the rocky seashore at night, which seems to be the only time the Formorians can leave the sea.

Where to Find Them: At seashores.

How to Contact: Contact not advised!

Magickal and Ritual Help: None.

Fossegrim

Land of Origin: Norway.

Other Origins: None known.

Other Names: None known.

Element: Water.

Appearance and Temperament: Fossegrim are smaller than humans, perfectly formed except for their feet, which tend to taper off into a misty nothingness. They can be either baneful or playful depending upon their mood of the moment.

Time Most Active: All year.

Lore: Fossegrim (Foe-say-grim) are guardian spirits of waterfalls. They are expert harpers and have beautiful singing voices. They appear as attractive, virile men and women, which makes them very alluring to young humans. This shell is merely an illusion, and in truth they appear to have no gender differentiation at all, and can change in a heartbeat from one sex to the other. While these faeries do not deliberately set out to hurt people, their playfulness can get out of hand. They do not seek human mates.

Where to Find Them: In and near Norway's waterfalls and fjords.

How to Contact: Unknown. If you run into one, approach with caution, because their mood and intent is often unpredictable.

Magickal and Ritual Help: Unknown.

Fylgiar

Land of Origin: Iceland.

Other Origins: None known.

Other Names: None known.

Element: Air.

Appearance and Temperament: A Fylgiar can only be seen by its human familiar just before the person dies. Their only human aid and concern goes to this one person, and they ignore all others.

Time Most Active: All year.

Lore: An Icelandic child born with a caul over its head was thought to be special, a sentiment not unknown around the world. But in Iceland this means that the child will go through life with a faery companion, a shadow familiar known as the Fylgiar.

The Fylgiar serves this person, and it is believed that the person also serves the Fylgiar while asleep or when making deliberate astral projections. This faery can be heard in the home of such a person banging and knocking around.

Their most disturbing quality is that they warn their human companions of their own deaths, at which time they can be seen. The condition of the Fylgiar at the time of the sighting indicates what sort of death it shall be. A mauled faery means a nasty, painful death, while a peaceful one means a calm, painless death.

The Fylgiar continues to live on after the human familiar dies, but it is believed that it accompanies its person to Valhallah, the Nordic Land of the Dead, where it remains until the human soul is comfortable and accepting of his or her demise.

Where to Find Them: Shadowing a person born with a caul.

How to Contact: Unknown, but you might look for one in Faeryland if you wish to see what they look like. You will be most successful in this attempt if you either were born with a caul yourself or are of Icelandic descent.

Magickal and Ritual Help: None known.

Gancanagh

Land of Origin: Ireland.

Other Origins: None known.

Other Names: In Scotland and Cornwall he is the Ganconer.

Element: Air.

Appearance and Temperament: The Gancanagh (Gon-cawn-ah) is a male faery who materializes in lonely places and attempts to seduce human females, who will eventually die of love for him.

Time Most Active: All year.

Lore: The Gancanagh is rarely seen any more, giving rise to rumors that he, the last of his kind, has died.

His trademark is an Irish clay pipe which he is always either holding in his hand or has clenched in his teeth. If you notice a man in a lonely place who has a pipe but he is not actually smoking, this may be the Gancanagh. Faeries hate smoke, and cannot inhale the stuff at all.

Feminists speculate that this faery is no more than a fear-form created to control women by frightening them into staying close to home.

Where to Find Him: Unknown.

How to Contact: He may not be able to be contacted because he is either dead or not a complete being.

Magickal and Ritual Help: None.

The Gandharvas

Land of Origin: India.

Other Origins: None known.

Other Names: None known.

Element: Earth.

Appearance and Temperament: The Gandharvas are extra small faeries who live underground and possess vast musical talents. They will cause humans no harm, but will avoid us if possible.

Time Most Active: All year.

Lore: Some of the few references to these native Indian faeries which still exist are in found old Sanskrit poetry. Most of the information which can be found about them discusses their musical talent and does not mention how or where to find them, their origins, or any other useful information.

Where to Find Them: Inside hillocks and caves in India.

How to Contact: They seem to shun human contact, but you might win their confidence if you share a love of music and are willing to spend the time to get to know them.

Magickal and Ritual Help: Undetermined, but some vague Sanskrit references hint that they may have once, long ago, joined humans in worship and praise of the deities.

Gans

Land of Origin: American Southwest.

Other Origins: None known.

Other Names: None known.

Element: Air.

Appearance and Temperament: The Gans are vaporous spirits who inhabit the mountains of the North American Southwest. They are neither good nor evil.

Time Most Active: All year.

Lore: The Gans are the faery folk of the Native American tribe we know as the Apaches, who have special dances and ceremonies to honor them.

These faeries represent the spirit of the mountains and the good or evil to be found there. The Apaches appeal to them through dances where they don black masks, white robes, and wooden headdresses to seek their favor in much the same way the Arabs curry favor from their Genies.

The Apaches believe that whatever befalls them in the mountains is a direct result of the Gans and their feelings about the way they were approached in ritual.

Where to Find Them: In the rugged mountains of the American Southwest.

How to Contact: The Apaches have kept most of their tribal rituals as much a secret as possible, so little is known about the exact way in which they appeal to the Gans. We do know the manner of dress used and that the ritual involves dancing at night.

Any sincere approach, even if it isn't exactly accurate historically, would probably be better than a half-hearted effort done in perfect detail. To ask a favor, try calling to the Gans after doing a ritual dance in their honor.

Magickal and Ritual Help: While you are in or near the mountains the Gans can help alter the weather, help you find shelter, protect you from falls and wild animals, or intercede with deities in your behalf. On the other hand, they can cause bad weather, missteps, falls, and encounters with wild animals.

Geancanach

Land of Origin: Ireland.

Other Origins: The Hebrides Islands of Scotland.

Other Names: None known.

Element: Fire.

Appearance and Temperament: The Geancanach (Gan-cahn-ock) is pixie-like in appearance, with huge eyes that curve upward on the ends and large pointed ears. They are always depicted as being very small, no more than a few inches in height, and having playful, if somewhat mischievous, smiles. They have small wings which do not seem functional, and they appear to move from place to place by dematerializing and reappearing quite rapidly. They may be mistaken for flickering lights or lightning bugs.

Time Most Active: At night.

Lore: These northern Irish sprites are the guardians of home hearths. They crave the warmth of the fireside and are quite harmless to have around, although they do have a tendency to play pranks. Repay any kindness from them with the warmth of your fire and with the fresh milk they obviously love so much.

In old Irish cottages the hearth was at the center of the home, with all other rooms being referred to by their relationship to the fireplace. Those are the hearths the Geancanach prefer.

Where to Find Them: Around a blazing fire at your hearthside.

How to Contact: Offer a simple evocation at your fireside, either physical or astral, with an offering of milk.

Magickal and Ritual Help: Guarding the flue opening and the house, and all things in the fire including fire-related spell work would be the province of the Geancanach. Catch them in a serious mood to work successfully with them.

Genie

See *Jinn.*

Ghillie Dhu

Land of Origin: Scotland.

Other Origins: None known.

Other Names: None known.

Element: Fire.

Appearance and Temperament: Like the Irish Lesidhe, the Ghillie Dhu (Gillee Doo or Yoo) are guardian tree spirits who are disguised as foliage and dislike human beings. Their name literally means "dark shoe."

Time Most Active: At night.

Lore: The Ghillie Dhu prefer birch trees to all others and jealously guard them from humans. Persons traversing enchanted woods must take care not to be grabbed by the long green arms of a Ghillie Dhu, or they could be enslaved into the service of the guardian forest spirits forever. These faeries once heavily populated the Scottish forests, but are not seen much anymore for reasons which are unclear to us.

Where to Find Them: In trees, especially birch trees.

How to Contact: Contact not advised!

Magickal and Ritual Help: None.

Gianes

Land of Origin: Italy.

Other Origins: None known.

Other Names: Elves adept at weaving are known all over Europe.

Element: Earth.

Appearance and Temperament: Gianes (Gee-ahwn-ayes) are solitary wood Elves who occasionally will aid humans. They wear old-fashioned peasant clothing and large, pointed hats made of animal skins. They are nearly always seen with small spinning wheel spindles in their back pockets.

Time Most Active: All year, mostly at night.

Lore: The Giane live in the forests of northern Italy. They are master cloth weavers, but they weave for fun rather than for anyone's benefit. Some say they can also weave potent spells. Divination is another of their talents, and they will aid you in seeing the future if you seek them out with your questions. But be warned that they don't believe in euphemisms when it comes to foretelling what they see, and they can sound very harsh or frightening when making predictions. Their usual method of divining is to scry into their moving spinning wheels.

Italian folklore says that possessing a small piece of their woven cloth is a powerful good luck talisman.

Where to Find Them: In woodlands, especially enchanted woods.

How to Contact: Call to them in the woods and ask them to appear, and seek them in Faeryland where they are easily found. Because of the astral nature of divination, it is best to find these faeries on their own home ground.

Magickal and Ritual Help: Divination is their forte, and they will answer your questions if you really want the answers. Do not ask them to do spells for you, as the price they command is much too steep. They will, however, offer their advice and suggestions on how you can do the spell for yourself.

Giants and Ogres

Land of Origin: Worldwide, but they are most populous in the Yorkshire region of England and in the mountains of Eastern Europe.

Other Origins: None known.

Other Names: A one-eyed Giant or Ogre is called a Cyclops.

Element: Air.

Appearance and Temperament: Giants look like humans but are much larger. Ogres are about the same size as humans but have deformed faces, excessive body hair, and sometimes a hump in their backs. Ogres are usually unfriendly, and Giants have been known to be both friendly and nasty.

Time Most Active: All year.

Lore: Giants and Ogres both figure largely in children's faery tales. The best known Giant is probably the one from the tale "Jack and the Beanstalk" where he is portrayed as evil, though in fact he is the victim of the story even though we are taught to identify Jack as the protagonist. Other popular faery tales from Yorkshire about giants are "The Brave Little Tailor" and "Jack the Giant Killer."

Perhaps because of their size and unappealing appearance Giants have been regarded as unfriendly, but some folklore exists which tells us this is not so. Continued persecution by humans may make them unwilling to trust us, but it is certainly possible to find Giants who would welcome some human interaction.

Ogres tend to be human-sized and have extreme deformities. They are usually quite stupid and have hateful dispositions. One of the most famous Ogres is Baba, a Slavic faery, who eats humans and has the power to turn people to stone.

Ogres are pretty fearless, but Giants are terrified of cats.

Where to Find Them: In Faeryland. In many folk tales they are said to live on clouds.

How to Contact: Approach both of these faeries with extreme caution when you find one to first ascertain his or her intent and mood.

Magickal and Ritual Help: Undetermined.

Gitto

Land of Origin: Wales.

Other Origins: None known.

Other Names: Griffith and Griffin—both of which are popular Welsh surnames. Also spelled Gryphon and Geetoe.

Element: Air.

Appearance and Temperament: Gittos (Ghee-toes) have the heads of horses and the bodies of goats, but they have human speech and laughter. Though they have no wings, they can fly for short distances. They do not like people.

Time Most Active: All year, but especially at harvest time.

Lore: Like their cousins, the Irish Phookas, the Gittos like to blight crops and claim for themselves all crops left in the field after sundown on Samhain. They have an intensely malevolent nature and would love to harm humans if given the opportunity. Fortunately for us, they don't seem to know just how to do this.

Where to Find Them: In fields after sundown between Samhain and Bealtaine.

How to Contact: Contact not advised!

Magickal and Ritual Help: None.

Glashtin

Land of Origin: The Isle of Man.

Other Origins: Possibly the Outer Hebrides Islands of Scotland.

Other Names: Hawlaa, Howlies, Howlers.

Element: Air.

Appearance and Temperament: The Glashtin (Glosh-teen) is a goblin who is half cow and half horse. If the head part is a cow he is stupid; if a horse, he is shrewd and cunning.

Time Most Active: During storms.

Lore: These faeries appear during storms in which they revel and play, seeming to take delight in the havoc they leave behind. Manx people have seen them riding on the winds, laughing as they are being battered about. At one time the Manx believed them to be the cause of their many storms.

They howl loudly just before storms hit, providing ample warning to those within earshot. But these are probably instinctive shouts of glee and not any deliberate kindness to humans.

Where to Find Them: In the sky during a severe storm.

How to Contact: Unknown and unadvised.

Magickal and Ritual Help: None.

The Glaistig

Land of Origin: Scotland.

Other Origins: None known.

Other Names: None known.

Element: Water.

Appearance and Temperament: The Glaistig (Clee-stickh) attempts to appear as a beautiful woman, but if one scrutinizes her closely, one can see her animal parts. Horses and goats in particular are part of her make-up, and she seems to have no control over shapeshifting them away. She is a complete misanthrope and should never be sought out by humans.

Time Most Active: At night.

Lore: The Glaistig preys mostly on human males, whom she appears to hate with a vengeance. But she has been known to be very tender and gentle to the elderly and towards children. Occasionally she has been given credit for aiding Scottish farmers, but all the same, they would rather not have her around.

Her methods of killing males include blood-sucking in the manner of a vampire, or drowning. It has been hypothesized by feminists that the Glaistig is not a real being, but a fear-form projected by men who fear women. The image of the evil, grasping virago sucking the life out of men has been an old standby excuse for female persecution since Biblical times.

Glaistig is attached to one particular locale, one usually associated with very old Scottish families.

Where to Find Her: Unknown.

How to Contact: Contact not advised!

Magickal and Ritual Help: None.

Gnomes

Land of Origin: Europe.

Other Origins: Scotland is the land from which most of the Gnome lore in North America comes from.

Other Names: Throughout Europe, each land has its own name for the Gnome. In Germany they are called Erdmanleins, except in the Alpine areas, where they are known as Heinzemannchens. In Sweden they are called Nissen, and Nisse in Denmark and Norway. In Brittany they are called Nains. The Finns call them Tontti, and in Iceland they are the Foddenskkmaend. The Polish word for Gnome is Gnom, but it is Djude in Bulgaria and Albania. In Hungary, Yugoslavia, and Czechoslovakia, Gnomes are called Mano. The Dutch word is Kabouter, the Belgian is Skritek, and in Switzerland and Luxembourg they are known as Kleinmanneken, which means "little men." In western Russia Gnomes are called Domovoi Djedoes, which roughly translated means "earth faery."

Element: Earth.

Appearance and Temperament: Gnomes are dwarf faeries who appear to be quite old because they mature very early, though their average life span is around a thousand years. They reach maturity in about a hundred years, at which time they stand about 12 inches tall and look well past middle age. They are male and female adults and

Gnomes live among the intricate root systems of old oaks.

children, wear old-fashioned peasant costumes, and are kind-hearted and will always aid sick or frightened animals.

Time Most Active: All year.

Lore: Much has been written about the Gnome, the most well-known account being the Dutch book *Gnomes* by Wil Huygen, which has been translated into English.

Gnomes live deep in ancient forests under old oak trees and make their dwellings among the intricate root systems. Their principal occupation is the protection and healing of wildlife, though they may occasionally help a human along on his or her spiritual quest.

Gnomes wear small pointed hats of red, their clothing is always green or blue in color, and their dimpled faces are merry and kind. They like to wear rainbow-colored stockings which they weave themselves. In general they are very smart and clever.

Sharing a tradition with the Amish and Orthodox Jews, married male Gnomes grow beards, and married women cover their hair.

They share their woodland homes with the animals they love and with whom they have a relationship of mutual trust and affection. Their only known enemies are martens and some owls, and humans who encroach on their homes.

The idea that a Gnome can bless or enhance a garden or wild place is stuck in our popular consciousness, as shown by the proliferation of the many ceramic or plastic "Lawn Gnomes" on the market.

An animated children's television series produced by BRB International called *The World of David the Gnome* has been seen on American cable television for several years. David, with his red hat and blue coat, lives with his wife in an oak tree and spends his time helping animals and fighting off evil Trolls. All in all, the scripts remain faithful to the European Gnome legends, including the libation of milk given to David's family each day by a kind townswoman.

In ceremonial magick, Gnomes are not only the archetypal earth elementals of the north who are called upon to witness all rituals, but in the Order of the Golden Dawn they are known as one of the four "Essential Spiritual Beings" who are called upon to "praise God" during a ritual known as Benedicite Omnia Opera. For information about the other elementals of high magick, see Salamanders, Sylphs, and Undines.

Where to Find Them: At the base of old oak trees. Look for them in the autumn of Faeryland.

How to Contact: A simple invitation may bring them to you. Try using the guided meditation in this book for an audience with the Gnome King, who will offer you guidance when you are in need.

Magickal and Ritual Help: Gnomes can help you protect yourself and your pets and lend their energy to any number of magickal purposes, especially healing spells, at which they excel. They may also be willing to teach you some secrets of medicinal herbalism. Gnomes love to dance to raise energy and might be persuaded to lend this energy to rituals celebrating the deities, especially the Gods and Goddesses of the woodlands.

Goblin and Gobelin

See **Boggart** and/or **Hobgoblin.**

Golem

Land of Origin: Israel.

Other Origins: Possibly ancient Canaan.

Other Names: None known.

Element: Earth.

Appearance and Temperament: A Golem (pronounced with a long 'o') is human in appearance, but is not a thinking creature and has no malice towards humans except as programmed by his creator.

Time Most Active: All year.

Lore: A Golem might best be described as a zombie—a staring, unthinking creature in a human body who is in no real way human or whole. They are well known by adepts in ceremonial magick as creatures created by magick rather in the same way that witches can create elemental beings (see Chapter 6). The Golem was written about by Jewish folklorist Yudl Rosenburg in his short story "The Golem, or, The Miraculous Deeds of Rabbi Liva."

Where to Find Them: Unknown.

How to Contact: Contact not advised!

Magickal and Ritual Help: None.

The Grant

Land of Origin: England.

Other Origins: None known.

Other Names: None known.

Element: Fire.

Appearance and Temperament: The Grant looks something like a small, oddly-formed horse, though he walks erect. He warns humans of approaching trouble and is said to be very friendly, if somewhat terrifying to see.

Time Most Active: At sunset.

Lore: Each Grant is attached to a particular English village, where he acts as lookout and guardian. If there is approaching trouble he runs through the streets at sunset stirring up the local dogs to bark and horses to whinny out a warning.

Sightings of the Grant are well documented. He has actually been seen at sunset in numerous villages, and during World War II a few English hamlets claimed they were warned by their Grant of approaching air raids.

English faery lore says that he is a very amiable creature, but quite bothersome to look upon.

Where to Find Them: Near the English villages they have adopted.

How to Contact: Unknown.

Magickal and Ritual Help: Undetermined. In times of national crisis he may be able not only to warn the English, but to lend his energy to the defense of his homeland.

Gremlin

Land of Origin: Germany.

Other Origins: Also a popular faery form in England.

Other Names: Grimblens, Gremlers, Sky Boogies, and Widgets. Fifenellas are female Gremlins, and Widgets are the children. Spandules are the ones who ice airplane wings.

Element: Air.

Appearance and Temperament: Gremlins range in size from very small to almost human-sized. They are hairy all over and tend to be dun to dark brown in color. They have wide grins that are anything but mirthful, and stubby little ears like those of terrier dogs. They do not like humans and seek to destroy them whenever possible.

Time Most Active: All year, especially at night.

Lore: Gremlins seem to have once had the power of flight, an ability which was lost for reasons unknown to us. Now they live high in the mountains of Europe where they can feel the winds and dream of the days when they could be airborne on a whim.

It is not surprising that the world's trouble with Gremlins began when we conquered the skies. During World War II, pilots from both sides flying over Europe would report seeing hairy creatures hitching rides on their wings. Shortly thereafter reports were being sent in to command headquarters all over Europe insisting that these creatures were actually damaging the planes. Leaders of neither the Axis nor the Allied powers were willing to believe these fantastic tales, but as more and more came in they felt the reports had to be kept in the official flight records.

Pilots who complained of Gremlin damage had wires pulled out of engines, holes punctured in wings, gas leaks, spontaneous fires, and wing ice even when air temperatures were well above freezing. Other Gremlins would pop up in front of the windshields just to frighten the pilots.

Gremlins are very strong and can tear through metal without any strain. They seem to not need water, air, and food for sustenance, or at least they can go for long periods without them.

They are cousins of the Irish Phooka with whom they share similarities. Their origins are hazy and very little folklore was recorded about them until World War II. This may simply be because we humans tend to ignore anything which doesn't directly concern us.

Where to Find Them: Unknown.

How to Contact: Unknown and unadvised.

Magickal and Ritual Help: None.

Griffins and Griffiths

See **Gitto**.

Grigs

See **Pixies**.

Gruagach

Land of Origin: Scotland.

Other Origins: None known.

Other Names: Gruaghach, The Herdswoman, The Firesitter.

Element: Earth.

Appearance and Temperament: The Gruagach (Grew-g'ac) is a solitary female faery, extremely grotesque in appearance, but with a heart of gold. She carries a shepherd's staff in her gnarled hands, and her gown is usually green in color, though it has been said to be corn-silk gold. She enjoys any brief human contact she can get and will offer whatever help she can in your spiritual pursuits if you do not show fear or revulsion.

Time Most Active: Summer during daylight hours.

Lore: Gruagach is derived from a Gaelic root word which means "hairy," and this profuse hair is part of her deceptively hideous appearance. She is primarily a protector of livestock, principally cattle. She leads cattle to water and guards these herds from the Buachailleen, the evil "Herding Boys."

She is always cold and loves a warm fire, but being a faery, cannot start her own. Therefore, to keep warm, she makes her home in the summer of Faeryland. When the Gruagach is traveling in the human world, Scottish folklore tells us that she will appear at the doorstep of Highlanders and ask to sit by the fire for a while. If she is allowed she will look after the home and herds; if refused, she will create trouble and steal animals.

In Scotland obligatory libations of milk were given to her at Imbolg and Lughnasadh by pouring it into a hollow stone called a Gruagach's Stone. This practice still persists as a folk ritual among many rural Scottish cattleherders, though its orginal meaning has been long forgotten by most of them.

Her Irish manifestation is somewhat less benevolent. In Ireland it is said that she is desperately searching for a son and is not above taking one if he catches her fancy. But the Gruagach is so compassionate that if the distraught parents come to her and beg for the child back, she will tearfully let him go.

On the Isle of Man the Gruagach is a male whose behavior is more like that of the mischievous Buachailleen (see separate entry).

Where to Find Her: In pastures and in the summer of Faeryland.

How to Contact: Go to her and ask her for advice or assistance. Be direct, as she has a very limited attention span.

Magickal and Ritual Help: She can aid in spiritual quests and in guarding herds. She will also lend her considerable magickal energies to your spells for human, animal, or plant fertility.

Guriuz

Land of Origin: Italy.

Other Origins: None known.

Other Names: None known.

Element: Air.

Appearance and Temperament: These Italian weather Elves have not been seen for a long time. They were said to look like other Italian Elves and to be friendly toward farmers.

Time Most Active: Spring through the end of harvest.

Lore: The Guriuz (Goor-ee-use) used to help bring the weather needed by Italian farmers. They may have died out, be in hiding, or not have ever existed as whole beings.

Where to Find Them: Unknown.

How to Contact: Unknown.

Magickal and Ritual Help: Unknown.

Gwragedd Annwn

Land of Origin: Wales.

Other Origins: None known.

Other Names: None known.

Element: Water.

Appearance and Temperament: The Gwragedd Annwn (Gwergeth Ai-noon) are beautiful blonde water faeries who love children and are helpful to human mothers, children, and the poor. They are human in size and are female only.

Time Most Active: All year.

Lore: These feminine faeries live in and near the lakes of the Black Mountains of Wales. Though they are helpful to women and children, they seem uninterested in males except as occasional mates. They are reputed to like female company, but are very temperamental and easily offended.

Gwragedd Annwns love dancing and have been seen enjoying their revels under the full moon. They are believed to be a very old group of faeries, and some mythologists believe that the Irish Faery Queen Fand may have been of this race. The marriages between these faeries and the men they take seem to be generally happy, and the offspring of these couplings are gifted in music. In rural Wales you can occasionally find someone who will point out entire families believed to be descended from these unions.

The underwater lakes they live near hold their palaces and treasures which have been unseen by all but a few of their half-human children. They can be distinguished from humans by their breathtaking beauty and by their inability to count past the number five, which is the number in which they collect everything except mates. They make loyal if somewhat distant wives and are excellent mothers.

Where to Find Them: In the Black Mountains of Wales.

How to Contact: Go to the Black Mountains, either physically or astrally, and seek them out. Approach with caution.

Magickal and Ritual Help: They can aid in protection spells for women and children and can even be called on to be temporary guardians in time of great need.

Gwyllions

Land of Origin: Wales.

Other Origins: None known.

Other Names: None known.

Element: Fire.

Appearance and Temperament: Gwyllions are mountain dwellers who care for the wild goats of Wales and are rarely seen. They dislike humans, whom they regard as arrogant, and so they keep their distance from us.

Time Most Active: All year.

Lore: It is said that Gwyllions once had the power of flight, but when and how they lost it is a mystery. They now content themselves with watching over goats. Occasionally a Welsh mountain climber or hiker has seen something staring at him thoughtfully from behind the rocks, something he is unable to identify. This may be a Gwyllion.

The female Gwyllions are nocturnal, and it is believed that exposure to sunlight would kill them.

Gwyllions fear storms and knives. One bit of Welsh folklore tells us that the Gwyllions often seek shelter in the homes of mountain dwellers during storms. While they are in your home you can corner them with a drawn knife and they must then grant you one wish. Unfortunately the price for doing this is the eternal ire of these faeries who will forevermore plague your mountain journeys with difficulties. On the other hand, allowing them the safety of your home will make them more disposed to guard the pathways to your house.

Where to Find Them: In the Welsh mountains and in Faeryland's mountains, but they will usually run away if they think you are looking for them.

How to Contact: They will not allow themselves to be found or approached by people.

Magickal and Ritual Help: None.

Hamadryadniks

Land of Origin: Yugoslavia.

Other Origins: Czechoslovakia. These are probably the same species as the Hamadryads of Greece and similar to the Dryads of Celtic lands (see entries for Lesidhe and Dryads).

Other Names: None known.

Element: Air.

Appearance and Temperament: Hamadryadniks are tree spirits who, like the Lesidhe, appear as living foliage. But unlike the Hamadryads and Dryads, they hate human beings.

Time Most Active: Daytime.

Lore: Unlike most guardian spirits of trees, the Hamadryadnik emerges from his perch during the day instead of at night to forage for food and secure its domain. They look like foliage, and when humans appear they can freeze and blend into the background. They detest people who so ruthlessly continue to destroy forest land and would like to do us harm, but they don't seem to be able to figure out how to accomplish this.

During the night they are bound to the tops of their tree homes from which they cannot emerge. For them to touch the earth at night is to vanish forever.

Where to Find Them: In trees.

How to Contact: Contact not advised!

Magickal and Ritual Help: None.

Hamadryads

See **Dryads.**

Heather Pixies

Land of Origin: Scotland.

Other Origins: The Yorkshire region of northern England.

Other Names: Moor Sprites.

Element: Earth or Air.

Appearance and Temperament: Like other Pixies, the Heather Pixies have clear or golden auras and delicate, translucent wings. But these faeries are attracted specifically to the moors and to the heather which covers them. They are not averse to human contact, but do not seek us out. They have a pranksterish nature.

Time Most Active: All year.

Lore: The word Pixie may be related somehow to the Picts, the early inhabitants of Scotland. Scottish faery lore says that Heather Pixies enjoy spinning flax.

Where to Find Them: In fields of heather, or on the moors of the Scottish Lowlands.

How to Contact: Approach them slowly and let them know you wish to befriend them.

Magickal and Ritual Help: Undetermined.

Hobgoblin

Land of Origin: England.

Other Origins: Germany, where they are called Gobelins.

Other Names: Hobgobs, Goblins, Hob-thrush, Billeeboinkers, Bloblins, Gooseys. Scottish Hobgoblins are often called Brags and they are excellent shapeshifters. Also see the entry under Boggart.

Element: Earth.

Appearance and Temperament: The appearance of the Hobgoblin can vary greatly, especially as it is used now as a generic term for an evil faery. Some appear only as dark blobs, and others as mean-looking Elves.

Time Most Active: Varies.

Lore: The English Hobgoblin loves to live in homes where he makes much trouble for the people who live there. Though he seems to have no moral code of his own, he is very happy to enforce the one by which he feels his human hosts should abide. The miserly and lazy are apt to feel his pinch or find their rooms and possessions in disarray.

They love the warmth of fire, and like most faeries cannot start their own. They are rarely seen any more but once were quite populous in England.

Their lore traveled to North America with English immigrants and they have become part of American and Canadian children's stories. Hobgoblins have been immortalized in Indiana poet James Whitcomb Riley's children's saga *L'il Orphant Annie,* where he tells us, " … an' the Gobble-uns 'll git you ef you/ Don't Watch Out!"

Where to Find Them: If you wish to risk the contact, search for them in Faeryland.

How to Contact: Contact not advised!

Magickal and Ritual Help: None.

The Holly King

See **Santa Claus.**

Huldrafolk

Land of Origin: Scandinavia.

Other Origins: None known.

Other Names: Huldras, Dark Elves.

Element: Earth.

Appearance and Temperament: These Elves are known as dark Elves not only because of their dark coloring, but also because of their nasty personalities.

Lore: Huldrafolk literally means "hidden people," and they live deep in the burghs and caves in the many mountains of Scandinavia. They have the ability to blight humans with deformities, especially with very small ones such as baldness or a crooked nose. They cause these deformities with a lick of their dark brown tongues. To be touched like this will eventually turn a person against the world of mortals.

Where to Find Them: Mostly in damp caves.

How to Contact: Contact not advised!

Magickal and Ritual Help: None.

Hyldermoder

Land of Origin: Scandinavia.

Other Origins: Guardian tree faeries are known all over Europe.

Other Names: None known.

Element: Earth.

Appearance and Temperament: The Hyldermoder is one-of-a-kind. She is the guardian spirit of the sacred Elder tree of the Norse tradition, and is always dressed in a flowing green gown. She has the appearance and countenance of an elderly and kindly but protective mother. She bears no malice toward humans unless they tamper with the Elder tree.

Time Most Active: All year.

Lore: The Hyldermoder literally means "Elder Mother," and she may in fact be a devalued Mother or Crone Goddess. She is the Elder Tree Mother who guards the sacred Elder trees.

Hans Christian Andersen, Danish folklorist and author, recorded a tale about this faery in his story "The Old Lady of the Elder Tree."

Where to Find Her: In the branches of the Elder tree, especially under a full moon.

How to Contact: Petition her as you would a Goddess.

Magickal and Ritual Help: If she is indeed a Mother Goddess she can offer help with any need, especially those related to tree magick, fertility, wisdom, prosperity, psychicism, or inspiration.

Hyters

Land of Origin: England.

Other Origins: Possibly Spain.

Other Names: None known.

Element: Air.

Appearance and Temperament: Hyters (High-ters) are shape-shifters who appear as birds. They are not predisposed to showing kindness to humans, though they have never harmed anyone.

Time Most Active: Late afternoon and early evening.

Lore: Hyters have been known to gather in groups and buzz humans for the sheer joy of frightening them, but no human has ever reported being hurt. They favor appearing as scavenger birds such as the buzzard or the vulture, which makes them particularly unappealing to humans. In Mexico there is a persistent belief that many of these scavenger birds have human faces, and this may be a carryover from belief in the Hyter.

Where to Find Them: In the skies of Faeryland just before sunset.

How to Contact: Contact not advised, but you can sit at a safe distance and watch them.

Magickal and Ritual Help: None.

Ieles

Land of Origin: Romania and Eastern Europe.

Other Origins: None known.

Other Names: None known.

Element: Earth.

Appearance and Temperament: Ieles (Ee-lays) look like large, bipedal cats. They are very dangerous and spend most of their time looking for human victims.

Time Most Active: At night.

Lore: Ieles will wait near a crossroads for a human victim to approach. Like vampires, they suck the blood from their human prey. Remember that Eastern Europe is the land of Dracula, and in the remote Carpathian Mountains belief in these night creatures is still strong.

Often they will sing or dance to help lure humans off the main road to them. They cannot get into the middle of the crossroads—long seen as a place of protection because they were made like an equilateral cross—or their power is forever grounded.

Where to Find Them: At crossroads, just off the main path.

How to Contact: Contact not advised, but if you come upon one, stay in the center of the crossroads until it leaves.

Magickal and Ritual Help: None.

Illes

Land of Origin: Iceland.

Other Origins: Also in other parts of Scandinavia.

Other Names: None known.

Element: Earth.

Appearance and Temperament: Illes (pronounced Eels) are Trolls who live underground and can only come out at night. Like other Trolls, they are hairy and dark in color and are completely unclothed. They are very confusing if not dangerous to humans because they can shapeshift into beautiful human forms for just long enough to lure humans into their underground world.

Time Most Active: At night.

Lore: Illes can cause death through suffocation and through making humans pine away for the beautiful temporary forms these Trolls can take. They are expert string players and use their music to attract humans. They can cause humans to grow sick just by touching them.

Illes are nocturnal but are not forced to be night creatures. They love to dance under the full moon and can keep this up tirelessly for hours.

Where to Find Them: In burghs of Scandinavia.

How to Contact: Contact not advised!

Magickal and Ritual Help: None.

Incubi

See *Succubi and Incubi.*

Irish Elves

Land of Origin: Possibly Germany.

Other Origins: Elf-like faeries are known all over Europe.

Other Names: The Little People, The Wee Folk, the Little Fellers.

Element: Earth.

Appearance and Temperament: Elf in Ireland is a generic term for non-winged faeries. They are comparable to the Gnomes of Scotland, a place which shares much of its folklore with the northern part of Ireland. Irish Elves are dwarf-like in appearance, usually sporting green or blue clothing and red caps. Males, females, and children have all been seen. They are friendly, but wary of humans.

Time Most Active: Usually at night.

Lore: These trooping faeries are beings who live within the earth among the tangled roots of sacred trees. They go abroad during the night to aid woodland animals and occasionally reward a virtuous or unselfish human being by some act of kindness. The faery tale of the kindly old cobbler who was assisted by Elves bears out this belief.

Irish Elves do their rare good deeds to humans out of the joy of giving, and any act of overt thanks will drive them permanently away.

Unlike the rest of Europe, Ireland has no native word for Gnome and these Elves are either Gnomes or their first cousins.

Where to Find Them: At the base of sacred trees in dense woodlands.

How to Contact: Ask them to appear to you in the physical when you are in your circle, or go to Faeryland and seek them out.

Magickal and Ritual Help: Irish Elves may be useful in spells for home protection, environmental help, and shoemaking. Care of wild animals seems to be their primary function and love, and they will be helpful in caring for sick or injured pets if asked. Ask them to guide you to healing herbs for your animals.

Irish Sea Water Guardians

Land of Origin: The Isle of Man.

Other Origins: Water guardian faeries are known throughout the world.

Other Names: Sea Sprites, Manx Undines, Undines.

Element: Water.

Appearance and Temperament: These Manx sea guardians are very small faeries, only a few inches high, who guard the stormy Irish Sea and are beloved of the Sea God Manann. They are both male and female and are beautiful to see. A green-blue aura of light is said to dance around them. They are fierce guardians but are still disposed to help all living creatures in need on the sea if they are specifically asked to do so.

Time Most Active: All year.

Lore: Irish Sea Water Guardians merit their own entry because their lore differs significantly from other Sea Sprites and Undines. They are quite definitively the guardians of the Irish Seas and not merely its elemental creatures. When not playing in the water they are in the service of the Sea God Manann.

The Water Guardians sail on broken eggshells through the Irish Seas and surf on seashells during storms. Sailors in the Irish Sea often feared nearing Man for all the faeries in its waters.

Irish Sea Water Guardians enjoy the company of playful marine life such as dolphins and groupers and will readily assist ailing fish. They have been known to come to aid humans, but they must first be asked for their assistance in clear and precise terms.

Where to Find Them: In the Irish Sea off the coast of Man.

How to Contact: Call them to you while in the sea surrounding the Isle of Man, a place which can be visited on the inner planes.

Magickal and Ritual Help: Ask them to lend their energies to safe travel spells over water, to aid sailors in need, to work for marine environmentalism, and to help in petitioning the God Manann.

Jack Frost

See **Snow Faeries.**

Jimaniños

Land of Origin: Mexico and Central America.

Other Origins: Possibly Aztec or Spanish in origin.

Other Names: Jimaniñas is the feminine form.

Appearance and Temperament: The Jimaniños (Heem-awn-neen-yo's) are the seasonal faeries of Mexico. They are winged, trooping faeries who look like pudgy children. They aid the Goddess in the turning of the Wheel of the Year.

Time Most Active: All year.

Lore: Jimaniños means "little children," which is how these faeries appear. They tend to shy away from people except on the Mexican festival El Dia de Muerte (the Day of the Dead, November 2) at which time they, like the people around them, dance in the streets and visit the cemeteries. This is also a day when they play pranks.

Some Mexican folklore says they are the souls of children who do not know they are dead.

Where to Find Them: Unknown, unless you are celebrating the Day of the Dead with them.

How to Contact: Unknown.

Magickal and Ritual Help: So far there is no known ritual in which the Jimaniños will participate, but given their love of the Day of the Dead festival, they might be persuaded to help out in Samhain rituals honoring your ancestors. If they are indeed discarnate human children, pagans have a duty to help them safely cross over to the land of the dead.

Jinn

Land of Origin: Saudi Arabia.

Other Origins: Persia.

Other Names: Genie, Jeannie, and Jeenie are other words which also mean Jinn that have been transliterated from Arabic. Sometimes they are euphemistically referred to as Spirits of the Lamp. In Egypt they are called Afreets. Djinn is another term for Jinn which was popular in England. It eventually came into the Victorian vocabulary to also mean an occult shop or a place where magick was performed, such as is seen in the 1877 Gilbert and Sullivan operetta, *The Sorcerer.*

Element: Air.

Appearance and Temperament: Jinns used to be both male and female, but in the staunchly patriarchal Arab countries, they came to be seen as wholly male. But because they were occasionally housed in receptacles such as bottles which are also chalices symbolizing the feminine principle of deity, they were certainly also female in equal numbers. Lamps, because they shed light, were sacred to Sun Gods, indicating that the faeries in these were male. They live in bottles and oil lamps from which they appear when summoned by their masters or owners and grant wishes.

Time Most Active: All year.

Lore: Thanks to the famous Persian folk tale "Aladdin and the Magical Lamp," westerners are familiar with the Jinn. When the lamp or bottle is rubbed, the Jinn is summoned forth and must do its master's bidding. Such lamps were the private property of sheiks and potentates and not for the common person. When such a lamp fell into the hands of an average person, a entire army would be called out to retrieve it.

In the late 1960s the American television series *I Dream of Jeannie* centered around an astronaut who found an old bottle containing a female Jinn named Jeannie.

These bottles and lamps seem to have disappeared over time, leaving both their whereabouts and the source of these legends shrouded in mystery.

Where to Find Them: Unknown.

How to Contact: Unknown.

Magickal and Ritual Help: If you can find one, anything you wish must be granted to you.

Kelpies

Land of Origin: Scotland.

Other Origins: None known.

Other Names: Irish Kelpies are called Uisges (Ech-ooshk-ya) or Fuath (Foo-ah), and they are also part of northern Irish faery lore, suggesting their migration from Scotland. A Cornish Kelpie is called a Shoney, a name derived from the Norse name Sjofn, a Goddess of the Sea. In Iceland they are called Nickers, which are similar to the Nix, the water sprites of Germany. In the Shetland and Orkney Islands they are called Nuggies.

Element: Water.

Appearance and Temperament: Kelpies are rarely seen anymore, and it is just as well. These small, bulbous-shaped faeries with huge teeth and pointed ears are sly, stupid, and extremely foul-tempered. Irish lore says they are web-footed water spirits with manes and tails like horses, and the girdled bodies of women.

Time Most Active: Unknown.

Lore: These cannibalistic faeries once densely populated the North Sea and all the lochs of Scotland. Deer who wandered too close to the lochs, other faeries, and humans were their favorite meals.

In northern Scotland there are stories of Kelpies who appear as friendly seahorses and allow passing humans to mount them so that they may be drowned.

Kelpies have limited shapeshifting powers and can appear as handsome young men to lure young girls to them. However, they can be detected because they are unable to keep their hair from appearing like seaweed.

Kelpies once made their principal home under the murky waters of the infamous Loch Ness, which was thought to be sacred to them. They were probably the forerunners of our current belief in the Loch Ness monster.

Where to Find Them: Unknown.

How to Contact: Contact not advised!

Magickal and Ritual Help: None.

Killmoulis

See **Brownie.**

Klaboutermannikins

Land of Origin: Germany and the Bel-Ne-Lux countries.

Other Origins: None known.

Other Names: Water Mannikins.

Element: Water.

Appearance and Temperament: These faeries are invisible. They inhabit the figurehead of any ships which they choose to protect.

Time Most Active: All year.

Lore: German sailors believed that the figurehead of any ship on which they sailed had to be very lifelike in order to attract a Klaboutermannikin to dwell inside.

In Flanders, where most German ships were once made, only the oldest and most sacred woods were used to carve the figureheads.

The Klaboutermannikin guarded the ship from sickness, rocks, storms, and dangerous winds. If a ship with one of these faeries aboard sank, the faery sank with it and then aided the souls of the sailors out of the waters and into the Land of the Dead. Dutch sailors once believed that to sink without a Klaboutermannikin meant your soul was condemned to the water for eternity.

The root word, mannikin, is often used as a generic term for elven faeries in Germanic lands.

Where to Find Them: In the figureheads of ships.

How to Contact: There has never been a known way to contact them short of creating a carved figurehead for them. But go ahead and try evoking them with a ritual designed to contact them. Let them know you have a boat you need blessed or that you desire protection during sea travel. Since there aren't a lot of carved figureheads to reside in anymore, they may show up.

Magickal and Ritual Help: They can help protect you on the sea or waterways. Ask them to come and participate in rituals to bless your boat or ship.

Knockers

Land of Origin: Cornwall.

Other Origins: South Central Europe.

Other Names: Knockers in Wales are known as Coblynaus (Koblee-nows), and they are called Black Dwarves in Scotland. A similar faery in Germany is called a Wichlein (Veek-line). In southern France they are called Gommes. In Finland they are called Paras.

Element: Earth.

Appearance and Temperament: Knockers are the most popular faeries in Cornwall, and will no doubt be familiar to readers of gothic mysteries. They are dwarf faeries who live in the mines and caves of the region and like to play games and aid respectful miners.

Time Most Active: All year.

Lore: Knockers live in mines and caves and get their name from the knocking sound they make when directing miners to a rich vein. They are always accurate, though sometimes they scatter their knocking just to play games with the miners who regard them as friends. Frantic knocking in any mine is a warning of imminent danger, and Cornish miners won't go into a mine after they are warned off by Knockers. Knockers have a reputation for frightening the miners by showing up unexpectedly and making silly faces. Afterward they can be heard laughing with glee. A miner must also laugh, for to show anger will only upset the Knockers, who can cause a lot of damage to the mine.

Because every miner knows that the Knockers can create as well as warn of mine disaster, they are treated with great respect, and food and drink are left for them regularly. If they are not fed they will find some other more hospitable mine in which to live. Their fits of rage are much feared, for Knockers are very strong and violent when aroused.

German miners will greet the Knockers verbally or with a doff of their miner's helmets upon entering a mine.

There are Cornish miners who swear that in some cave-ins the trapped miners have been located due to the knocking of these faeries, who have led the way to them. Some mines in Cornwall have been closed due to the Knockers who wish to keep a few of these underground places to themselves, and all but a few greedy persons begrudge them this quirk. One famous mine left to the Knockers is a rich Dartmoor mine said to still contain heavy veins of tin, copper, and gold. No Cornish miner will swear or whistle while underground. These are two things that the Knockers hate, and to indulge oneself could bring disaster to the whole mine.

In Czechoslovakia, Knockers warn the family of a miner who is going to die in a mine accident by pounding on the miner's house until morning.

Some lore traces the origin of the Knockers to the souls of Jews who used to work there.

Where to Find Them: In caves and mines.

How to Contact: Call to them, ask their aid, or make a simple evocation to your circle. But keep in mind that these faeries have a strong will of their own, and they are not likely to respond unless they choose to do so. People who have access to caves can start to build a relationship with them by leaving libations.

Magickal and Ritual Help: Call them to help you find your way out of a mine or cave. Then follow the knocking to be led out. If you work in any type of underground facility, leave out food for them. Befriending them will induce them to warn you of impending disasters.

Kolbalds

Land of Origin: Germany.

Other Origins: None known.

Other Names: Poltersprites. Sometimes spelled Kobauld, Cobald, or Kobolde. In Scandinavia they are called Hutchens or Heinzelmannchens and are distinguished by their red felt hats.

Element: Earth.

Appearance and Temperament: Kolbalds (Coe-bolds) are dwarf faeries usually seen wearing little brown knee pants and caps. They can be very helpful but will turn abusive if ignored or belittled.

Time Most Active: At night.

Lore: Kolbalds are a German version of the Scottish Brownie, though they have a less helpful nature. Alone or in small groups they adopt homes where they will live, expecting the full benefits of the household even if they do not choose to work for their keep. When not in human homes, Kolbalds live in hollow trees.

Kolbalds have pipes clenched in their teeth, but they do not smoke. In fact smoke seems to upset them greatly, and smoking up a room may be a good way to drive them away.

If they feel ignored or belittled they can turn abusive and will behave with poltergeist activity by making noise and throwing things about. There are very few of them left today, and they are nearly impossible to remove from your home once they take up residence. In such cases a series of exorcisms is the best course of action. Burning smoky incense will also discourage them.

Where to Find Them: In infested homes and in hollow trees.

How to Contact: If you really want a Kolbald in your home, leave out food and milk and make an evocation to them. Otherwise visit them in Faeryland, making sure they do not follow you home.

Magickal and Ritual Help: Undetermined, but may be able to help with home protection spells if they are feeling charitable. In general they are too untrustworthy to be of much use to humans.

Kornbocke

See **Phooka**.

Korreds

Land of Origin: Brittany.

Other Origins: None known.

Other Names: They are also called Korrs or Kores. A similar faery in Cornwall is called the Pyrenee.

Element: Earth.

Appearance and Temperament: These elven creatures always appear to be male. They have hairy bodies, spindly legs, and bird-like arms, but sport huge heads in comparison.

They have wild spiky hair and long pointed noses. Compared to the rest of their body, their facial features are huge. Their hairy bodies resemble those of monkeys, and they have cloven feet and loud hooting laughter. Scaring humans is a big part of their life, and they take their task seriously.

Time Most Active: All year.

Lore: Korreds are the faery guardians of the dolmens (stone altars) and standing stones of Celtic Brittany. Faery lore in France says that it was the Korreds themselves who brought the stones to Brittany and erected them.

They are frightening to look at, and they like it that way so that they can scare away humans who come to disturb the stones, who are on insincere spiritual quests, or who confuse spiritual enlightenment with personal power and ego boosting. These are one of the very few faeries impervious to the grounding power of metal, which they are said to feed upon.

If you approach standing stones with reverence and an open mind and heart, you have nothing to fear from the Korreds.

Where to Find Them: In the standing stones of Brittany, an easy trip in the inner planes.

How to Contact: Call to them at the stones and make yourself known as a friend.

Magickal and Ritual Help: Possibly they could lend energy to protection spells and help you gain knowledge of the civilizations that used the standing stones. Breton legends say they will aid any sincere seeker who comes to learn the lessons and share the power of the stones.

Korrigans

See **Corrigans.**

The Lady of the Lake

Land of Origin: Cornwall.

Other Origins: Wales.

Other Names: None known.

Element: Water.

Appearance and Temperament: The Lady of the Lake is part of the Arthurian myths. Her arm, holding the famous sword Excalibur, is most frequently seen by human eyes.

Time Most Active: All year.

Lore: The Lady of the Lake lives in Dosmary Pool, a lake in Cornwall. She is the woman who gave Arthur his famous sword Excalibur, and to whom it was returned upon his death.

Many pagans and mythologists have speculated on whether this Lady is really a Mother or Maiden Goddess-form, and have wondered if she may still have been expressly a Goddess had not the Arthurian stories been so adulterated and altered over time to suit each new generation.

Underneath Dosmary Pool she is said to preside over a magnificent and wealthy faery kingdom forever shielded from humans by the illusion of water.

Where to Find Her: In Dosmary Pool, an easy trip on the inner planes.

How to Contact: Try making an invocation to her as you would make to a Goddess.

Magickal and Ritual Help: She can help direct you along your spiritual pathway. Listen for her messages to come telepathically. If you actually see her arm rise from Dosmary Pool, consider yourself highly favored.

Leanansidhe

Land of Origin: The Isle of Man.

Other Origins: There is said to be only one of her, and she has migrated to Ireland's eastern coast.

Other Names: A similar faery of Hebrew legend is called Estrie.

Element: Water.

Appearance and Temperament: The Leanansidhe (Lan-awn-shee) is a beautiful female vampire faery. She is said to give inspiration to poets, but the reward for her services is death or, at best, captivity in her kingdom.

Time Most Active: At night all year long.

Lore: There is only one Leanansidhe, and she lives under the Irish Sea off the eastern coast of Ireland.

Like all vampires, she is a blood-sucker. But rather than drinking the blood of her victims, she collects it in a huge red cauldron which is said to be the source of her beauty and powers of poetic inspiration. This may connect her with the Celtic Crone Goddesses who preside over the great cauldron of life, death, and rebirth.

One Manx legend says that calling for protection from the Sea God Manann ruins her hopes of gaining power over you.

Where to Find Her: Unknown.

How to Contact: Contact not advised!

Magickal and Ritual Help: She can aid you in the creation of majestic poetry, but it is probably not worth the effort. Many inspiring Gods and Goddesses are available to assist with poetic motivation who do not extract so high a price for their services. Try calling upon the Irish Goddess Brigid rather than the Leanansidhe to overcome your poetic writer's block.

The Leanansidhe may be the remnants of a demonized Goddess, but the form has been so grossly distorted over time that it is pointless to try to approach her as such.

Leprechauns

Land of Origin: Ireland.

Other Origins: Europe has many treasure-hoarding faeries, all of them similar in appearance.

Other Names: The Gentry. Jewish folklore had a similar character called the Sheedem or Shedim, who was demonized during the Jews' initial patriarchalization and is now used derogatorily in reference to pagan deities.

Element: Earth.

Appearance and Temperament: The Leprechaun (Lep-rah-kahn) is a solitary faery and a trickster who loves to play pranks on the humans he meets. He always appears as a male, and no sighting of a female Leprechaun has ever been recorded. They are always seen wearing green clothing of costly material and green tri-cornered hats. They are mischievous, but will be helpful to humans if approached with respect. They are very quick-witted unless they are drunk.

Time Most Active: All year.

Lore: The most well-known of all the faery folk of Ireland is the Leprechaun. He guards a pot of gold, which is in fact a cauldron associated with the Crone Goddess. If one can gain control of one of these wily creatures one can have the cauldron, and three wishes along with it. The origin of this belief is rooted in Crone worship and is a symbol of spiritual attainment.

Leprechauns are shoemakers by trade, but their clientele is limited to the faery world and they only work on one shoe—never a pair.

The Leprechaun is a solitary faery who does not enjoy working with his fellow creatures and keeps to himself unless there is a party, at which time he gets very drunk and very social. There are numerous stories of persons who have accidentally come upon an open burgh and witnessed these Leprechaun revels. Occasionally they feel moved to invite humans to join them. Feel free to accept their invitation, but do not drink, eat, or dance with them.

Music, dancing, fox hunting, and drinking Irish whiskey are said to be the Leprechauns' favorite pastimes. They love to dance and are attracted to the folk music of their land. Legend says that if you start one dancing he cannot stop until you quit playing your tune. In this frenzied state he may gladly lead you to his crock of gold, if you will please only allow him to stop dancing. Also catching a Leprechaun's eyes and staring at him unblinkingly will give you power over him. Whatever you do, do not grab the little fellow. Remember that he is a creature of another dimension. If you grab him he will fade, still very much in your grasp, but unseen in our world. You will think you have lost him and inadvertently set him free.

But even if you are sly enough to capture this elusive faery, the lucky Leprechaun still has his ways to trick you out of both the crock of gold and the three wishes. If he can trick you into making a fourth wish by sundown, you lose all your wishes and the crock, too. This is certainly not hard for him to do, given the propensity we humans have for wistfully voicing wishes. The poem "The Three Wishes" by Mark Shapiro tells of this legend:

I caught me a Leprechaun,
> *and you know what that means!*
I got me three big wishes,
> *and I wanted so many things.*
I wanted silver and I wanted gold,
> *and riches beyond my place,*
And castles all in clover,
> *and love and a beautious face.*
"So what it be, your wish number one?"
> *asked the Leprechaun all in green.*
"I wish I might have beauty,
> *the most bewitching ever seen."*
"Done!" said the green little Leprechaun,
> *all with a wave of his hand.*
"And I wish," I said, "to have riches,
> *the greatest in this land."*
With a flourish and a flutter they did appear,
> *great beauty and my gold,*
And then I wished for a lover fair,
> *all that my heart could hold.*
Bedazzled I was when I saw him there,
> *my knight in armored bob.*
"Thank you, Leprechaun," I gushed with glee,
> *"You've done a most splendid job."*
But the Leprechaun stood near me,
> *seeming unanxious to leave.*
"I'm glad you know your mind, lass.
> *So many waste wishes, you see."*
So enraptured I was with my bounty
> *that I hardly noticed when*
That wee little, green little Leprechaun
> *began chattering away again.*

> *"'Tis a bonnie day, is it not, my lass?*
> > *Don't you wish, lass, it would bid*
> *To stay like this all year long?"*
> > *And I replied … I did.*
> *The little Trickster laughed with mirth,*
> > *and then my face did fall.*
> *"The rules be, lass, if a fourth wish you make,*
> > *then you lose them all!"*

Leprechauns love to match wits with people, and are fond of riddles and word games which they will attempt to use to gain the upper hand in their dealings with humans.

Where to Find Them: In the physical, try seeking them in wild areas with large grassy hills. You will have a better chance of finding them if you seek them in Faeryland as they rarely come to the earthly plane anymore.

How to Contact: They will not respond to any known evocations or invitations.

Magickal and Ritual Help: Leprechauns can help guide you to the cauldron, or crock of gold, which symbolizes spiritual attainment. In this it is not unlike the Grail quests of the Arthurian tradition. Because of this long association with gold, Leprechauns may be helpful in giving energy to prosperity spells. They can also be persuaded to look after your finer horses. In the guided meditation in this book you met the King of the Leprechauns.

Lesidhe

Land of Origin: Ireland.

Other Origins: India.

Other Names: In Slavic lands they are known as Leshes and in Russia as Zuibotschniks (Zoo-botch-nicks), whose cries are audible and who appear to travel in a small whirlwind. A similar faery in Germany is called a Leshiye and can assume the shape of an owl or a wolf. In Russia this faery is called a Vodyaniye and loves to drink.

Element: Air.

Appearance and Temperament: The Lesidhe (Lay-shee) is a guardian of the forests who is always disguised as foliage. They appear to be androgynous and, even though they are usually found in groups, they seem to have little to do with one another. Therefore they can be classified as solitaries rather than trooping faeries. Unless one gets up and walks about it is hard to distinguish them from the green plants and trees they hide among.

Time Most Active: Spring and summer, especially at dawn and dusk. They are active day and night, but seem to prefer being nocturnal.

Lore: Lesidhes like to mimic mockingbirds to confuse hikers and travelers, and over time they have learned to make even more confusing human sounds. It is believed that they have come to dislike humans for their callous treatment of the environment. The recorded reports of contact with them have all been unfavorable. Though no Lesidhe has ever actually harmed anyone, their pranks are nasty, usually involving trying to lose people in deep woods.

Where to Find Them: Caution is advised when attempting to approach a Lesidhe, for little is known about how they will interact with humans. In the physical or in the astral go to a wild wood and wait until you sense their movements in the trees. If you look and seem to see foliage itself moving in an anthropomorphic way, you're probably seeing a Lesidhe.

How to Contact: While in the protection of a circle call to them and explain what you would have them do, then wait and see what sort of response you get. However, contacting them is not a wise practice. Extreme caution is advised.

Magickal and Ritual Help: They might possibly be persuaded to aid in magick and ritual to aid the planet and the environment.

Limniades

Land of Origin: Greece.

Other Origins: They may have once been sun deities.

Other Names: None known.

Element: Fire.

Appearance and Temperament: Limniades (Leem-nee-od-ayes), a word from which we derive our word illuminate, are small blobs of pure light. Like their cousins, the English Will-O'-the-Wisps, they avoid humans.

Time Most Active: At night.

Lore: Limniades are still seen out in the Greek countryside, and no one can explain them. Greeks once thought them to be discarnate humans condemned to walk the earth by night in repentance of some misdeed.

Where to Find Them: In the Greek countryside.

How to Contact: Unknown.

Magickal and Ritual Help: None known.

Lob

Land of Origin: Wales.

Other Origins: Possibly Germany or England.

Other Names: None known.

Element: Air.

Appearance and Temperament: The Lob is a small dark blob that looks rather like a rain cloud with arms who spends all his time deciding how he can make the most trouble. Fortunately for us, he is lazy and rarely carries through with his ideas, though he delights in human misery.

Time Most Active: Possibly at night.

Lore: The Lob is a goblin, and the name may have been a contracted form of the English word Hobgoblin. The Lob is attracted to ugly, raw emotions and to arguments and fighting. Occasionally psychic persons have reported seeing a little "black thing" whenever they have been at the scene of an argument, fight, or wherever there is a build-up of negative emotions.

Lobs most likely stay alive by feeding off these energies, needing them as if they were food. As he feeds he starts a chain reaction. His negativity feeds the discord which he was initially attracted to, and then he can feast again off the escalated tension.

Where to Find Them: They are most likely to be found wherever there is human discord or violence.

How to Contact: Contact not advised!

Magickal and Ritual Help: None. If you have been part of a quarrel or violent scene, it is a good idea to do a banishing ritual in the area to rid it of the negative vibrations accumulated there. Focus especially on dispersing any Lobs who have been attracted to the scene. Then mentally infuse the area with pink light, a color known for its peaceful, calming effect.

The Lorelei

Land of Origin: Germany.

Other Origins: England.

Other Names: The English call her Mary Player. Merewipers, Meerweibers, Sirens, and Havfrues are all groups of faeries of the same looks and disposition as the Lorelei.

Element: Water.

Appearance and Temperament: The Lorelei (Lore-ah-lie) is a lovely young woman faery who sits on the cliffs above the Rhine River and sings, luring sailors to their deaths in the rocks below.

Time Most Active: All year.

Lore: The Lorelei is a one of a kind, a personification of all the female water spirits of Central Europe. Her beauty and cunning have been much celebrated in the songs and folk tales of Germany.

The English have a similar faery, called Mary Player, who is classed as a type of mermaid. She has but to circle a ship three times to sink it. A sailor's doggerel adapted from an old German poem which tells her tale has become a Mother Goose rhyme:

> ... *Three times she went 'round our gallant ship,*
> *And around three times went she.*
> *And three times more she went 'round our ship,*
> *And sank us to the bottom of the sea.*

Where to Find Her: In the Rhine River.

How to Contact: Contact not advised!

Magickal and Ritual Help: None.

Lunantisidhe

Land of Origin: Ireland.

Other Origins: Possibly ancient Rome.

Other Names: None known.

Element: Air.

Appearance and Temperament: The Lunantisidhe (Loo-nan-tee-shee) are thin and wizened in appearance and look like small, bald, old men. They have pointed ears and long teeth, and long arms and fingers which enable them to climb easily through the blackthorn trees which are their home. They are found in groups, but they are neither trooping nor solitary. They are said to hate humans with a fervent passion.

Time Most Active: At night.

Lore: Lunantisidhe is an odd blending of the Latin word *luna* which means "moon," and the Gaelic *sidhe* which means "faery." They are the guardians of the blackthorn tree from which humans and Leprechauns make shillelaghs, a walking staff indigenous to Ireland.

Their sole purpose for existing seems to be to protect the blackthorn trees from human encroachment. The only time they leave the trees is to pay homage to the Moon Goddess at the Esbats.

Where to Find Them: In blackthorn trees.

How to Contact: Contact not advised!

Magickal and Ritual Help: None.

Lutins

Land of Origin: France.

Other Origins: None known.

Other Names: Follet.

Element: Air.

Appearance and Temperament: The Lutins are expert shapeshifters who have not held one form long enough for any human to characterize their appearance. They are extremely capricious, being useful one minute and destructive the next.

Time Most Active: All year.

Lore: Some Lutins live in human homes and others in trees near water, but they are believed to change homes as often as they change their outward forms. They shapeshift constantly into both animals and inanimate objects, but never into the form of humans. One of their favorite games is to shapeshift into a nugget of gold and watch humans chase after them.

They move from place to place with a little flash of light which makes them appear momentarily like fireflies.

Lutins are usually benign in their intentions towards humans, but they have such changeable tempers, ones which can accidentally result in physical or psychic harm, that prolonged contact with them is not advised.

Where to Find Them: Uncertain, as they move about constantly.

How to Contact: Unknown.

Magickal and Ritual Help: Undetermined.

Ly Erg

Land of Origin: Scotland.

Other Origins: None known, though he shares some in common with the Beansidhe, the Erlkonig, and the Fylgiar.

Other Names: None known.

Element: Water.

Appearance and Temperament: There is only one Ly Erg. He dresses like a soldier and can only be distinguished from a real one by his small size and his red right hand.

Time Most Active: Unknown.

Lore: The Ly Erg is seen as a portent of death, but unlike so many such portents, this is one with whom you have a second chance at life. It is reported that he will stop his mark on a road or path (especially if it is near water) and challenge you with a raising of his red right hand. The best thing to do in this instance is to retreat, because if you allow him to engage you in combat you will die within a fortnight.

His red hand is said to be the result of many years of bloodstains from those he has killed in combat.

The Ly Erg is a part of Scottish folklore which has almost been forgotten, and there are fewer and fewer accounts of him in extant texts over the past two centuries.

Where to Find Him: On lonely roadsides near water. Since he has not been reported as having been seen in many years, the only place you are likely to find him is in Faeryland.

How to Contact: Unknown and not advised.

Magickal and Ritual Help: None.

Mal-de-Mer

Land of Origin: Brittany and Cornwall.

Other Origins: None known.

Other Names: None known.

Element: Water.

Appearance and Temperament: No Mal-de-Mer has been described or even seen by a human. They live in the sea near Cornwall and Brittany and prey on ships.

Time Most Active: At night, and during storms at sea.

Lore: Mal-de-Mer is a French term which means "evil of the sea." Once again these may not be a true faery type, but only a fear-form.

When ship travel in Cornwall and Brittany became commonplace, groups of criminals known as Wreckers prowled rocky coasts and lured ships to their doom by falsely projecting lights along the coastlines, which made the ship's crew think they were safe harbors. The wooden ships would break up on the rocks and the crews would be forced to abandon ship or be killed. Wrecked ships abandoned by their crew were legally considered fair game, and the Wreckers made themselves rich from the bootleg cargo. Mal-de-Mers were accused of causing many of these wrecks, though it is doubtful they ever had anything to do with them.

Where to Find Them: Unknown.

How to Contact: They are probably not able to be contacted because they most likely lack existence.

Magickal and Ritual Help: None.

Mannikins

See **Elves.**

Mary Player

See **The Lorelei.**

Masseriol

Land of Origin: Northern Italy and Iberian Peninsula.

Other Origins: None known.

Other Names: Masseriols who prefer city life to the country are called Barabaos and are native to Venice.

Element: Earth.

Appearance and Temperament: The Masseriol (Mahs-air-ee-oel) dresses all in red, has an elderly face, and a booming laugh that is somewhere between the cry of a horse and a goat. He can be helpful, but he has a very high opinion of himself. He is plump, but always impeccably well dressed and groomed. They are always male.

Time Most Active: All year.

Lore: Masseriol means "little farmer," and they have been known to occasionally help out on farms as long as they don't have to get themselves dirty. They can also be of help in the kitchen when one of them has taken a shine to the lady of the house.

The Masseriol fancies himself a ladies' man, and has a fetish for young girls whom he woos to his mountain lair to dance for him. No harm comes to these girls, though the experience can be unnerving.

Where to Find Them: In rural Italy and on farms in Faeryland.

How to Contact: Make an invitation while in a circle.

Magickal and Ritual Help: He can help tend livestock, pets, and gardens. Females, keep yourself protected if you wish to contact a Masseriol. Males should not hesitate to try to communicate with him.

Mazikeen

Land of Origin: Middle East.

Other Origins: Possibly India.

Other Names: This may be the origin of the Germanic word Mannikin, which means "little man," and is used in the Middle East to describe a host of forever-partying faery life.

Element: Air.

Appearance and Temperament: Mazikeen are winged faeries who cannot fly. They are often mistaken for angels, but they are faeries whose sole purpose is to steal food and drink for their endless revelries.

Time Most Active: All year.

Lore: The Mazikeens do not need sleep and can party all the time.

Where to Find Them: Unknown.

How to Contact: Unknown.

Magickal and Ritual Help: None. They are much too self-absorbed to aid humans.

Melch Dick

See *Churn Milk Peg and Melch Dick.*

Menehunas

Land of Origin: Polynesia.

Other Origins: None known.

Other Names: Menahunes.

Element: Earth.

Appearance and Temperament: Menehunas are the most well-known faeries in Polynesia, and are seen as Elves in native dress who live in the tropical forests. They can be tricksters, but they will also serve humans.

Time Most Active: All year.

Lore: The Menehunas (Mi-nee-hoo-nahs), like the Leprechauns, guard a crock of treasure and can grant wishes if they are caught. They have also been known to help lost travelers find their way out of the jungles, and some accounts say they have even provided fresh water and food for these people.

Where to Find Them: In the jungles of the islands of the South Pacific, especially in places near waterfalls.

How to Contact: They must come to you. They will not appear by invitation or evocation.

Magickal and Ritual Help: If you are lucky enough to see a Menehuna, he may aid you on your spiritual quest and answer questions about what you need to know about yourself. Call to them if you are lost in the tropics. They have tremendous stores of magickal energy which they can direct your way if they wish.

Merewipers

See **The Lorelei.**

Merpeople

Land of Origin: Worldwide.

Other Origins: None.

Other Names: Fish-Folk, Mermaids, Mermen, Water Dancers, Blue Men. In Ireland they are called Merrows.

Element: Water.

Appearance and Temperament: Merpeople are more commonly called Mermen or Mermaids depending upon their gender. They have the lower bodies of fish and the upper bodies and heads of humans. They appear as adult males and females of great beauty, but no children have ever been sighted. They are usually friendly and are slow to anger, but their ire can be aroused by persons who desecrate and pollute their home.

Time Most Active: All year.

Lore: Sailors have recorded many tales of Merpeople who have saved drowning people or who have steered their ships clear of disaster. Around areas of known faery islands sailors would report seeing entire colonies of them frolicking in the water. Breton sailors even believed dolphins to be friendly Merpeople playing in the wakes of their ships. Ghost ships and sunken wrecks, all well known to the world's sailors, are thought to be their homes. Occasionally

Mermaids wish to take human mates, such as in the popular faery tale "The Little Mermaid." Mermen rarely take human brides. They seem to have trouble reproducing themselves and may need human males to further their race. Merpeople are excellent parents who cherish and protect their young.

One malevolent race of Merpeople are the very strong Blue Men of the Muir from Scotland, who have been accused of causing storms in the North Sea and throwing boulders at ships. The best way to dispatch them is by reciting rhymes, which is said to confuse them.

Where to Find Them: At sea or at the seashore.

How to Contact: Call out to them with your mind and ask for their aid. Feed fish and care for marine life to win their trust. Seek them in the waters of Faeryland for best results.

Magickal and Ritual Help: They may offer help in finding things or persons lost at sea, or in discovering faery islands. They may be called upon to help save someone who is drowning, or to help navigate your boat through storm or fog. They can be counted upon to help care for marine life and in spells aiding water environmentalism. Begin forming a relationship with them now if you think you may ever want to work with them. They give their trust slowly, but fully.

Merrows

See **Merpeople.**

The Moerae

Land of Origin: Greece.

Other Origins: These faeries may have been native to India.

Other Names: There are numerous other triplicities which are less than Goddesses and more than merely faeries. Among these are the Furies (Roman), the Norns (Teutonic), the Gorgons (North African), the Erzulie (Voodun), and the Zoryas (West African).

Element: Earth.

Appearance and Temperament: These faeries of Greece usually appear in groups of three representing a young girl, a middle-aged woman, and an old woman, or else they appear just as three middle-aged women. They are neither helpful nor harmful to humans, but dispense fate as they see fit.

Time Most Active: All year.

Lore: The Moerae determines the fate of children, and the fact that she appears as a threesome relates her strongly to two ancient pagan images. One is the Triple Goddess who is Maiden, Mother, and Crone in one, and the other is the Three Fates, a Greek triple demigoddess who determined the life's course of every human being.

While paganism has rejected these doctrines of predestination, preferring instead a concept of total self-responsibility, the Moerae still functions as a helper who can soften our fate, even though it comes of our own making. One example of this softening of fate is seen in the classic story of Sleeping Beauty. After Sleeping Beauty's birth, a group of faeries come to bless the child with gifts of beauty, riches, etc. One evil faery cursed her to die at age 16. But instead of being stuck with this fate, another faery, whom we can equate with the Moerae, decrees that she will not die, but will only fall into a long slumber.

Where to Find Them: Deep inside dark caves.

How to Contact: Make an invitation to your circle and petition their aid as you would that of a Goddess.

Magickal and Ritual Help: Help out of difficult situations, inspiration. Love spells, matchmaking, and divination are also their province, and she is one of the few faeries who will concern herself with human romantic love.

Monaciello

Land of Origin: Italy.

Other Origins: None known.

Other Names: None known.

Element: Earth.

Appearance and Temperament: Monaciello (Moe-nah-see-ail-oh) means "little monk," which is how their hooded cloak-dress makes them appear. He always wears red and is always drunk, but is not unfriendly. A similar Italian faery who lives in caves is called a Monachicchio, but he is a mean drunk.

Time Most Active: All year.

Lore: These faeries are native to Calabria, an area known for its fine wines. He is like the Irish Clurichaun in that he inhabits and guards wine cellars, but like the Irish Leprechaun he also guards a treasure.

The hoods that they wear with their little cloaks are necessary to their survival. Italian legends say that if you can steal the hood you can gain the Monaciello's treasure, for he will be desperate to get back his hood or else he will soon die.

They have merry personalities and they like to steal human clothing for sport.

Where to Find Them: In wine cellars.

How to Contact: Set out wine for him in your basement or wine cellar.

Magickal and Ritual Help: He can possibly be useful in home protection spells, but basically is a useless and fun character.

The Moss People

Land of Origin: Germanic lands and Switzerland.

Other Origins: Faeries which appear as butterflies are also known in Polynesia and Africa.

Other Names: All of these are other terms for Moss People translated from the German: Monarchs of the Forest, Butterfly Faeries, Flying Leaves, and Greenies.

Element: Air.

Appearance and Temperament: Moss People are both male and female and have large butterfly wings attached to lithe bodies that look mostly human. They are very beautiful creatures, though hard to detect in the wild, where they tend to hide in moss and other dark wood foliage. They are shy of people and very capricious.

Time Most Active: Late spring and summer.

Lore: Moss People are seen less and less, but this may be because they have learned it is safer to hide from us. They have a very timid and humble nature. In Switzerland they have been reported asking to borrow an occasional tool from a woodsman or farmer.

Moss People are good luck to have around. Keep their environment clean and natural if you wish to continue to have them.

Where to Find Them: In dense woodlands in the summer.

How to Contact: Unknown, but try acknowledging their presence with friendly conversation and offerings of fresh milk.

Magickal and Ritual Help: Undetermined, but these shy faeries may yet surprise us with their abilities. While they have never been known to aid any pagan magick, they may do so if approached correctly by someone who has won their trust.

Mother Holle

Land of Origin: Germany.

Other Origins: Many faeries in the world enjoy spinning.

Other Names: None known.

Element: Earth.

Appearance and Temperament: Mother Holle is an older woman, but not elderly. Her hair is long and black and she wears a dark green robe. There is only one of her and she is neither good nor evil, but dispenses justice fairly as she sees fit.

Time Most Active: All year.

Lore: Mother Holle was probably once a German Goddess, and in her legends we can still see the blurred images of both Mother and Crone. Most of what we know about her comes to us through German folk tales, the most well-known being "Mother Holle and the Two Sisters."

Mother Holle spends her days at her spinning wheel, which also relates her to the Goddess who, in some cultures, was thought to have created the world from her wheel. She gives advice when asked and can instantly divine the future. She rewards those who are industrious, especially while in her service. Gold is her most frequent form of payment, which again may be a metaphor for spiritual attainment. She is most disposed to aiding young women.

To those who do her bidding she gives rewards and an open invitation to visit her world, which exists in a verdant meadow at the bottom of a wishing well. In the above-mentioned faery tale, one of the sisters stumbles into Mother Holle's world when she falls into a well. In this case the well functions as a birth-canal image, and offers new life (an image of rebirth) to those who will take her advice. She is stern but not mean, and is wise like the Crone Goddesses.

Mother Holle likes a well-made bed, and this is one of the tasks she is likely to ask of a human petitioner. When one shakes out the huge feather tick, white down flies everywhere and covers everything. This image is so pervasive in the popular mind of the German people that when it snows they are still heard to say, "Mother Holle is making her bed."

Where to Find Her: In Faeryland and in meadows, and at the bottom of old wells.

How to Contact: She responds best to evocations made at wishing wells. Evoke her with care and respect, remembering that she may in fact be a Goddess. Astrally venture down a wishing well to seek her.

Magickal and Ritual Help: Divination and spiritual guidance, help with pressing problems.

Muireartach

Land of Origin: Scottish Highlands.

Other Origins: None known.

Other Names: Hag of the Seas.

Element: Water.

Appearance and Temperament: There is only one of her. She is an old woman who is bald, has jagged teeth, a blue-gray complexion, and one great eye. Her intent has always been painted as malevolent, but this is unclear.

Time Most Active: During winter, night, and storms.

Lore: The Muireartach, whose name means "one of the sea," is sometimes said to be the ruler of the great sea storms which frequently bash the Scottish coast. She shares some characteristics with the Cailleac Bhuer, and may, like her, be some sort of distortion of the Crone Goddess rather than a faery.

Where to Find Her: Unknown.

How to Contact: Unknown.

Magickal and Ritual Help: Undetermined.

Murdhuachas

Land of Origin: Ireland.

Other Origins: None known.

Other Names: Walrus People, Sea Cows.

Element: Water.

Appearance and Temperament: Murdhuachas (Mer-oo-khas), one of several races of Irish sea faeries, are often mistaken for Merpeople (Mermaids and Mermen). Like them they possess fish-like lower bodies, but rather than having humanoid upper bodies, they have the upper bodies and heads of other mammals. Their temperament is ambivalent.

Time Most Active: Dawn and dusk.

Lore: They have been known to be helpful in locating fish or in finding one's home port on a fog-shrouded night. And they have been just as well known to turn nasty and lure sailors to their death on coastal rocks, like the German Lorelei, with their haunting songs. They are never seen in the Irish Sea, only off the west coast in the Atlantic Ocean. Some believe them to be a cousin of the Formorians.

Where to Find Them: At seasides, especially near rocky shores.

How to Contact: Contact not advised!

Magickal and Ritual Help: Undetermined.

Neck

Land of Origin: Scandinavia.

Other Origins: None known.

Other Names: Neckan, Necker. A Nakki is a Neck from Estonia or Latvia.

Element: Water.

Appearance and Temperament: A Neck is a shapeshifting water faery who is an expert harper and singer. It is likely they possess no gender or concrete form, but usually appear to humans as poor reflections of themselves. They are seductive and cunning and should be avoided.

Time Most Active: All year.

Lore: Necks are very alluring to human males. They are usually seen lounging beside the edge of a lake or stream. They have been credited with the drowning of many people.

Where to Find Them: In lakes and streams.

How to Contact: Contact not advised!

Magickal and Ritual Help: None.

Nereides

Land of Origin: Greece.

Other Origins: Sweden, Albania, Crete.

Other Names: Exoticas.

Element: Water.

Appearance and Temperament: Nereides (Nair-eye-deez) are beautiful and graceful female water faeries most usually seen in the Aegean Sea. They are dangerous to humans, especially children.

Time Most Active: At noon and midnight.

Lore: Nereides live in the warm coastal waters of Greece, and their list of human injuries is lengthy. They inflict insanity on anyone who sees them under a full moon, and they cannot bear children, so they steal them instead. Greeks believe that they haunt childbirth, hoping to take the baby away. The only thing they love more than children is milk and honey, and setting some out will distract them from their mischief. But don't get used to feeding them or they will hang around like stray animals. They can shapeshift into the bodies of swans and like to sing while swimming in this form. Nereides wear white shawls when they are on land, and if a human man can capture one of these, he can gain control over the faery. In Sweden a folk tale exists of a lad called Edric who stole away a Nereide named Godda from a dance when she dropped her shawl.

Their lives are short in faery terms, no more than a hundred years.

On many of the Greek islands it is believed that Nereides have mated with the human population, and in one of these villages the locals will point out to you persons they believe descended from these unions.

Where to Find Them: In the sea near Greece or Sweden.

How to Contact: Call to them at seasides. Approach with some caution. Males should carry extra protection; females need not overly fear them.

Magickal and Ritual Help: None known.

Nibelungen

Land of Origin: Germany, Norway, and Denmark.

Other Origins: None known, but there are many tales of faeries who hoard gold all around the world.

Other Names: Nibelung (Neeb-el-loong) is the singular spelling. A similar faery in India is called a Raksha, and is very poorly groomed, smells bad, and is excessively stupid.

Element: Earth.

Appearance and Temperament: These Teutonic dwarf faeries live in a hidden subterranean crystal palace. They come to woodlands when the mood strikes, and this is where humans have seen them. They are tricksters and quite capricious, with a temperament most resembling that of the Irish Leprechaun.

Time Most Active: All year.

Lore: The Nibelungen's gold is guarded when they are not around by a dragon named Fafnir. Humans can obtain the gold only in the astral world; it will not travel back to the physical realm. Those who try to take it lose everything they have gained spiritually. Some Norse mythologists believe this to be a metaphor for obtaining or losing the blessings of the Nordic Sun God.

Nibelungen are mentioned in German composer Richard Wagner's ring cycle of operas, a series based upon German folklore and myths. They are featured in *Der Ring des Nibelungen*.

These faeries are goldsmiths who make golden rings with magickal properties. They are best known for their rings of fertility which many a barren human has sought but failed to obtain. The Nibelungen seem to take great delight in the failings of humans who seek their magick and their world, and their merry laughter is often heard just as some hapless human falls, trips, or loses the prize they believe they have just won.

Where to Find Them: The location of their crystal palace is a secret, but it may be in Valhallah, the Nordic Land of the Dead. Seek them in Faeryland.

How to Contact: They will not respond to any known evocation or invitation.

Magickal and Ritual Help: Nibelungen may be able to assist you as spiritual guides if you find them on the inner planes, but be on the lookout for their endless pranks. Let them know you are aware of the true nature of their golden treasure if you wish to gain their respect.

Nicker

See **Kelpies.**

Nis

See **Brownie.**

Nixen

Land of Origin: Germany and Switzerland.

Other Origins: River and water sprites are common throughout the world.

Other Names: Nixie. The singular form is Nix. Child Nixen are called Urchins, a word which has come into English usage to mean an unruly or delinquent child.

Element: Water.

Appearance and Temperament: Nix are water sprites who primarily live in the rivers of Germany and Switzerland. They are seen in both genders, but the females seem to predominate. The females are very lovely, and the males are quite handsome except for their green teeth. Their temperament runs somewhere between mischievous and dangerous.

Time Most Active: All year, but they are less visible in winter.

Lore: Nixen have been known to lure swimmers and sailors to their deaths on rocks and to invoke storms in the rivers they inhabit. Germans once believed they did this to hide their periodic gatherings.

The Rhine River used to be their primary home and is held sacred by them. They have a utopian under-lake kingdom which is wealthy and beautiful and is ruled over by a king and queen with equal power. They are master fiddlers who have composed many catchy tunes that humans are warned not to play on human fiddles for fear of being unable to stop until the strings are cut. Some of these Nixen tunes survive as German folk songs which usually contain the word Nix in the title. Austrian composer Franz Schubert, who used Germanic folk songs and tales as the basis for many of his famous *lieder* (songs), set to music the Wilhelm Muller poem *Wohin*, which mentions the singing Nixen dancing down the Rhine to the sea.

In the last century, reported sightings of Nixen have been scarce. It is believed that they still live in their underwater world, but rarely surface.

Metal is an especially potent weapon against them, which renders them powerless and can even kill them if they are exposed for too long a time.

When Nixen were numerous, they were considered the Succubi and Incubi of the waters and would often seek out human mates to take underwater with them. But sadly for the human involved, this was not a permanent mating and the abused bodies of these victims would eventually be found near the river.

Nixen have on a few occasions been helpful to humans by warning of drownings and approaching storms, but this is rare.

Where to Find Them: In and under the Rhine River, or in any river of Faeryland.

How to Contact: These faeries will not come when called; you will have to seek them out. Approach them with extreme caution, as they have a history of being more harmful than helpful. If you meet one and begin to feel uncomfortable, simply walk away from the water. They cannot live long on land.

Magickal and Ritual Help: None known.

Noggles

Land of Origin: Western Europe.
Other Origins: None.
Other Names: None known.
Element: Water.

Appearance and Temperament: The Noggle is a solitary faery who lives near the edge of inland streams, which he jealously guards against human encroachment. They look like small gray horses, complete with miniature tack.

Time Most Active: Spring and summer.

Lore: The Noggle is a mischievous faery who lets it be known that he does not appreciate humans building on his waterways. His two favorite pranks are jamming mill wheels and chasing people into the water.

Where to Find Them: In rural areas near sylvan streams.

How to Contact: Calling to them will have little effect, but if you hang around long enough and show no fear they may find you just for the challenge of trying to scare you off.

Magickal and Ritual Help: Ask the Noggles to lend energies to spells and rituals designed to protect their environment. If you live near a stream where you suspect the presence of a Noggle, attempt to befriend it by not polluting the water and leaving libations of fresh straw for it. In exchange for your kindness and your protection of the steam, it will help protect your land from intruders both physical and astral.

Nokke

Land of Origin: Sweden.

Other Origins: From Sweden they came to the Shetland and Orkney Islands of Scotland.

Other Names: None known.

Element: Water.

Appearance and Temperament: This is a musical river sprite who is often heard but never seen.

Time Most Active: Evening.

Lore: Nokkes (Noe-keys), both male and female, can be heard singing at dawn and dusk. They avoid humans completely. When humans try to find them by following the sound of their voices, they either stop singing or move somewhere else and take up the song again, leaving the frustrated follower behind. Whether this is done for sport or because they really don't want humans around is unknown.

Where to Find Them: Nokkes can be heard near rivers in their native land. Seek them at dusk.

How to Contact: Unknown.

Magickal and Ritual Help: Unknown.

Nucklelavees

Land of Origin: Scotland.

Other Origins: None known.

Other Names: Nucklelavees is the Anglicized spelling, the one most commonly seen today. The original spelling was Nuchlavis.

Element: Water.

Appearance and Temperament: Nucklelavees (Nuke-lay-lah-veez) are Scottish sea faeries native to the Hebrides Islands. They are ill-tempered in the extreme; are hideous; have large, powerful bodies; and can take almost any form they wish—but they always appear very ugly to humans. When not shapeshifting, they appear as half-human and half-horse with fins for feet. If cut, they bleed black blood.

Time Most Active: All year.

Lore: Nucklelavees enjoy coming out of the sea and chasing humans just to frighten them, but no one has ever been reported to be actually captured by one. They are easy to escape by crossing over running water such as a creek or river, because this is as far inland as they can travel. Nucklelavees also prey on other faeries.

These foul faeries can be smelled approaching long before they show up. The odor they emit has been described as a cross between spoiled fish and rotting eggs all covered with mildew.

Some pagans believe these faeries are either earth-bound human discarnates or wicked pirates who died at sea and are now stuck between the worlds of the dead and the living, unable to move firmly into either.

Where to Find Them: At seashores.

How to Contact: Contact not advised!

Magickal and Ritual Help: None.

Nymphs

Land of Origin: Greece.

Other Origins: None known.

Other Names: None.

Element: Can be any.

Appearance and Temperament: Nymphs are diminutive female faeries known to be very seductive.

Time Most Active: All year.

Lore: Nymph is a classification of faeries rather than a single type. There are wood nymphs, water nymphs, sea nymphs, tree nymphs, grove nymphs, etc. They are all on good terms with the Greek deities, and other mythical animals such as Pegasus and the Satyrs.

They have a reputation for excessive sexuality. The word nymphomaniac, a medical term for a woman with an enormous sexual appetite, was derived from the name of these Greek nature faeries.

Where to Find Them: Nymphs exist in every conceivable place in nature, and are all over Faeryland.

How to Contact: Depends on the type of Nymph. Go to the place where you want to find one and call to them.

Magickal and Ritual Help: Most Nymphs are too playful to be useful as working partners, but they will invite you into their games, which you should feel free to join. Human males have been known to have sexual relations with them and report that directing this energy outward to a specific goal is an excellent magickal device.

The Oak King

Land of Origin: Europe.

Other Origins: None known.

Other Names: Robin Redman, King of the Waxing Year.

Element: Earth.

Appearance and Temperament: The Oak King is usually depicted as wearing a small breech cloth and a crown of oak leaves and acorns. In his right hand he carries a staff of oak wood.

Time Most Active: From Yule to Midsummer.

Lore: The Oak King exists in the pagan lore of western Europe as something more than a faery but less than a God. He is the king of the waxing year and the other half of the Holly King, the king of the waning year. From Yule to Midsummer the Oak King reigns, taking over the mantle of rulership from the Holly King.

In many pagan Yule rituals this struggle is acted out between two coven members who portray the two kings, who are really only reflections of each other. Though they fight and one pretends to die, it is merely the other half of himself resting until it is his turn to reign again.

The robin, a spring bird, is the symbol of the Oak King, just as the wren represents the Holly King. The first stanza of the English nursery rhyme "Jenny Wren and Robin Redbreast" reflects the old belief in these two nature spirits and their struggle for supremacy twice a year. The "merry time" referred to in this ditty is the Yule Sabbat, and the cake and wine is the cake and ale ceremony usually associated with Esbats:

> *Jenny Wren fell sick*
> > *Upon a merry time.*
> *In came Robin Redbreast and*
> > *Brought her cake and wine.*

The Oak King shares similarities with the Horned God of Europe, and he may in fact be a devalued pagan God whose origins have been long forgotten.

Where to Find Him: Look for him in Faeryland and sense his presence at the Yule and Midsummer Sabbats. His spirit can be called to your circle at those times. This is one faery you should not fear inviting into your circle space.

How to Contact: Try making an invocation to him at the Yule and Midsummer Sabbats.

Magickal and Ritual Help: Undetermined, but if he is a God-form, then he may aid you in your spiritual quests. Seek an audience with him in Faeryland.

The Oakmen

Land of Origin: Germany and Scandinavia.

Other Origins: Guardian spirits are known worldwide.

Other Names: None known.

Element: Fire.

Appearance and Temperament: Oakmen are male dwarf faeries with huge heads who are the guardians of sacred oak groves. They are not very friendly towards people, but no one has ever been harmed by one.

Time Most Active: At night.

Lore: The Oakmen may have actually been some type of humans who worshipped in tree settings like the Druids of the Celtic lands. Because of the need for secrecy they may have gathered only at night and in the guise of non-human beings, in much the same way witches once gathered in secret. But the fact that they have come into legends as Dwarves means we have to take their existence as faeries seriously, also.

Where to Find Them: In oak groves, especially in the Black Forest of Germany.

How to Contact: Approach with caution and respect on their home territory and identify yourself as a friend.

Magickal and Ritual Help: Undetermined.

Ogres

See *Giants and Ogres.*

Orculli

Land of Origin: Italy.

Other Origins: None known.

Other Names: They are called Norrgens in the Swiss Alps.

Element: Air.

Appearance and Temperament: Orculli are giants with a mean disposition and a cannibalistic diet. On the rare occasions that they are seen, they appear as bearded males.

Time Most Active: All year.

Lore: Orculli live on clouds just like the Giant in the fable "Jack and the Beanstalk" and descend to earth only to obtain food. They prefer to eat their own kind, but will settle for beef and human meat if they must. Their touch alone can sicken cattle to death, and they are adept thieves.

One Alpine legend says that, like the elephant who fears a mouse, these giants fear cats and will flee in terror from them.

One can always tell when an Orculli is around because of the vile smell they produce, said to be like that of a rotting carcass. Despite their size they are slow and clumsy, and humans can easily get away from them.

The Swiss giants, the Norrgen, prefers to eat human children and young faeries.

Where to Find Them: On clouds over the Alps.

How to Contact: Contact not advised!

Magickal and Ritual Help: None.

The Paian

Land of Origin: Scandinavia.

Other Origins: None known.

Other Names: They may be the origin of the Seelie Court of Scotland.

Element: Earth.

Appearance and Temperament: This is the dwarf faery congress of Scandinavia.

Time Most Active: At the Sabbats.

Lore: The Paian is not an individual or even a single type of faery. It is a faery gathering, a congress or forum, of all the dwarf faeries of Scandinavia. They meet in secret at the Sabbats to worship, play, and discuss business. No known human has ever witnessed this gathering.

Their most famous ruling was against a dwarf named Ammaze who was censured and then excommunicated for trying to live as a human.

Where to Find Them: Their meeting place is a secret.

How to Contact: The congress is completely hidden, but some of the individual faeries are accessible. How to contact them depends on what type of dwarf faery they are.

Magickal and Ritual Help: Varies with each dwarf race.

Painajainen

Land of Origin: European Alps.

Other Origins: None known, but horse faeries and deities are common to Europe. The most familiar such creatures to western pagans are the Shopiltees of the Shetland Islands and the Celtic/Gaulic horse Goddess, Epona.

Other Names: In Italy they are called Linchettos.

Element: Earth.

Appearance and Temperament: These faeries look like small white horses who ride through the Alps.

Time Most Active: At night.

Lore: Painajainen like to tease and sometimes harm children, but they never steal them, and no child has ever been killed by one. Bringing nightmares is their most usual way of tormenting. Even today their tiny, ghostly hoofbeats are occasionally heard echoing though the Alps, though no horse and rider can be seen.

No explanation has been given for why the Painajainen dislike children so much, but it may have to do with their difficulties in reproducing themselves. An effective Alpine remedy against them is to place a broom or some iron under a child's pillow.

They live long, for as many as 4000 years.

Where to Find Them: In the Alps.

How to Contact: Contact not advised!

Magickal and Ritual Help: None.

Pamarindo

Land of Origin: Northern Italy.

Other Origins: None known.

Other Names: None known.

Element: Earth.

Appearance and Temperament: This Italian male dwarf faery is very small, mean, and obese. He is a scavenger who kills animals. He wears a hat of fur and red clothes which are stained with animal fat. He is lazy and disliked by other faeries.

Time Most Active: All year.

Lore: The Pamarindo is a carnivore who is either forbidden or unable to make his own kill. Therefore he must engage in creative ways of obtaining his meat, such as running animals off cliffs or causing them to fall and impale themselves on fallen tree branches.

He has ghastly table manners, and his clothes are usually streaked with grease and animal fat. He will not move out of the way for anyone, and has been known to knock down travelers he meets on the road. He is extremely rude and antisocial.

Where to Find Them: Unknown.

How to Contact: Contact not advised!

Magickal and Ritual Help: None.

Penates

Land of Origin: Ancient Rome.

Other Origins: None known.

Other Names: A Lare (Lahr-ay) is a Penate who is solitary and cannot be exposed to daylight.

Element: Earth.

Appearance and Temperament: Penates (Pay-not-ayes) are dwarf faeries who wear peasant costumes and small tool belts. They always are seen as males.

Time Most Active: At night.

Lore: The Penates and the Lares were very likely house deities of ancient Rome who were later demoted to faery folk. In fact the word Lares is similar is origin to the Latino-Etruscan word for Lord, *Lar*.

They are similar to the house Brownies of Scotland in that they adopt a home and do good deeds for their adopted family by night.

The Penate can go abroad by daylight if he chooses, but he prefers to be out only at night. The Lare is a night-bound creature who cannot be exposed to sunlight or he will perish.

Where to Find Them: When he is not in an adopted home his whereabouts are unknown.

How to Contact: Leave them wine and bread and make a formal invitation for them to share your home.

Magickal and Ritual Help: They are useful in home protection spells and for aid in getting tedious chores finished faster.

Phi-Suk

Land of Origin: Thailand.

Other Origins: Possibly India.

Other Names: None known.

Element: Fire.

Appearance and Temperament: The Phi-Suk wears the ancient native dress of southeast Asia. They are neither good nor bad to humans, but are dispensers of justice and lessons in much the same way as the Moerae of Greece.

Time Most Active: All year.

Lore: Phi-Suks were regarded as pagan Gods in the days before the Buddhist religion came to Thailand. They are still viewed in some remote regions as minor deities, as well as nature spirits whose job it is to help teach humans the lessons they need to learn in life so they can get out of the cycle of reincarnation.

Where to Find Them: The whereabouts of their home has been lost in the turbulent history of the region, and they are now thought to live in heaven with the patriarchal God Buddha. They are available to you only between incarnations.

How to Contact: They are not able to be contacted.

Magickal and Ritual Help: None.

Phookas

Land of Origin: Ireland.

Other Origins: Wales and Scandinavia. It is possible that the Phooka was originally a Nordic faery who was brought to Ireland, where it retains its strongest identification.

Other Names: They are known as Kornbockes in Scandinavia, where they have the bodies of goats, and Bookhas or Bwcas in Wales, where they have the bodies of horses or pigs and a more pranksterish nature.

Element: Air.

Appearance and Temperament: Phookas (Pook-ahs) are the Hobgoblins of Ireland. They have heads resembling human males, but the bodies of horses. They can fly for limited distances, though they have no wings. Phookas are trooping faeries who run in destructive packs. They are said to be extremely ugly and ill-tempered and to have frequent quarrels among themselves.

The Irish Phookas have never been known to enter human homes, but the Welsh Bookhas have been known to come in through chimneys.

The Kornbockes of Scandinavia and Germany tend to be helpful on occasion and will actually help in the growing of their favorite grain, corn, for which they were named. But they are not averse to stealing or spoiling it if they feel the inclination.

Time Most Active: Samhain to Bealtaine, especially at night.

Lore: Wreaking havoc is their favorite pastime, and they will go out of their way to harm children and crops. The Phookas lay claim to any crop which is not harvested by Samhain night, and to cut a plant after this time risks provoking these dangerous faeries and their malevolence. In spite, for taking what they believe to be theirs, they have been known to kill herd animals, particularly cattle. In Ireland a mysteriously dead cow is sometimes said to have been "poofed" or "pooked," a term derived from belief in the Phookas.

They especially love human babies and are always on the lookout for a newborn to steal. And because of their limited powers of flight they are jealous of airplanes and will do them harm whenever they can.

Phookas love potatoes, and at night they come to harvest them from the untended fields. In Ireland, a folk legend says that potatoes dug after sunset are the tastiest and they never rot, but to get at them one risks encountering a Phooka.

Between Midsummer and Samhain the Phookas seem to go into a hibernation of sorts and are seldom seen. The Old Irish proverb—never count your crop until July is over—was a malediction against Phookas.

Where to Find Them: Unknown.

How to Contact: Contact not advised!

Magickal and Ritual Help: None.

Phynnodderees

Land of Origin: The Isle of Man.

Other Origins: Wales.

Other Names: Bugganes. Fenoderee is the Anglicized spelling.

Element: Water.

Appearance and Temperament: The term Phynnodderee is actually Welsh, and sometimes these Manx faeries are called Bugganes instead. The Phynnodderees go completely naked, revealing wizened, emaciated male bodies. Their skin is leathery, and they have small patches of silver hair tucked here and there all over themselves. By human standards they are very ugly.

Time Most Active: All year, but are only visible to humans at twilight and dusk.

Lore: The Phynnodderee are believed to have been expelled from faery society and now are solitary beings condemned to their watery realm and their hideous form for all time by the curse of an offended Faery King. They live in the shallow edges of the water on the Manx coast and seem to have no problem with their nudity. They are very ill-tempered, but have never caused humans any harm.

Where to Find Them: In shallow coastal waters.

How to Contact: Contact not advised!

Magickal and Ritual Help: Generally these faeries should be avoided, though in Dora Broome's *Fairy Tales of the Isle of Man* she tells of a man who called upon a Phynnodderee to heal a sick calf, but after the faery did his job he carried off the man because he had not adequately protected himself. If you come upon one it is best to quietly walk away.

Pillywiggins

Land of Origin: England and Wales.

Other Origins: Forms of flower faeries are known worldwide.

Other Names: Flower Faeries, Spring Faeries.

Element: Air.

Appearance and Temperament: Pillywiggins are seasonal faeries associated with spring. They are small winged creatures who resemble Pixies, and they are very playful. Their sole purpose seems to be to tend to spring flowers.

Time Most Active: Spring and early summer.

Lore: Pillywiggins live among wildflowers which grow at the foot of huge oaks. They are trooping faeries who have no ill will toward humans, and they seem only mildly interested in us. They have been seen mimicking human behaviors such as weddings and dances, but do not lower themselves to playing pranks.

These faeries are seasonal helpers to the spring Goddess and God who nurse along the tender flora each spring. They are quite diminutive and like to ride bees from flower to flower.

The Pillywiggin queen, Ariel, often rides bats, and is blonde and very seductive. She wears a thin, transparent garment of white, sleeps in a bed of cowslip, and can control the winds. She cannot speak, but communicates in beautiful song. Though she is not seen any more, she is still believed to exist in Faeryland.

Where to Find Them: In wildflower fields, especially if there are oaks nearby, and in the spring gardens of Faeryland.

How to Contact: Look in the spring of Faeryland. The guided meditation in this book provides a brief audience with the Queen of the Spring Faeries.

Magickal and Ritual Help: Undetermined.

Piskies

See **Pixies.**

Pixies

Land of Origin: Scotland.

Other Origins: None known.

Other Names: They are sometimes called Grigs or Dusters in the part of England known as East Anglia, and they are known as Piskies in Cornwall. Other names are Pisgies, Pechts, Pechs, and Pickers. The term Pixie is sometimes used incorrectly as a generic term for all British faery folk.

Element: Air.

Appearance and Temperament: Pixies (Pixy in the singular) are small, winged creatures with heads too large for their bodies. They have pointed ears and noses and arched eyebrows. Their wings are shiny and translucent, and they are usually seen wearing seasonal colors and flora. Pixies are generally friendly but are extremely capricious and given to nonmalicious mischief. The little caps they wear are the tops of foxglove or toadstool, plants they hold sacred. No gender differentiation seems apparent.

Time Most Active: Spring.

Lore: The word Pixy may relate to the word Picts, the early inhabitants of Scotland, whose spirits the Pixies were once thought to be. Like these faeries, the Picts would not touch iron even though they were superb metalsmiths. Excessive contact with iron can kill Pixies.

These faeries are wildly attracted to flowering gardens and are often seen around Bealtaine. Their queen is said to be a tiny woman of sublime beauty who has created a spring world in Faeryland which few humans can resist.

They loathe human laziness and have been known to pinch a couch potato until he springs into action.

Pixies are trooping faeries who love playing, dancing, and music above all else. They like to have large gatherings known in northern England as Pixie Fairs. A few humans have come upon these revels and have been allowed to watch briefly, but never asked to join in.

There exists an old Scottish folk tale about two fishermen walking home one evening on the Isle of Iona in the Hebrides when they spied an open burgh covered with partying faeries. So entranced they were, that they raced over to join in. Luckily one of the fishermen remembered metal was a protection against these faeries and embedded a fishhook in the side of the burgh. The fishermen were able to partake fully of the festivities and still leave when they wanted.

While Pixies do not seem overanxious for human contact, they have been known to be very helpful to deserving people. An old English folk tale recorded by E.M. Wright in *Rustic Speech and Folk-lore* tells of a woman married to a lazy man who would not go to his job as a thresher. Disguised as a man she went to do his job, only to find it done for her when she arrived each day. She later found out that a band of friendly Pixies had taken pity on her situation and had done the work themselves.

Legends about Pixie Dust, a sparkling material seen wherever these faeries have walked (often seen in cartoons and fantasy films as coming from the ends of magic wands), are as old as the faeries themselves. It was once believed that one could tell if a Pixie had been around by the silvery gold footprints they left behind. Some have tried to explain away this phenomenon as being either some type of naturally occurring fluorescent gas or else some sort of etheric residue picked up when traveling between the physical and astral worlds. It is more likely that the belief in the dusty footprints dates back to the first contacts between the Picts and the Celts. The Pictish people's greatest achievement was their extensive work in gold, silver, and bronze. Residual dust and small shavings from their efforts would logically collect on their feet and be tracked about where they walked. The Celts, who first coined the term Pixie Dust, may have actually been calling this substance "Pict's Dust" or "Pictish Dust."

Where to Find Them: In flower gardens, in wildflower preserves, and in the spring of Faeryland.

How to Contact: Approach with caution and let them know you wish to befriend them. But don't be surprised if your overtures are met with tricks of a harmless nature. They will not respond to invitations to your circle.

Magickal and Ritual Help: Undetermined.

Poleviks

Land of Origin: Poland.

Other Origins: None known.

Other Names: Polevikis.

Element: Air.

Appearance and Temperament: Poleviks (Poh-leh-vicks) look more like bipedal goats than anything resembling a human. They aid in the growing and harvesting of crops.

Time Most Active: Spring through autumn.

Lore: Poleviks hitch rides on the breezes above the grain fields of Poland. Generally they are benign where humans are concerned, but they are not to be trusted. If they aid with your crops, they expect excessive payment at the harvest's end. This can be combated by drawing up a contract stating just what you will give them and leaving it in the fields overnight for them to find. They will then usually decide your fields are not worth the trouble and move on. Even today some Polish farmers who wish to have no trouble with them leave extra grain in the field each week as a libation. This way they know their next year's crop will be looked upon favorably by them.

Farmers in the field using sickles are protected because this is an instrument which the Poleviks fear and will flee from. Polish farmers often hung their sickles up over their front doors each night to ward off the Poleviks.

They are attracted to blue cornflowers, and if you would avoid Poleviks, then get rid of any of this flower near your home.

Like the Phooka of Ireland, they lay claim to all that is left in the fields after a certain date. In this case it is not Samhain, but some time in late September.

They have a reputation for liking to spin flax, but will not do this for human benefit.

Where to Find Them: In fields of grain from Spring to September.

How to Contact: Contact not advised!

Magickal and Ritual Help: The trouble they bring outweighs any help they might be as farmhands.

Portunes

Land of Origin: England.

Other Origins: None known.

Other Names: Wish Makers.

Element: Earth.

Appearance and Temperament: Portunes look like old men and are among the smallest of all faeries, less than an inch tall. They have a trickster's nature.

Time Most Active: All year.

Lore: Portunes are best described as English Leprechauns. They are superb horsemen, grant wishes if captured, and guard a treasure. But unlike Leprechauns, they can be persuaded to help with farm chores. The Portune can grant wishes—one per customer—if he can be physically captured.

Where to Find Them: In burghs and woodlands.

How to Contact: Try using an invocation, but they will respond only if they want to.

Magickal and Ritual Help: May aid you along your spiritual quests. Other help they provide is unknown, as they avoid humans except for the occasional trick.

Puck

See *Robin Goodfellow.*

Pyrenees

Land of Origin: Cornwall.

Other Origins: None known.

Other Names: None known.

Element: Earth.

Appearance and Temperament: No one has actually seen a Pyrenee, but their energy can animate the ancient standing stones of Cornwall.

Time Most Active: At the Sabbats.

Lore: The megaliths and standing stones of Cornwall have always been surrounded with legend and mystery, one such tale being that they can rise up and walk, dance, and sing. Whether this is because of some ancient spell or from some sentient energy, such as that of a Pyrenee, living inside them is unknown.

Where to Find Them: In the megaliths of Cornwall by night.

How to Contact: Call to them at the site and ask to join their Sabbat rituals.

Magickal and Ritual Help: Pyrenees may share the secrets of the ancient megaliths and the magick once used among them.

The Red Cap

Land of Origin: Scotland.

Other Origins: Red-capped faeries are common throughout Europe, though unlike this one, most are friendly to humans.

Other Names: In Northern Ireland he is called Fir Larrig.

Element: Fire.

Appearance and Temperament: The Red Cap, an emaciated man with a leathery body and little or no hair, carries a sharp wooden scythe to strike down all who invade the area he has decided to guard for the time being. Solitary and hateful in nature, we can all be grateful there is only one of him.

Time Most Active: All year.

Lore: The Red Cap moves from place to place on a whim throughout the extreme lowlands of Scotland along the English border. He haunts the ruins of old castles and cairns which he guards with his life. The Red Cap he wears, and for which he was named, is said to be made of dried human blood.

Some sources say he is a cannibal who will consume faeries and humans alike.

The Red Cap may be a fear-form stemming from the dangers of old castle ruins and cairns. If this is true, then he is a fear-form who is very strong: there have been documented sightings of him.

The first cousins of Red Cap are the Dunters, who live in the keeps of old castles and defense towers. They are very noisy, and their moaning and whining will usually keep an entire castle awake on nights when they choose to cry. They do not attempt to harm human beings like their cousins, and seem often not to notice our presence. Modern folklore says the Dunters are the earth-bound ghosts of ancient Pictish victims.

If you meet up with Red Cap in your Faeryland travels it is wise to turn the other way.

Where to Find Him: Unknown.

How to Contact: Contact not advised!

Magickal and Ritual Help: None.

Roanes

See **Selkies.**

Robin Goodfellow

Land of Origin: England.

Other Origins: Greece, Celtic Lands, and possibly Germany.

Other Names: Puck, Pan. He is also called Jack Robinson, as in the expression, "Before you can say ..."

Element: Earth, but he may be any and all of them.

Appearance and Temperament: Robin Goodfellow looks like a Greek Satyr, with the head of a young male and the body of a goat. He has a playful, lusty nature, and loves to play pranks on humans. He has small horns on his head, and he carries with him pan pipes which he loves to play while he dances.

Time Most Active: All year, except between Samhain and Ostara.

Lore: In Greece Robin Goodfellow was probably the God Pan, as their appearance is virtually identical. In Shakespeare's play *A Midsummer Night's Dream,* Robin becomes Puck and again displays the frolicking nature of Pan.

But above all else, in pagan circles he is very much associated with the Great Horned God, the most well-known and persistent of the European pagan God-forms. The fact that he is never seen between Samhain (when the God dies) and Ostara (when he is again an adolescent) underscores this association.

Robin Goodfellow is always seen with a legion of animal follow-ers dancing merrily to his pipes. The Great Horned God has also been known as Lord of the Greenwood, and this may be another of his guises. A popular Elizabethan ballad called "Robin Has to the Green-wood Gone" may have been a thinly disguised song about this deity.

In the English legends, Robin is the son of a faery father and a mortal mother who loves to play tricks on humans who venture into his woods. Some have claimed to hear his laughter after the trick is successfully completed. He is also adept at animal and bird calls.

As the Greek Satyr, he symbolizes the faery folk of Greece.

Where to Find Him: Look for him at the spring Sabbats and in the spring of Faeryland. Look for him in woodlands which are populated with animals.

How to Contact: Evoke him as you would a God, petition him with a ritual designed for that purpose, or approach him in Faeryland.

Magickal and Ritual Help: If Robin is indeed a disguised Horned God, he can offer you any help a God could. Invite him to your circle and request his aid with whatever you need.

Rubezahl

Land of Origin: Germany.

Other Origins: Eastern Europe.

Other Names: Hey-Hey Men, Hoioimann, He-Manner, Ropenkerl, Huamann, Schlocherl, Rubheyzahl.

Element: Air.

Appearance and Temperament: These are male dwarf faeries in short black cloaks who each carry a thin, spiky walking stick. They are mean to human travelers. They wear large cloaks which hide their faces and seem to not want humans to know just what they look like. Because of this it is believed that they cannot shapeshift.

Time Most Active: All year.

Lore: The Rubezahl (Roo-bee-zahl) was once credited with being able to summon the wind or the rain, if only for a brief time. They would bring whichever one would most annoy a human traveler in their woods. If the human had no water they would summon a hot sun, and if he or she had no shelter they would summon a cold rain. They like to yell confusing noises so that travelers lose their way. They make their homes in the mountains.

Where to Find Them: In the German and Eastern European mountains and dense woodlands, and near little-used roads.

How to Contact: Contact not advised!

Magickal and Ritual Help: None.

Rusalki

Land of Origin: Russia.

Other Origins: None known.

Other Names: None known.

Element: Water.

Appearance and Temperament: Rusalkis are lovely female water faeries with long green hair who like to play water games with people. They do not seem deliberately malicious, but sometimes their games get rough and dangerous.

Time Most Active: Evening.

Lore: Rusalkis share similarities to the other beautiful female water faeries in both Europe and the Orient, and the concept may be one which originated in India or northern Africa.

Where to Find Them: In shallow pools.

How to Contact: Approach them with caution on the inner planes. Leave their presence if their games get rough or frightening.

Magickal and Ritual Help: Undetermined.

Salamanders

Land of Origin: Middle East.

Other Origins: Ceremonial magick, China.

Other Names: Fire Elementals, Guardians of the South.

Element: Fire.

Appearance and Temperament: The elemental Salamanders look identical to the lizard-like amphibians of the same name. They are regarded as powerful beings who are well aware of their value to magicians.

Time Most Active: All year.

Lore: Salamanders, indigenous to both Iberia and Asia, are water-dwelling animals. But somewhere in the Middle East, around 3000 years ago, the Jewish and Egyptian mystics declared the Salamander's astral version to be the archetypal elemental being of the south and therefore representative of fire. The choice probably had much to do with their ability to withstand hot desert climates, and with their chameleon-like adapability which made their appearance as ephemeral as a flame. It was from there that they came into ceremonial magick.

Many pagans see these elemental beings in and around their candle flames and hearths when doing spells and rituals involving fire. Their energy is thought to be disruptive if allowed to remain after ritual work is done, and most witches and magicians formally banish them after such workings.

For more information on the elemental beings of high magick, see Gnomes, Sylphs, and Undines.

Where to Find Them: You automatically call them to your circle when you invoke the four directions.

How to Contact: See above.

Magickal and Ritual Help: Because of their association with ceremonial magick, Salamanders are thought to be able to lend their energies to any ritual or spellworking, especially those involving fire. And because they are extremely powerful, gaining their good will through positive works can be a boon to magick of any kind.

Saleerandees

Land of Origin: Wales.

Other Origins: May be from the Salamanders of ceremonial magick and the Middle Eastern traditions.

Other Names: None known.

Element: Fire.

Appearance and Temperament: Saleerandees are scaled faeries resembling bipedal lizards.

Time Most Active: Daytime.

Lore: Saleerandee may be a corruption of Salamander, the elemental fire archetype of ceremonial magick. Saleerandees are nude and always cold, so they seek out human fires. They do not harm humans, but their sudden appearance can be frightening. It is said they can start no fires of their own.

Where to Find Them: Near fireplaces.

How to Contact: Unknown.

Magickal and Ritual Help: Though they do not seek out human contact, they might be persuaded to lend their energy to fire spells. Try asking their help just before you perform magick with a candle or at your hearth, and see if you can feel their presence.

Santa Claus

Land of Origin: Europe, Turkey, Western Asia.

Other Origins: Unknown.

Other Names: St. Nicholas, Kris Kringle, Father Christmas, Sinter Klass, The Holly King, King of the Waning Year.

Element: Air.

Appearance and Temperament: Santa Claus, a one-of-a-kind faery, is always portrayed as portly, a condition indicative of abundance. He wears a red or green winter suit and has a sprig of holly in his hat. He is also shown as smiling and happy. He is benevolent, especially to children.

Time Most Active: From Midsummer to just after Yule.

Lore: Many pagans are somewhat surprised by Santa Claus's inclusion in the pagan pantheon of seasonal and elemental entities, yet who could argue that he is not wholly a part of astral reality? Long before he was adopted as a saint and benefactor by Christianity, he was the pagan Holly King who reigned over the waning year from Midsummer to Yule when his counterpart, the Oak King, took over.

He is symbolized by the bird known in Europe and the Americas as the wren. Deer are sacred to him, which may have been the reason for their inclusion in the Santa Claus myth. Elves are said to be in his service, and this may have been the source of those famous little workhorses known as Santa's Elves.

The modern Christmas Santa came from a combination of Turkish folklore and some hard facts about a kindly old bishop who gave gifts to children. This historical Santa was a bishop of Myra in Asia Minor in the sixth century.

Old Dutch and Norse custom calls him Sinter Klass, and he rides a white horse, a symbol of many pagan Goddesses, on his nightly rounds. He came into Dutch folklore through a story which is probably apocryphal about a time when he left Asia Minor (or Spain, in some legends) to visit Holland and liked it so much that he returned every year in December.

He was canonized by the Christian church, adopted as the patron saint of Russia, and his fame and word of his good deeds spread. His feast day was placed near Yule in order to detract from the Sabbat festivities. Eventually he had grafted on to him the looks, behavior, and motivations of the pagan Holly King, probably in an effort to make his story more appealing to the pagans the early church wished to convert.

As the Holly King, he may once have been an actual God whose place in the pagan pantheon was devalued and eventually lost.

Where to Find Him: Look for him in Faeryland, and sense his presence at the Midsummer and Yule Sabbats.

How to Contact: Call him at the Midsummer and Yule Sabbats with the same reverence you would reserve for a God. Many covens enact the struggle between him and the Oak King at these Sabbats.

Magickal and Ritual Help: Undetermined, but he would probably help you along in spiritual quests. For best results, attempt to work with him during the waning of the year.

Satyrs

See **Robin Goodfellow.**

Sea Sprites

See **Undines.**

The Seelie Court

Land of Origin: Scotland.

Other Origins: Possibly these faery forms were derived from old Indian legends about god-like air spirits of both good and evil who did great battles in the heavens.

Other Names: The Blessed Ones, the Sluagh.

Element: Mostly Air, but can be any.

Appearance and Temperament: The Seelie Court are the blessed trooping faeries of the winds who have been heard but never seen. Scottish folklore presents them as a huge host of light and benevolence riding on the night air.

Time Most Active: Anytime, but mostly at night and on the Sabbats.

Lore: The Seelie Court and its counterpart, the Unseelie Court, are a rare example of duality—completely separated opposing forces—in paganism. The Seelie Court is thoroughly good and benevolent, made of the most heroic and beautiful faeries of Scotland. They ride the winds looking down at the earth for any good which they can do. They acquired the title "Court" because they also act as arbiters and judges in faery disputes.

    Scottish mythology tells us that the Seelie Court once interacted very much with humans. There is one legend which shows their great compassion for human misfortune when the Queen of the Seelie Court removed a curse from a man destined to live his life in reptilian form.

    Some accounts place the Seelie Court underground when not in trooping flight. One family who was supposed to have stumbled upon this underground abode was the MacCrimmons, whose fame as pipers is known throughout Scotland. They were supposed to have been granted this marvelous musical gift from the Seelie Court in return for their unselfish desire to serve their fellow countrymen. Incidentally, they found the Seelie Court's burgh on the Isle of Skye.

Where to Find Them: Unknown.

How to Contact: Unknown.

Magickal and Ritual Help: Undetermined. It seems that they only approach humans whom they choose, and humans cannot command their presence or their aid.

Selkies

Land of Origin: Scotland and the Orkney Islands.

Other Origins: None known.

Other Names: They are called Roanes in Northern Ireland.

Element: Water.

Appearance and Temperament: Selkies are seaside faeries native to the Hebrides and northern Scottish islands. They appear as seals with some human characteristics, but legend says that they can shed their sealskin and appear with perfect male or female forms which are very alluring to young men and women. Their attitude and intent towards humans is an incomplete and foggy picture.

Time Most Active: All year.

Lore: Some Selkies have been lured into the human world where they live as mortals, but more often they lure mates into their realm. They cannot steal human mates as some sea faeries do, but must induce them to come willingly.

It was once believed they could control the coastal storms, and they may have aided the magick which brought about the defeat of the Spanish Armada in 1588.

They are capricious, but less so than many of their kind, and humans who mate with them must always keep their jealous natures in mind. When they tire of their human mates, as they inevitably do, they will leave them to die of broken hearts. One Hebridean legend says that the males used to come on shore, father half-human children, and then disappear into the sea again.

In *Scottish Faeries and Folk-Tales* there is a story about a young man who comes upon some Selkies at play. Hurriedly, they all don their seal skins and slip into the sea, all except one. The young man, who grabbed up that skin, finds it belongs to a lovely, young female Selkie. He begs her to marry him and be a faithful wife. She agrees and always keeps her word, but is never happy in the human world, and pines away for longing to return to the sea.

Where to Find Them: In the ocean and lochs of northern and western Scotland, and along the coast of the Hebrides Islands.

How to Contact: Because much of their intent is unknown, contact them cautiously. If you feel well enough protected, you could mentally call out to them at the coasts where they are known to live.

Magickal and Ritual Help: None known, but they may lend their energy in times of natural crisis to protect Scotland. They are credited with knowing all the secrets of the world's oceans and may someday be persuaded to share them.

Servan

Land of Origin: Switzerland.

Other Origins: None known.

Other Names: A similar faery in the Shetland and Orkney Islands is called a Trow.

Element: Earth.

Appearance and Temperament: No one has actually seen a Servan, but we know they have very mischievous natures.

Time Most Active: At night.

Lore: Though Servans have never been seen, we know of them because they leave behind their mischief and their footprints. Like the Trows of the Shetlands, they like to go abroad at night and hide things in odd places. Servans may merely be a blame-taking manifestation of the human psyche and not a faery at all.

Where to Find Them: Unknown.

How to Contact: May not be a complete being and therefore is not contactable.

Magickal and Ritual Help: None.

Shellycoats

Land of Origin: Scotland.

Other Origins: Not known, but this faery shares similarities with other inland water faeries of Europe.

Other Names: None known.

Element: Water.

Appearance and Temperament: Shellycoats are small faeries who dwell in pools of shallow fresh water and in woodland lakes. They are fish-like in appearance but have huge mouths and huge eyes which enable them to see very well at night. They have very round bodies with very few scales and are usually dark red or purple in color. They bob near the surface like large beach balls, usually with only their big eyes showing. Shellycoats like to play harmless pranks.

Time Most Active: All year.

Lore: These water faeries like to baffle travelers who are looking for water to drink or in which to recreate. They are not evil, but their pranks are sometimes mean. One Scottish legend says that Shellycoats do not wish to be mean, and if one merely tells them their prank was not funny, they go away and sulk until they feel forgiven. Stories abound of swimmers on a hot day starting to get into cool highland waters and being scared off upon seeing a Shellycoat watching them with huge, mischievous eyes.

Where to Find Them: In shallow freshwater pools, especially those in woodlands and in the Scottish Highlands.

How to Contact: Deliberate contact is probably not a good idea and serves no useful purpose. But if you are determined, seek them in the places they are known to live. It is quite possible that, with a little effort, witches can befriend these creatures.

Magickal and Ritual Help: Unknown.

Shoney

See **Kelpies.**

Shopiltees

Land of Origin: The Shetland and Orkney Islands.

Other Origins: They may have come to the islands from Norway.

Other Names: Sea Horses.

Element: Water.

Appearance and Temperament: Shopiltees are playful little water horses which have not been reported as having been seen for more than a hundred years.

Time Most Active: Unknown.

Lore: It is believed that these playful sprites of the North Sea have died out. But once they heavily populated the Sea and were playful and friendly with both sailors and with persons along the seashore.

Where to Find Them: Seek them in Faeryland. Use your energy to create thought-forms of them which may enable us to astrally repopulate their species.

How to Contact: Seek them in Faeryland. Visualize them clearly and call to them while offering your aid in helping them to exist once more. See Chapter 6 for ideas on creating these and other thought-form faeries.

Magickal and Ritual Help: It has been so long since humans have had contact with Shopiltees that it is hard to say what aid they might be to us. But they are likely to look with great kindness and gratitude to anyone who can help repopulate their species.

Silvani

Land of Origin: Italy.

Other Origins: Possibly Greece.

Other Names: None known.

Element: Air.

Appearance and Temperament: Silvani are winged wood nymphs who have a very filmy appearance, almost ghostly. They are of no use to humans, but do not seek to harm us. They wear red clothes and animal furs, particularly goat skins.

Time Most Active: All year.

Lore: These harmless faeries do not look whole when they are seen, but this may simply be the way they look when manifesting on the physical plane. Humans appear much the same way in the astral world.

Silvani, whose name means "wooded," love the color red. They wear it all the time and are very attracted to anything of this color. They used to be considered protectors of the Alps, but have never done anything to earn such a title. They are rarely seen any more.

Where to Find Them: In the Italian Alps.

How to Contact: Undetermined.

Magickal and Ritual Help: Undetermined.

Skogrsa

Land of Origin: Sweden.

Other Origins: None known.

Other Names: None known.

Element: Earth.

Appearance and Temperament: Skogrsa are short, hairy, large-nosed wood elves who are very dangerous.

Time Most Active: All year.

Lore: These shapeshifting wood elves usually appear as owls. In the past they were often sought out as oracles, but the price they demanded for their services was very high and dangerous. Do not let them lure you into playing their game by believing their claims that they know something important which they have to tell you.

Though they are rarely seen anymore, they still have the reputation of being a hazardous contact.

Where to Find Them: In the woods of Sweden.

How to Contact: Contact not advised!

Magickal and Ritual Help: None. There are safer methods of divination than to approach a Skogrsa.

Sleigh Beggy

Land of Origin: The Isle of Man.

Other Origins: None known.

Other Names: Squinters.

Element: Earth.

Appearance and Temperament: Little is known about these shy, stocky Manx faeries who live in underground burghs. It is known that they hate the taste of salt and do not like ashes or artificial light, so you are unlikely to find them in your modern home. They are believed to anger easily. The Beggys go nude and have crow's feet which make their footprints easily recognizable.

Time Most Active: Unknown.

Lore: Manx people believe the faeries called Sleigh Beggy to have been the original inhabitants of the island, like the better-known Tuatha De Danann of Ireland. They are always spoken of in flattering terms to avoid raising their anger, though no legends state just exactly what an angry Sleigh Beggy is likely to do.

Ashes, which are hated by these faeries, are your best protection against them. Because of their hatred for ashes they also shun fire and are believed to enjoy the cold.

Where to Find Them: It is probably not advisable to seek them out, but if you want to try, look in the winter regions of Faeryland.

How to Contact: Contact not advised!

Magickal and Ritual Help: Unknown.

Snow Faeries

Land of Origin: Europe and Asia.

Other Origins: Unknown.

Other Names: Frost Faeries, Winter Faeries, Jack Frost, The Frost King, Old Man Winter. In Scandinavia and Japan she is the Snow Queen. In Russia he is sometimes known as Father Frost who brings death to winter travelers in his realm.

Element: Water.

Appearance and Temperament: Snow Faeries take on many different appearances depending in which land they live in. In some lands they are trooping faeries like the Pillywiggins, who collectively help bring winter to the world. In this instance they are small, winged creatures, dressed in white. As an individual being, such as Jack Frost, he is a solitary male. No record has ever been kept of their attitudes towards humans, but they appear to have no interest in us at all.

Time Most Active: Late autumn to early spring, and mostly at night.

Lore: Snow Faeries are not just faeries but a single pervasive personification of winter which is part of the faery lore of the entire northern hemisphere. These faeries bring on winter, encourage the snow, and paint frost on windowpanes.

In Russia the bringer of winter is an old man called the Frost King, who is a Slavic version of the English Jack Frost. In Scandinavia and Japan the bringer of winter has a female personification known as the Snow Queen, who may have descended from a Crone Goddess. The Snow Queen of Denmark has her own kingdom with a large white palace from which she rules the winter season. Danish pagans often make libations or offerings to her to see them safely through winter. But she is a childless beauty whom Danish lore tells us is always seeking a child who would not be missed to take as her own.

Before science was able to understand the simple principles of condensation, no doubt the picturesque frost left on windowpanes during the night took on a magickal quality. For that reason, and because of the great variations in descriptions and lore about Snow Faeries, they may be no more than thought-forms.

Where to Find Them: In the winter of Faeryland, in a night winter woods, or near winter streams and lakes.

How to Contact: Unknown.

Magickal and Ritual Help: None known.

Snow Queen

See **Snow Faeries.**

Spriggans

Land of Origin: England.

Other Origins: Also known in Cornwall, where they are believed to be bodyguards to the Unseelie Court.

Other Names: None known.

Element: Air.

Appearance and Temperament: Spriggans are small and round, but can inflate to enormous proportions by sucking in large amounts of air. On the ground they are often mistaken for sharp rocks, and they live both in the mountains and in the sky. They are dangerously malevolent.

Time Most Active: At night all year long.

Lore: In Cornwall Spriggans are bodyguards of the Unseelie Court, a flying host of evil faeries. In England they are the most unpleasant faery beings one could meet. In centuries past they were accused of leaving changelings, blighting crops, and being superb thieves, and they can command destructive winds at their will. Though they are immensely greedy, they do not like human misers and will save their worst for them.

Where to Find Them: Unknown.

How to Contact: Contact not advised!

Magickal and Ritual Help: None.

Spunkies

Land of Origin: Scotland.

Other Origins: Celtic counties, and all countries where changelings were thought to be a problem.

Other Names: None known.

Element: Air.

Appearance and Temperament: Spunkies have never been seen, but they are not friendly faeries. Reports of their appearance varies, but they are all said to be short, ugly, and long-armed.

Time Most Active: All year.

Lore: Spunkies are stealers of "unprotected" children. In the place of the stolen infant they leave an ugly faery changeling. Spunkies may be another faery form that is merely an incomplete thought-form stemming from the unexplainable infant deaths in which a child simply failed to thrive.

Unprotected, in this sense, may mean both magically and spiritually. In more modern times the term most certainly meant without benefit of Christian baptism, and in pagan times it meant without formal dedication to the Goddess and the bestowal of a secret name.

Modern folklorists are quick to point out that Spunkies are almost unknown today. Robert Burns, Scotland's poet laureate, wrote of Spunkies, saying, "… in some miry slough he sunk is Ne'er more to rise."

Where to Find Them: Unknown.

How to Contact: Spunkies probably cannot be contacted because they most likely were never more than projected fear-forms.

Magickal and Ritual Help: None.

Succubi and Incubi

Land of Origin: Middle East.

Other Origins: India and the Orient.

Other Names: Succubus and Incubus are the singular forms.

Element: Air.

Appearance and Temperament: Neither faery has ever been seen by human eyes, but their presence has been keenly felt by many unfortunate persons. They see humans as existing for their own perverse amusement.

Time Most Active: All year, but fortunately their attacks are few and far between.

Lore: The Succubus is a female faery who sexually attacks human men, and the Incubus is a male faery who sexually attacks human women. Their unprovoked attacks have been documented throughout human history. It was once believed that anyone claiming such contact was mad and they were summarily incarcerated. But the evidence for their existence is well-documented, and their assaults are still going on today. Pick up any popular work on modern hauntings and there will be at least one story of a frightening sexual attack by an astral entity which has occurred in the last few years.

Persons who have been attacked by these malevolent spirits display mild to severe bruises and bite marks, many of them in places where they could not be self-inflicted. Women may also show torn vaginal tissue after an attack.

There are two folk remedies which may help keep them from you. A peony flower taken to bed or a cauldron in the room is said to keep away the Incubus, and bluebells or phallic-shaped magickal tools are supposed to ward off the Succubus.

Where to Find Them: Unknown.

How to Contact: Contact not advised!

Magickal and Ritual Help: None.

Sylphs

Land of Origin: Greece and Egypt.

Other Origins: Ceremonial magick.

Other Names: Windsingers.

Element: Air.

Appearance and Temperament: Sylphs appear as very small, winged creatures whose features are vaguely human. They are so light in color and body as to be virtually transparent. The wings they bear seem only to be there for show, because they appear so buoyant as to defy gravity, and they can hold themselves aloft for long periods without ever moving their tiny wings. In fact, the wings may be no more than human thought projections intended to justify to our rational minds the appearance of flight. Sylphs can be helpful to humans who seek them out.

Time Most Active: All year.

Lore: Sylphs are native to Greece and Egypt, but they may have originally come from the Middle East, where Jewish, Arab, and Egyptian mystics declared them to be archetypal representatives of air and of the east. Today they are still the representatives of air and the east in ceremonial magick. For more information on the elementals of high magick, see Gnomes, Salamanders, and Undines.

Where to Find Them: You automatically call them to your circle when you call upon the four directions.

How to Contact: See above.

Magickal and Ritual Help: Because of their long association with ceremonial magick, Sylphs are thought to be able to aid with any ritual or magickal undertaking, especially those concerning the element of air.

Sylvans

Land of Origin: Greece.

Other Origins: None known.

Other Names: None known.

Element: Earth.

Appearance and Temperament: Sylvans are beautiful faeries who lure humans to their deaths in the woods.

Time Most Active: All year, especially at night.

Lore: As the name suggests, Sylvans are wood faeries, but they may be only fear-forms which grew out of the dangers of the woods, especially of the deep woods at night. There is a bit of Greek folklore about a young man named Hylas who tricked the Sylvans into letting him go by offering to bring his brothers to them.

Where to Find Them: Unknown.

How to Contact: They may not be able to be contacted since they may not exist as more than an almost forgotten thought-form. Remnants of their energy may be found in remote regions of Faeryland.

Magickal and Ritual Help: None.

Tengu

Land of Origin: Japan.

Other Origins: None known.

Other Names: None known.

Element: Air.

Appearance and Temperament: Tengu (Tin-goo) are winged faeries who characteristically carry a fan of feathers. They do not aid humans or seem to want any human contact.

Time Most Active: All year.

Lore: The Tengu are nature spirits which are part of the old Shinto religion of Japan. These winged wood elves are not apt to aid humans, though they seem to bear us no grudge. They are reputed to have great magickal powers which they keep to themselves, and they can shapeshift with great ease, usually going into animal forms.

Where to Find Them: In Japan's dwindling woodlands.

How to Contact: They will not respond to any known evocation or invitation.

Magickal and Ritual Help: None known.

Thussers

Land of Origin: Norway.

Other Origins: None known.

Other Names: Called Vardogls in Iceland.

Element: Earth.

Appearance and Temperament: Thussers are a community of small faeries of both genders and their children who live in earthen mounds near the fjords of Norway. They tend to avoid humans, but they are not malicious.

Time Most Active: At night, particularly during the full moon.

Lore: At night the mounds of the Thussers open to the moon, and the little people wake up to celebrate their moon Goddess in whatever phase she is in. They love to dance, and are expert fiddlers who specialize in the folk music of Norway. Humans have seen their revels and tried to join in, but these shy little faeries flee when people approach. Thussers live in family communes headed by the eldest member of that family, whether that is a male or female.

Some sources claim they are metalsmiths by trade, a radical departure from other faeries, for whom metal is a deadly taboo.

Where to Find Them: At night near the earthen mounds of coastal Norway.

How to Contact: Thussers are very shy, but you can ask them to join in your own Esbat rituals. They may not be visible, but chances are they are nearby celebrating with you.

Magickal and Ritual Help: They may join in Esbat rituals. If you ask them to come to your circle and you Draw Down the Moon, you should be able to feel them paying you homage as their Goddess. For those who have experienced this, it is an unforgettable verification that their magick has worked.

Tighe Faeries

Land of Origin: The Isle of Man.

Other Origins: The Bean-Tighe is an Irish faery which shares similarities with the Tighe Faeries of Man, but there is no evidence to indicate which may have originally migrated to where, or if they sprang up simultaneously.

Other Names: None known.

Element: Earth.

Appearance and Temperament: No one has ever seen a Tighe (Tee or Teeg), but they are believed to be relatives of the Scottish house Brownie and, like their Scottish cousins, they attach themselves to the service of one home.

Time Most Active: At night.

Lore: Tighes will go abroad in the night in pairs and take care of household tasks which were not accomplished. during the day. They are especially careful of the fireplace and porch and get along well with animals, except for cats. If you have a cat, you will not have a Tighe Faery.

They are very delicate of feeling, hate loud noises, and abhor any display of gratitude other than food offerings.

It is believed that the Tighe race is dying out, for fewer and fewer can be accounted for. If you can thought-form create a few and offer them a safe place to live, you may reap some unexpected thanks.

Where to Find Them: At your hearthside at night.

How to Contact: These faeries will not appear at your will nor do your bidding by your asking. A Tighe does a task out of the joy of doing a kindness and will balk if asked to perform.

Magickal and Ritual Help: Undetermined, but may participate in general house blessing rituals.

Tomtra

Land of Origin: Finland.

Other Origins: None known.

Other Names: None known.

Element: Earth.

Appearance and Temperament: The Tomtra is a Brownie with a somewhat less likable disposition. He always appears as a male wearing a small green cap and brown clothing.

Time Most Active: All year, especially at night.

Lore: The Tomtra, like the Scottish Brownie, adopts a human home as his own, but he demands a neat and orderly environment, which he will help maintain. If the people of his house are sloppy, he can torment them until they either mend their ways or until he gives up and moves on. The ground of his home must also be kept clean or this sprite will become disgusted and leave, taking all his good luck away with him.

Thursday is their holy day, during which time they rest, treating it like a sabbath. They work and play hard and feel they owe themselves one day a week.

Even though he shares the bounty of your home, a Tomtra feels he must be paid for his assistance around the house and asks warmth and food. He loves to look after horses, and he hates cheats and will not tolerate being treated stingily. Give him Yule gifts to keep him around.

The Tomtra will steal hay and milk. He is an expert fiddler, though he is not known to entrap dancers. Dance with him without worry.

Where to Find Them: In homes, but it is unknown where they live when they are not with human hosts.

How to Contact: Leave out food for him and invite him in.

Magickal and Ritual Help: The Tomtra will gladly join in celebrations of the Goddess, and can lend energy to home protection spells and spells for physical energy and stamina. Dance with him to raise a potent cone of power.

Trolls

Land of Origin: Germany and Scandinavia.

Other Origins: They are also known in northern Scotland and northern Italy.

Other Names: Called Trolds in Sweden, and Hill Men or Berg People in Denmark.

Element: Earth.

Appearance and Temperament: Trolls vary in size, but they are larger than most faeries. They are hairy and bipedal, and some are quite grotesque. Trolls hate humans, animals, and other faeries.

Time Most Active: All year.

Lore: Trolls have been part of Germanic and Nordic folklore as long as humans have been able to relate them as part of an oral tradition. The well-known children's faery tale, "The Three Billy Goats Gruff," tells of how a Troll guards a bridge and will not allow three goats to cross. The first two goats are eaten by the Troll, but the third is able to overcome this obstacle by poking the Troll in his most sensitive organ—his eyes.

Trolls have been best known as guardians of byways, though their help seems arbitrary and dubious. They are more like neighborhood bullies who decide upon a territory and then stake it out for the sheer meanness of doing so. Sometimes they do this all alone, but like all bullies they are really cowards who prefer to run in packs. They have little or no loyalty to these packs, and fighting among themselves is a frequent occurrence.

One of their favorite pastimes is throwing rocks at other creatures, and they love to laugh for long periods of time for no reason at all. Other faeries and wild animals tend to avoid them if possible.

Trolls are said to find humans ugly and are often more afraid of us and of our power than we are of them. But they are the "macho men" of the faery world and will not back away from a showdown.

They never steal human mates or human babies, whom they regard as worthless and smelly. They are carnivorous as well as nocturnal, but do not eat human flesh. Goat and mutton are their favorite meats, and they are noted for having abysmal table manners. They also hate any bright light and are extremely stupid.

In England, the most famous Troll is Grendl of Chaucer's *Beowulf*. In America, Trolls can be seen on television as the antagonists in the animated children's series *The World of David the Gnome*.

Fortunately for humans, Trolls never go into human homes, which they believe all smell terrible, and they rarely manifest these days outside of the inner planes.

Where to Find Them: Unknown, but they may find you in Faeryland. If you come upon one, do not run from them. Like any bully they can sense fear and you will only make your situation worse. Outsmarting them is your best defense and, fortunately, this is not difficult.

How to Contact: Contact not advised!

Magickal and Ritual Help: None.

Trows

Land of Origin: The Shetland and Orkney Islands.

Other Origins: Probably Scandinavia.

Other Names: Night Stealers, Creepers.

Element: Air.

Appearance and Temperament: Trows (pronounced to rhyme with row) are squat, round, and misshapen faeries who have no legs. They are not wicked, but love to prowl about in the night and move things around or hide things in odd places.

Time Most Active: At night.

Lore: Trows are native to the Shetland and Orkney Islands and possibly to the Upper Hebrides. They are completely nocturnal and sneak around at night moving things around just for the fun of aggravating humans. A Shetland proverb says, "If it be moved by morrow, blame not hand but Trow."

The name Trow is Norwegian in origin, suggesting that Trows may have once been Nordic faeries who found their way into Scottish mythology.

Since Trows have no legs, they move about by rolling on their bulbous forms or by bouncing like rubber balls.

Where to Find Them: Look in the Shetlands, Orkneys, or upper Hebrides at night when they are playing games. Where they make their homes is unknown.

How to Contact: Unknown.

Magickal and Ritual Help: Undetermined, but it is doubtful if Trows will ever aid humans.

The Tuatha de Danann

Land of Origin: Ireland. One of the five myth cycles of the island is the Invasion Cycle in which the Tuatha de Danann take a leading role.

Other Origins: None.

Other Names: Irish Faeries, the Royalty, the Gentry.

Element: Can be any.

Appearance and Temperament: The Tuatha De Danann (Too-ah day Thay-nan) figure largely in the myth cycles of the Irish people. They were among the earliest conquerors of the island, and their Goddess Dana is one of the earliest named Great Mother Goddesses of western Europe. She was later renamed Brigid, a name by which she is better known today. The Tuatha are trooping faeries, warrior-like in temperament, but fair and just. They are male, female, and children, and look exactly like humans only somewhat smaller.

Time Most Active: All year.

Lore: When the Milesians, ancestor cousins of the Celts, arrived to conquer the island somewhere between 3000 and 1000 BCE, the Tuatha were driven underground into the faery burghs which they still inhabit. Hurling, the national game of Ireland, is a popular sport among them, one which was said to need human participation to be successful. Finvarra, a Tuatha King, was very fond of it and chess and he had his favorite human opponents. Much folk music of the island was said to be composed by them.

The Book of Leinster, a seventh-century collection of Irish myths, records that the Tuatha De Danann were "faery" peoples, while *The Book of the Dun Cow* describes them as being "gods, but not gods." The early Celtic illuminated manuscript known as *The Book of Invasions* recounts their conquering and dividing of the island.

The construction of the ancient stone megaliths of Ireland is sometimes credited to them, since their origins remain a mystery. Another stone in their possession was the Lia Fail, or Stone of Destiny, on which the High Kings of Ireland stood as they took the crown. The stone was said to cry out in agony if a wrongful ruler stood upon it, while it roared with leonine pride when the rightful one stepped up. The current royal family of Britain is believed by many English to be descended from the Milesian kings who once stood on this stone.

The Tuatha also possessed the invincible sword of the Sun God Lugh and the cauldron of the God Dagda, which was taken from the Land of the Dead.

Legends about the Tuatha are recorded in many other early books of Ireland, and most books on Irish mythology and folklore give a great deal of space to the exploits of these faery creatures. The Tuatha were the first to divide Ireland into four provinces and set up governments for each. The Tuatha then subdivided themselves into four groups, which were once the names of these cities. Each city corresponds to a different direction. The two principal groups of this subclassification are the Gorias and the Finias. A number of the Tuatha's rulers have become pagan deities, including Etain, Midhir, Finvarra, and Daniel O'Donoghue of Connacht.

Where to Find Them: The Tuatha can go almost anywhere they wish, but make their homes in the burghs of Ireland.

How to Contact: Call them to your circle, go to them in trance, or go to a faery burgh. One legend says that if you approach a burgh on Midsummer evening, knock on it three times, and request it to open in the name of Dana, that it will open to you. But be cautious with this practice. Like most faery contact, this experience is best and most easily accomplished on the inner planes.

Magickal and Ritual Help: Anything and everything.

Twlwwyth Tegs

Land of Origin: Wales.

Other Origins: None known.

Other Names: None known.

Element: Earth.

Appearance and Temperament: Twlwwyth Tegs are small anthropomorphic faeries of all ages and genders. They are trooping faeries and appear to be friendly towards humans, though they seem to want little to do with us.

Time Most Active: All year.

Lore: The term Twlwwyth Teg is sometimes used as a generic name for all the faeries in Wales, but this is an improper use of the label. The name roughly translates as "fair family," and they live in family structures not unlike our own were several thousand years ago. The principal difference would be that the female Twlwwyth Tegs are equal to males in both stature and in their society. They live in clan groups which are determined by the eldest female member of the family, and the eldest male is the primary defender of the clan and its namesake, much like the ancient Celts of Wales.

The Tegs' children mature at age one hundred and go off to live in small groups with other young people until they pick mates. Twlwwyth Tegs have intermarried with other Welsh faeries, and their offspring are known as the Bendith y Maumau, the native elves of Wales.

The Tegs live off the Welsh coast on faery islands which are connected to the mainland by deep tunnels. They, or a patron Goddess, protect their islands with fog and storms. They are harmless unless you attempt to invade their islands, in which case they will try to defend themselves. These faeries love to garden, and their islands are said to be a paradise of flowers and foliage. Night Rades to the mainland are common occurrences and have been observed by travelers. On the mainland they have burghs which they stay in, rather like faery hotels, until they are ready to return to their islands. One of the reasons given for their Rades to the mainland is that they come in search of food and fresh water. At one time the Twlwwyth Tegs were accused of stealing children, especially the fair-haired, fair-skinned ones, but this does not seem to be something which interests them anymore.

Welsh folklore says their chief ruler is Gwyn ap Naud, an ancient British God of the Dead.

Where to Find Them: At the Welsh seashore.

How to Contact: Evoke them to a circle on the beach. Use food and fresh water as an inducement and a sign of friendship.

Magickal and Ritual Help: Undetermined, but they may be useful in weather spells and in protection rituals.

Uilebheist

Land of Origin: The Shetland and Orkney Islands.

Other Origins: Probably this Scottish faery form is actually Norse in origin, but has been lost in Nordic folklore.

Other Names: Draygan.

Element: Water.

Appearance and Temperament: The Uilebheist are faeries who appear as multiheaded sea monsters who guard the inlets and waters around the rocky coasts of the Shetland and Orkney Islands.

Time Most Active: Unknown.

Lore: The Uilebheist probably came to these remote islands with the Norse invaders. In Norse literature there exist some vague references to faery guardians of the fjords. who were probably the prototype for these Scottish faeries.

Island seamen often spoke of sea monsters off the coast of northern Scotland whose purpose seemed to be the protection of the islands rather than the destruction of sailors and ships.

Uilebheists are also known as Draygans, and the word's similarity to the English "Dragon" cannot be discarded. They may have once been thought of as sea dragons associated with the water element rather than fire.

Where to Find Them: In the North Sea near the Shetland and Orkney Islands.

How to Contact: Unknown. Try calling to them in a ritual or going to them in the seas of Faeryland.

Magickal and Ritual Help: Undetermined, but they may lend their aid to rituals and spells involving the protection (both physical and environmental) of the northern lands of Scotland.

Uisge

See *Kelpies.*

Undines

Land of Origin: Greece.

Other Origins: Germany, Britain, Indonesia, the Middle East, and ceremonial magick.

Other Names: Sea Sprites, Water Watchtowers, Watersingers, Sea Guardians, Water Elementals.

Element: Water.

Appearance and Temperament: Undines appear like small sea-horses with human faces. They are stern and yet playful, depending upon what they feel is their appropriate role at the time. They are also thought to have a somewhat seductive nature, though their very small size in relation to humans makes them little threat in that regard.

Time Most Active: All year.

Lore: Undines were first recorded in the annals of human folklore by the Greeks, who reported seeing them frolicking in the Aegean Sea. In the Middle East they came to represent the element of water in the mystic rites of the Kabbalists and the Sufis, both mystic traditions of the patriarchal religions of the region. When Rome adopted the Greek pantheon and, along with it, much of its folklore, they also adopted the Undines, whom they regarded as demigods.

In Ceremonial Magick, Undines are the archetypal elementals of water and of the west. They are called upon to witness all rituals and, in the Order of the Golden Dawn, to "praise God" in a ritual known as Benedicite Omnia Opera. For information on the other elementals of high magick, see Gnomes, Salamanders, and Sylphs.

Where to Find Them: They are automatically called to your circle when you do an invocation to the direction of the west.

How to Contact: See above.

Magickal and Ritual Help: Because of their close association with ceremonial magick, Undines are credited with the power to enhance the energy and efficacy of any ritual or spell, especially ones associated with water.

The Unseelie Court

Land of Origin: Scotland.

Other Origins: Possibly this faery form was derived from old Indian legends about god-like air spirits of both good and evil who did great battles in the heavens.

Other Names: None.

Element: Mostly Air, but can be any.

Appearance and Temperament: The Unseelie Court, like the Seelie Court, has never actually been seen. Attempts by humans to describe them paint them as a massive dark cloud which rides upon the wind. They are thoroughly evil.

Time Most Active: Mostly at night, especially from Samhain to Ostara.

Lore: The term Unseelie is most often said to mean "unblessed," but is probably best described in this context as meaning "damned." Some Scottish legends say they were all once members of the Seelie Court who fell from Grace.

The Court travels on the night winds from where their unnerving cackles and howls can be heard. They have no method of reproduction, so they enslave mortals whom they think would never be missed and carry them along to become one of them.

The nature of the Unseelie Court has given rise to speculation that this legend is of Christian origin and represents a type of purgatory, but it is more likely that Christian Scots adapted the legends of the Unseelie Court to fit their needs.

Where to Find Them: Unknown.

How to Contact: Unknown, and contact is not advised! If they are like the Seelie Court, they will not respond to any evocations or pleas from humans.

Magickal and Ritual Help: None.

Urchins

See **Nix.**

Urisks

Land of Origin: Scotland.

Other Origins: None known.

Other Names: None known.

Element: Earth.

Appearance and Temperament: Urisks are extremely ugly, so much so that they have been credited with actually frightening people to their deaths. They are wrinkled, hairy in patches, and emaciated; have duck feathers on their backs and necks; and are topped with huge, misshapen heads. Despite their appearance they are quite friendly and seem to crave human companionship.

Time Most Active: All year.

Lore: Urisks often used to seek out human company, but their ghastly appearance frightened all would-be companions away. For that reason we see very few nowadays. They will be glad to be helpful in almost any endeavor in exchange for brief company. They are known to be very intelligent and highly psychic.

Where to Find Them: Best to find them in isolated woodlands, or to ask them to your circle.

How to Contact: Ask them to appear, or seek them out in Faeryland. Calling them to your circle as you invoke the four directions will also work. If you are psychically sensitive enough to see faeries at your circle, just make sure you are prepared for the Urisks' revolting appearance.

Magickal and Ritual Help: Undetermined, but they may offer their aid and energy for any positive purpose or aid in divinations.

Vasily

Land of Origin: Russia.

Other Origins: Faeries who love and care for horses are known throughout Europe.

Other Names: None known.

Element: Earth.

Appearance and Temperament: Vasilys are dwarf faeries that are both male and female, though there seem to be more males. They live in barns and make their beds in the hay. They shun human contact, so we have absolutely no knowledge of their feelings toward us.

Time Most Active: All year.

Lore: Vasilys are the greatest horse lovers on any plane of existence. They care for horses at all times, and are especially tender to the ones who are elderly or ill. No human has been harmed by them, but it is believed that they could be quite mean to anyone who abuses their favorite animal.

The Russians believe that if you hear sleigh bells when there is no sleigh it means they are looking after your horses.

Where to Find Them: In barns where horses live.

How to Contact: Vasilys will not respond to evocations or invitations.

Magickal and Ritual Help: Undetermined, but a persistent witch may persuade them to work magick for a sick animal.

Vilas

Land of Origin: European Alps and Poland.

Other Origins: The Balkans have faeries called Vilys who are male and share similar traits.

Other Names: Vily, Vilishkis.

Element: Earth.

Appearance and Temperament: Vilas (Vee-lahs) are female faeries, mistresses of the forest, and are so beautiful that once they are seen by human males, they are longed after forever. They do not like to get involved with humans, but they have rescued them from Alpine disasters by guiding rescue teams and dogs.

Time Most Active: All year.

Lore: Vilas may have once been a single Goddess of the Alps rather than a group of faeries. They are mountain nymphs who can heal all ills and will foretell natural disasters if moved to do so. They emit a cry similar to that of a woodpecker, which is a warning of avalanche or other Alpine catastrophes.

Vilas love animals, especially dogs, and they are thought to watch over the famous rescue dogs of the St. Bernard Monastery. They speak every known animal language.

Where to Find Them: They never leave the Alps. Either physically or astrally you must travel there to find them, but remember that they are not likely to show themselves to you.

How to Contact: Unknown.

Magickal and Ritual Help: For an act of kindness towards them or the dogs they look after, they will forever assist you in magickal matters. They are great healers and might be persuaded to lead you to healing herbs if asked.

Vodianoy

Land of Origin: Russia.

Other Origins: None known.

Other Names: None known.

Element: Water.

Appearance and Temperament: Vodianoy (Voe'd-ee'ah-noi) are small male faeries who have green hair and are bloated and wet as if recently drowned. They are dangerous and can cause sickness.

Time Most Active: At night.

Lore: Vodianoy live in the cold waters in and around Russia. They are completely nocturnal and bring sickness to humans, especially sicknesses associated with polluted water such as cholera.

This may not be a complete entity, but rather a fear-form caused by the frequent outbreaks of cholera in this region which ancient peoples couldn't understand.

Where to Find Them: In cold waters, if they exist at all.

How to Contact: They probably cannot be contacted, because it is doubtful that they exist as whole beings.

Magickal and Ritual Help: None.

Wag-by-the-Way

Land of Origin: Scottish Lowlands.

Other Origins: None known.

Other Names: None known.

Element: Earth.

Appearance and Temperament: The Wag-by-the-Way got his name because he used to guard the byways of the Lowlands for the noble families of Scotland. He has a long, cat-like tail which wags when he is irritated or angry. He is an extra small-sized dwarf faery usually covered in cinders. Only males have been reported. The Wag is generally friendly.

Time Most Active: Mostly at night.

Lore: This Scottish boarder sprite is similar to the Scottish house Brownie. He adopts a home where he is most domestic and friendly, almost like a family pet. He is intensely loyal to his family, but tends to throw things at visitors. They are always cold and love to get as close to fire as possible. It was long a custom in the Lowlands to swing cooking pots out from the fire when not in use so that the Wag-by-the-Way could get into the hearth and warm himself over the banked coals. For reasons unknown, the Wags are almost a vanished race, and there are very few left now.

Where to Find Them: In homes and near ancient roads in the Scottish Lowlands.

How to Contact: Keep a warm fire going whenever possible, even if it is only an astral one. Invite them in to your home, set out food for them, and send them healing energy in the hopes of repopulating their species.

Magickal and Ritual Help: Home protection, especially from physical intruders. Protection to travelers.

Water Leaper

Land of Origin: Wales.

Other Origins: None known.

Other Names: None known.

Element: Water.

Appearance and Temperament: The Water Leaper looks like a small bat bouncing along the surface of the Irish Sea. They are quite vicious and have been credited with killing humans.

Time Most Active: Unknown.

Lore: The Water Leaper mostly preys on fishermen, whom they lure into rocks or coerce overboard to drown. They may be another fear-form rather than a complete faery being.

Where to Find Them: In the sea off Wales.

How to Contact: Contact is not advised, but it is doubtful if one could be contacted because they may not fully exist.

Magickal and Ritual Help: None.

Well Spirits

Land of Origin: Ireland.

Other Origins: England and Norway. Ireland has no corner on the market of Well Spirits, but the pagan use of sacred wells there as magickal spots leads to my classification of them with Irish faeries.

Other Names: Well Guardians.

Element: Water.

Appearance and Temperament: Well Spirits are water sprites and well guardians who are very sympathetic to human needs, but asking their help often carries a huge price. They are superb shapeshifters who usually take the form of human beings whose bodies they envy, and are then dangerously beautiful.

Time most active: All year.

Lore: Ireland is a land covered with sacred wells, and each well has its resident Well Spirits. It is this guardian spirit to whom you make a petition when you drop a coin in a wishing well.

If you allow a Well Spirit to embrace you, you risk being dragged into the well with him or her to live forever as his or her consort in their watery world. Luring humans to their underwater world as mates is often the price for their aid.

So steadfastly are these wells protected that it was often considered dangerous to approach them without protection. The nursery rhymes of Jack and Jill and their fate while fetching water may be derived from the belief in Well Spirits.

Very few Well Spirits are not dangerous, but plain respect and a few protection charms will often turn the tide in your favor. The best way to know if a well is safe or not is to ask the local people. Irish mythology tells of a young woman who taunted the spirit of a sacred well and was sucked into it. While this may be a metaphor for some mental blockage, it is best to be respectful around these wells.

In England and parts of Norway, Well Dressing is part of Sabbat rituals which have come into popular custom.

Where to Find Them: At the side of sacred wells or wishing wells, or at hot springs.

How to Contact: Make a simple evocation at the places they are likely to be. Extreme caution is advised.

Magickal and Ritual Help: Undetermined.

Wichleins

See **Knockers.**

Wichtln

Land of Origin: Germany.

Other Origins: Also known in other central European countries.

Other Names: They are called Vattaren in Switzerland and Wights in England.

Element: Earth.

Appearance and Temperament: Wichtln (Veech-l'n) look like very tiny elves all dressed in brown fur coats. Their bodies are very bulbous and their arms and legs are much too long for their bodies. Their mischievous nature borders on downright meanness.

Time Most Active: All year.

Lore: Some persons who are acquainted with Wichtlns claim that they never sleep. While this is probably a gross exaggeration, these elves are tireless in their pursuit of fun, which is always at the expense of some unsuspecting human being or animal. Like the Scottish Brownie they adopt a human home and can do many of the household tasks and will gladly guard and protect their home, but most people feel that putting up with their poltergeist nature is just not worth it. Some of their favorite pranks are pinching, tripping, letting livestock loose, causing spills, and moving things about. Wichtlns love gifts, and such displays of affection will keep them in your home and generally keep them placated.

Where to Find Them: Unknown.

How to Contact: Invoke them into your home if you really want one, otherwise confine your contact to Faeryland. Make sure they do not follow you home.

Magickal and Ritual Help: They can probably aid you with home protection spells and general household chores, but their help is rather unreliable.

Wilde Frauen

Land of Origin: Germany.

Other Origins: Scandinavia.

Other Names: Called Elles and Elle Maids in Sweden.

Element: Earth.

Appearance and Temperament: Wilde Frauen (Veel-duh Frow-in) literally means "wild women," and they are the female wood sprites of the Germanic and Scandinavian forests. They stand about three feet high and represent all the ages of women from childhood through old age. Wild in this context does not describe their temperament any more than it does that of any other wood faery. Wild in this case refers to their living conditions among the roots of the oldest trees in the deepest part of the forests.

Time Most Active: All year.

Lore: Wilde Frauen are seen year 'round, but fewer have been seen in this century due in part to the diminishing of untouched forest

Look for the Wilde Frauen near the oldest trees in the forest.

lands. They dress seasonally and will always be found wearing the flora, foliage, and colors of the current season.

They have a powerful queen about whom little is known, and it may be speculated that she is a female version of the God called Lord of Greenwood, who in turn may be a version of the Horned God.

Where to Find Them: In unspoiled woodlands.

How to Contact: Invite them to your circle, or approach in their natural habitat. Some caution is advised.

Magickal and Ritual Help: Wilde Frauen are less capricious than most wood sprites and may be persuaded to help you raise energies for any positive endeavor, especially ecological ones.

Will-o'-the-Wisp

Land of Origin: England.

Other Origins: The faery lights are seen all over the world, and each land has a different name for them.

Other Names: Faery Lights, Hobbedy's Lantern, St. Elmo's Fire, Elf Fire, Jack-o-Lantern, Will-o'-the-Whisp, Willowisps, Will-o'-Light, Bob-A-Longs, Night Whispers, Fire Faeries. Jenny Burnt-Tail and Hunky Punky are the Cornish names. In the Shetland and Orkney Islands they are called Teine Sith, which means "Fire Faery." In Germany they are called Huckpoten. The Swedes call them Irrbloss. In France they are known as Les Eclaireux, and in Italy they are called Candelas. In Russia they are known as Ruskaly and are thought to steal unbaptized infants.

Element: Fire.

Appearance and Temperament: The Will-O'-the-Wisp appears as a collection of flickering, wavering, glowing lights low to the ground near marshes, meadows, and grassy hillocks. They are most easily seen an hour or so after sundown.

Time Most Active: From before sunset until just before dawn.

Lore: These golden lights which are seen glittering enticingly in the distance have never been explained by science. Many pagans believe them to be the lights of faery revels, or even of an open burgh. Other explanations are that these are the lights of trooping faeries on their Rades, or that they are the wandering souls of discarnate humans. When one approaches them they vanish, often appearing again just out of reach as if playing a game of tag.

It is arguable whether these lights are actual faeries or merely manifestations of a faery game, or the lights of a faery revel. The belief in faeries holding parties at night has long been part of human mythology, with more than a few persons claiming to have witnessed these gatherings, led to them oftentimes by the Will-O'-the-Wisp.

They were once seen as offering protection when they were near and may have been one origin of the Halloween Jack-o-Lanterns, which were first carved from Irish turnips.

Where to Find Them: Try looking in grassy meadows and parks on summer nights.

How to Contact: Unknown.

Magickal and Ritual Help: Undetermined.

Yann-An-Od

Land of Origin: Brittany.

Other Origins: None, though faeries who tend animals are known everywhere.

Other Names: None known.

Element: Earth.

Appearance and Temperament: The Yann-An-Od appears as a kindly old shepherd complete with long robe, shepherd's staff, and long white beard. Little is known about his feelings towards humans because he tends to fade from view when approached.

Time Most Active: Spring through autumn.

Lore: Yann-An-Od is actually the name of a faery king who guards flocks of sheep. He is a one-of-a-kind, and one has to wonder where his legions are if he is a king.

Where to Find Him: Among sheep herds.

How to Contact: Unknown, but you might try a simple evocation, though keep in mind that he shuns human contact and will probably not appear.

Magickal and Ritual Help: Undetermined.

The Yeti

Land of Origin: Asia.

Other Origins: May have been first known in northeast Asia and migrated across the Bering Straits to North America.

Other Names: Sasquatch, Bigfoot, the Abominable Snowman, the Snow Monster, the Gorilla Man.

Element: Earth.

Appearance and Temperament: The Yeti (Yet-ee) is a large, bipedal, hairy creature of light brown or white fur who is occasionally sighted throughout east Asia and North America. Rather gorilla-like in appearance, he tends to run away from humans.

Time Most Active: Possibly winter.

Lore: The Yeti is not a faery in the true sense of the word, no more so than the Loch Ness monster or Dracula. But as an entity of nature, the Yeti has a long history across two continents. Sightings of this creature have been numerous, some of them even committed to film. But the search for him has so far been a fruitless one.

Long before Europeans came to North America, the Native Americans told stories of a huge and powerful man-creature they named Sasquatch who roamed the wild and remote areas of the northwestern part of the continent, stories which are identical to those found among the indigenous peoples of eastern Asia.

In the last several decades there has been a new interest in the Yeti, who has been the subject of several documentaries, television specials, and even feature films. The movie and television adaptation known as *Harry and the Hendersons* is a story about a family who found and befriended a Yeti.

Though the Yeti wisely shies away from human beings, it is hopeful that someday we can contact this being and his kind for our mutual benefit.

Where to Find Him: Unknown.

How to Contact: Unknown. Send him healing, loving energy and let him know that not all humans want to approach him with a gun.

Magickal and Ritual Help: Undetermined. If humans would stop running in error from this being or beings, we may find we have a lot to learn from each other.

Zips

Land of Origin: Mexico and Central America.

Other Origins: None known.

Other Names: None known.

Element: Earth.

Appearance and Temperament: Zips (pronounced Seeps) are thin male faeries of very small size who wear tiny helmets and carry tiny spears. For all their fierce and battle-ready appearance, they are very shy and have always avoided people.

Time Most Active: All year, especially at night.

Lore: The Zips' sole function is to protect and care for deer, especially stags. It is unknown whether these faeries came over with the Spanish conquerors, were part of the native Mexican belief system, or a combination of the two. If they did travel from old Spain they may, at one time in the long-forgotten past, have been associated with the pan-European belief in the Great Horned God (i.e., Pan, Cernunnos, Faunus) and his sacred animal, the stag. In Mexican folklore there are stories of herds of wild deer impervious to human weapons who are believed to be protected by the Zips.

Where to Find Them: Unknown.

How to Contact: Unknown.

Magickal and Ritual Help: Probably animal protection and aid spells.

Zuibotschnik

See **Lesidhe.**

Afterword

Faery lore is plentiful but is often partially hidden; it is complex, and yet is very straightforward. Even within the perimeters explored in this guide there no doubt abounds much other faery life, and new variations on the old.

Because of these regional differences you may know the faeries I have mentioned to be something other than what they have been presented here to be, especially if you are part of either the Elven Tradition or of the highly secretive Fairy Tradition of Wicca.

I would be pleased to hear from anyone who has comments, criticisms, or additions to make to this guide. We as pagans are each of us students, and we are each of us teachers with an abundance of wisdom and knowledge to share. Please write to me in care of the publisher.

Bright Blessings!

EDAIN McCOY
Midsummer, 1992

Resource Guide

*T*he following are addresses of mail order suppliers who carry items of interest to pagans. When contacting any of the businesses listed here it is best to include a self-addressed stamped envelope (SASE) to ensure a speedy and direct reply. If you are writing from outside the United States, you will need to include instead an International Reply Coupon (IRC) available from your local post office.

Suppliers of Herbs and Oils

American Herb Association
P.O. Box 353
Rescue, CA 95672

> This umbrella body does not sell herbs. Instead, they seek to promote knowledge and use of herbs and can recommend reliable dealers throughout the United States. Be sure to include a SASE.

Companion Plants
7247 N. Coolville Ridge Rd.
Athens, OH 45701

> Sellers of herbs. Catalog $2.00.

Mountain Butterfly Herbs
106 Roosevelt Lane
Hamilton, MT 59840

> Write for current information and prices.

Herbal Endeavors
3618 S. Emmons Ave.
Rochester Hills, MI 48063

> Sellers of herbs. Catalog $2.50.

Indiana Botanical Gardens
P.O. Box 5
Hammond, IN 46325

> Sellers of herbs, charcoal blocks, herbal medicines, and some books. Request a free catalog.

Leydet Oils
P.O. Box 2354
Fair Oaks, CA 95628

> Sellers of fine essential oils. Catalog and price list $2.00.

Music

Southern Music Company
1100 Broadway
San Antonio, TX 78212

> Publishers and sellers of printed music, including much folk music. This busy company is often better contacted by phone. Their number is (512) 226-8167.

Postings
Dept. 654
P.O. Box 8001
Hilliard, OH 43026–8001

> Send $3.00 for a year of video and audio catalogs. They are sellers of videos and offbeat audio tapes and CDs. Their audio catalog usually includes a good selection of international folk music.

The Music Stand
1 Rockdale Plaza
Lebanon, NH 03766

> Sellers of gifts and novelties inspired by the performing arts. The Music Stand sells the Clark Pennywhistle with an instruction booklet and cassette tape for a very reasonable price. Catalog $2.00.

Valley of the Sun

> See listing under Periodicals.

Circle Network

> See listing under Periodicals.

Environmental Groups

Clean Water Action Project
317 Pennsylvania Ave. SE
Washington, DC 20042
(202) 745-4870

> This organization has chapters all over the country seeking to clean up and protect water resources.

Earth First!
P.O. Box 5871
Tucson, AZ 85703 (602) 662-1371

> Publishes *Earth First* Magazine. Is involved in many environmental causes.

Greenpeace
1436 U Street NW
Washington, DC 20009
(202) 462-1177

> This is a worldwide organization concerned with all aspects of the environment. They are a nonviolent but aggressive organization which has done a lot to increase awareness of our environmental woes.

Catalogs of Pagan Interest

Llewellyn's New Worlds of Mind and Spirit
P.O. Box 64383-733
St. Paul, MN 55164-0383

> Sellers and publishers of books on metaphysics, magick, paganism, astrology, and alternative spirituality. Write for a free copy. One year's subscription $10.00.

Pyramid Books
35 Congress Street
P.O. Box 4546
Salem, MA 01970-0902

> Sellers of metaphysical, pagan, and magick books. Catalog $2.00. Pyramid also sells beautiful pagan jewelry.

Ritual Tools and Other Pagan Items

Craft of the Wise
45 Grove Street
New York, NY 10014

> Sellers of herbs, oils, books, tapes, magickal tools, and other occult paraphernalia. Request free catalog.

Isis Metaphysical
5701 E. Colfax
Denver, CO 80220

> Write for information; catalog price varies. Isis carries books, jewelry, incense, oils, herbs, and periodicals. It is also a pleasant gathering center for local pagans and other "New Age" thinkers. Be sure to obtain a list of their upcoming workshops, lectures, and classes.

Moon Scents and Magickal Blends, Inc.
P.O. Box 1588-C
Cambridge, MA 02238

> Sells all manner of magickal paraphernalia, but their specialty is herbs and ritual oils. Request free catalog.

Mystic Moon Magick
8818 Troy St.
Department C
Spring Valley, CA 91977

> Suppliers of all types of magickal tools and accessories. Those with modems can call their BBS at (619) 466-5403. Catalog is $1.00, refundable with your first order.

Sacred Spirit Products
P.O. Box 8163
Salem, MA 01971-8163

> Sellers of books, magickal tools, herbs, incense, and other occult items. Catalog $3.00.

Periodicals

Circle Network News
P.O. Box 219
Mt. Horeb, WI 53572

> This quarterly pagan publication is nothing less than excellent. It is full of well-written articles and contacts. Circle also sells pagan musical recordings and songbooks. Send a self-addressed stamped envelope for full subscription information. Sample copy $4.50.

Winners!
Valley of the Sun Publishing
Box 3004
Agoura Hills, CA 91301

> Publishers and sellers of "New Age" music and mind/body video and audio tapes, including tapes to aid meditation and astral projection. First copy of their mag-a-log is free, and will be sent free for up to a year if you order from them.

The Green Egg
Box 1542
Ukiah, CA 95482

> Pagan periodical which was very popular in ther 1970s. Sample copy $5.50. Send a self-addressed stamped envelope for full subscription information.

Tides
P.O. Box 1448
Littleton, MA 01460
> Pagan journal published eight times a year. Sample copy $4.50.

About Ethnic Cultural Societies

These organizations can be found in virtually every city and town in the United States, and they can be a great help to you in finding out more about the folklore of your heritage—including any faery lore. Look in your phone book or the phone book of a nearby city for a contact number. More often, though, you will have to keep an eye on the local newspaper for news about where and when the local organization meets. If you have no luck there, go to your library and ask a librarian to help you locate them.

Appendix Two

The Elements of
Spell Construction

In an earth religion a spell can utilize virtually anything which comes from nature. Remember that the power is not as much in the object as within the deep mind of the witch. Remember too that elemental representations are less a concern than the will and force of the magician who draws on them.

Once you decide to create a spell for any need, follow these basic steps:

1. Clearly understand and define your magickal goal.

2. If you wish to use a specific element, then decide which one is most appropriate and collect items to represent that energy.

3. Gather candles, stones, or whatever else you intend to use to focus and send the energy you will raise. Empower those items with your personal energy as you focus upon your goal.

4. Decide upon your words of power. You may write them out or remember the key phrases you wish to use as you improvise.

5. If you wish to use a special deity in your magick, decide on who, and on how you will petition and connect with him or her. You may want to write out special prayers and invocations and memorize them.

6. If you wish to use a faery or elemental being in your magick, decide which one you would like to call on and have ready its favorite foods or other items which will induce it to stay and help you.

7. Plan how you will visualize your goal. This is the essence of the magick and very important to your outcome. The moment you start visualizing the resolution of a magickal need is the moment you begin to create the changes in your deep mind necessary for the magick to manifest. Don't skimp on visualization. Enjoy it!

8. Decide when and where you want to do the spell. Where will depend largely on your own resources. When can be any time you like, or you may consider astrological influences.

9. At the appropriate time, gather what you will use and go to the place where you will perform the spell.

10. Cast your protective circle or use some other form of protection which you can count on.

11. Your ritual is now beginning. Invite whatever elementals, faeries, spirits, or deities you wish to have present as you work. They should always be welcome, but they are not necessary for spell work. If you wish to use them for spell work, then have ready a speech telling them what you'd like from them.

12. Clear your mind and begin clearly visualizing your goal.

13. Raise energy within yourself and pour it into the magickal object(s).

14. Use your words of power, light your candles, charge your stones, dance or sing. Do whatever you have decided to do to focus your attention and raise energy. If you are working with

other beings, encourage them to raise energy with you. Get them to dance and infuse the area just outside your circle with as much energy as possible.

15. Take advantage of natural phenomena which can help you raise energy. A storm, for instance, is an excellent source of energy which any witch can draw on to help feed a spell. Just feel yourself becoming a part of the storm, and feel yourself psychically drawing on the storm's vast stores of energy as you seek to raise your own energies or cone of power.

16. When you feel you have put as much energy into the spell as you can, send the energy out to do your will. Relax, throw up your arms, raise a tool, kneel, or do whatever else makes you feel the energy being sent. Be sure to direct it out from you visually, as well. Also send out any energy raised for you by other entities at your circle side.

17. You should finish your spell with words such as "So Mote It Be." Mote is an obsolete word for "might" or "must." These words are synonymous with "Amen," "So It Is," and "It is Done." It is a statement of completion and an affirmation that you know your magick is successful. All magick is worked from the point of view that the desired goal is already manifest—it will not come to be, but IT IS. Always phrase your magickal desires in the present tense, such as "I have love in my life now" or "My bills are now paid in full." Talking of magick happening in the future will keep it forever in the future, always just out of reach.

18. Meditate briefly on your goal. Visualize it as already manifest. Smile, and know the magick is at work.

19. Thank and dismiss all faeries, spirits, and deities who have come to witness or aid in your magick.

20. Ground your excess energy and open your circle.

21. Record your spell in your Magickal Diary or Book of Shadows with the date, time, weather conditions, and any astrological data you wish to include. This will be useful later when you

have done enough spells to look for patterns. For example, you may see that your most efficacious spells were done on Sundays, or when it was cloudy or snowing, or when you had Gnomes present. Everyone has different affinities. These patterns will help you pick the best times for your own spell work.

Appendix Three

Outline for Ritual Construction

*B*elow is a step-by-step guide for creating pagan rituals which can be adapted to almost any need and can work for either covens or solitaries.

1. If you wish to use an altar, have it set with items of the season. Acorns, apples, and gourds in fall; flowers in spring; herbs, fruits, or greenery in summer; holly and evergreen in winter, etc. The direction your altar faces is up to you. Every coven and solitary has their own views on this. Many change directions with the seasons. If you are undecided, place the altar in the center of your circle facing north until you work out your own system. West is the direction of the crone's cauldron wherein all things begin and end and begin again.

2. Cast a circle of protective energy with an athame, your creative mind, or with any other ritual tool you feel comfortable using. See it clearly in your mind as a perimeter of protective blue-white light.

3. Invite, but never command, friendly spirits, faeries, or elementals to join you as you wish. In some traditions it is common to invite ancestors to join you, especially during the dark days from Samhain to Imbolg when it is believed that the portal between our dimensions is at its thinnest.

4. Call on the directional quarters or faeries if you wish, and light a candle to them. This is often done by ringing a bell in each direction and asking that the spirits of that quarter join you. However, remember that bells frighten away faeries. If you want faeries at your ritual, forgo the bell. Be sure to walk clockwise as you call the quarters. The direction with which you choose to begin is a personal one, though some traditions dictate one for you. The Celtic traditions usually begin with the west, where it is believed that the Land of Death and Rebirth is. Middle Eastern traditions begin in the east, the direction of the rising sun. And the English and Norse traditions usually begin rituals in the north, the dark land where—in the northern hemisphere—the sun never travels.

5. Definitely use a candle to honor each deity whom you invite into your circle. Goddess candles are traditionally white, and God candles are orange or red. Or you can use a white, red, and black candle for the Triple Goddess. Once again, this is a matter only you can decide. If you only have plain white candles available, then use them for both the God and Goddess, marking them with male and female symbols for distinction.

6. State out loud the purpose of your ritual: Sabbat observance, personal enrichment, rite of passage, honor of a deity, magick, or whatever. Sing, dance, chant, meditate, and/or offer praise and thanks to your deities. Let the words come from your heart. Singing (feel free to make up your own words and melodies as you go) can quickly tap your inner states of consciousness, and dancing can raise your personal power and energies. You can write out and memorize your rituals, or you can speak spontaneously as would have been customary in many ancient rituals. You can have certain set phrases you use, but be creative and celebrate with feeling. You will get more

out of your ritual by being spontaneous than you will with most prepared speeches. And if you find you have done something you really liked, then by all means write it down after you have closed the circle.

7. If you choose to work magick, have with you whatever materials you need for your spell. Once a circle is cast it is unwise to break it until it is grounded. Making a "hole" in the protective energies allows the energy you've worked to raise seep out, and can allow who-knows-what to enter. When I began my path in witchcraft I tended to ignore the sanctity of the circle, feeling myself too rational to believe some nasty entity was just waiting to get in. I had a few surprising and unpleasant experiences. Don't learn the hard way. The energy you raise will attract things you don't want around. With your circle properly cast they can't get in, and will go when the energy they are attracted to is grounded. Respect your circle.

8. If your purpose is a rite of passage, then you should have already worked out with the family of those involved just what words, gestures, or materials will be used. Keep these as simple as possible without losing the meaning of the event.

9. Raise and send your cone of power if you wish. If you have no magickal need for it you might send it out to heal the polluted and ailing Mother Earth. If you have just celebrated a rite of passage then you can send loving energy to the persons or spirit involved. But remember that magick is generally not worked on a Sabbat unless absolutely necessary.

10. If it is a Sabbat, enact whatever drama you wish to honor the holiday and use whatever seasonal rituals seem appropriate. The Great Rite, a symbolic union of the male and female principles of deity, is appropriate at all spring Sabbats, but can be done at any of them if you wish. At Samhain many circles enact the death of the God and mourn for him. At Yule we celebrate the rebirth of the God. Adapt seasonal songs for these holidays and thank the Goddess for the bounty of the earth at all seasons.

11. There is no rush to close the circle once you have finished your ritual. You may sit inside it and sing, meditate, scry, or just feel in communion and at peace with nature and your deities. If you are with a group, you can eat, tell stories, or play circle games. Don't dismiss the circle until you feel ready. Just being in this sacred space has a healing effect on the mind and body.

12. When you are ready to close the circle, thank the elementals and spirits who have joined you, and thank your deities especially. If you have called the quarters, then dismiss them in a counterclockwise movement beginning again with the west. Dismiss all whom you have called upon with the traditional phrase, "Merry meet, merry part, and merry meet again."

13. Ground the energy from your circle—always! See it dissipate and return to the earth.

Bibliography and Suggested Reading

Abrahams, Roger D., ed. *Afro-American Fairy Tales.* New York: Pantheon Books, 1985.

Arrowsmith, Nancy, and George Moorse. *A Field Guide to the Little People.* New York: Hill and Wang (A Division of Farrar, Straus and Giroux), 1977.

Bonwick, James. *Irish Druids and Old Irish Religions.* Dorset Press, 1986.

Brennan, J.H. *Astral Doorways.* Bungay, Suffolk, England: Aquarian Press, 1986 (first published in 1971).

Briggs, Katherine. *The Vanishing People: Fairy Lore and Legends.* New York: Pantheon Books, 1978.

Buck, Pearl S. *Fairy Tales of the Orient.* New York: Simon and Schuster, 1965.

Bulfinch, Thomas. *Bulfinch's Mythology.* Garden City, NY: Nelson Doubleday, Inc., 1968 (first published as *The Age of Fable,* 1855).

Campbell, Joseph. *The Masks of God: Primitive Mythology.* New York: Viking Press, 1959.

Cole, Joanna, ed. *Best-Loved Folktales of the World.* Garden City, NY: Doubleday and Company, Inc., 1982.

Colum, Padriac. *A Treasury of Irish Folklore.* New York: Bonanza Books (A Division of Crown Publishers, Inc), 1967.

Crichton, Robin. *Who Is Santa Claus?* Edinburgh, Scotland: Cannongate Publishing Limited, 1987.

Cunningham, Scott. *Cunningham's Encyclopedia of Magical Herbs.* St. Paul, MN: Llewellyn Publications, 1986.

_____. *Earth Power: Techniques of Natural Magic.* St. Paul, MN: Llewellyn Publications, 1987 (these natural, elemental spells are all perfectly adaptable to working with faeries).

._____. *Earth, Air, Fire and Water: More Techniques of Natural Magic.* St. Paul, MN: Llewellyn Publications, 1991 (this sequel to Earth Power is another book of elemental spells which are easy to adapt for faery participation).

Delaney, Mary Murray. *Of Irish Ways.* New York: Harper and Row, 1973.

Denning, Melita and Osborne Phillips. *The Llewellyn Practical Guide to Astral Projection.* St. Paul, MN: Llewellyn Publications, 1987.

Encyclopedia Judaica, Vols. 6 and 7. Jerusalem: Keter Publishing House, 1971.

Erdoes, Richard and Alfonso Ortiz, eds. *American Indian Myths and Legends.* New York: Pantheon Books, 1984.

Evans-Wentz, W.Y. *The Fairy Faith in Celtic Countries.* New York: University Books, 1966 (First published as *The Fairy Mythology,* 1911).

Froud, Brian, and Alan Lee (Edited and Illustrated by David Larkin). *Faeries.* New York: Harry N. Abrams, 1978.

Frazer, Sir James. *The Golden Bough,* Abridged Edition. New York: Macmillian, 1956.

Guerber, H.A. *Legends of the Rhine.* New York: A.S. Barnes and Company (Fourth Edition), 1895.

Hahn, Emily, and Barton Lidice Benes. *Breath of God.* Garden City, NY: Doubleday and Company, Inc., 1971.

Hazlitt, W. Carew. *Faiths and Folklore of the British Isles,* Volumes I and II. New York: Benjamin Blom, 1965.

Hodson, Geoffrey. *Fairies at Work and at Play.* London: The Theosophical Publishing House, 1982.

Huygen, Wil. *Gnomes.* New York: Peacock Press (A Division of Bantam Books), 1977 (translated from the Dutch).

Keightley, Thomas. *The World Guide to Gnomes, Fairies, Elves and Other Little People.* New York: Avenel Books, 1978 (originally published as *The Fairy Mythology,* 1880).

Langley, Jonathan, illus. *Rain, Rain, Go Away! A Book of Nursery Rhymes.* New York: Dial Books for Young Readers, 1991.

Lobel, Arnold, ed. and illus. *The Random House Book of Mother Goose.* New York: Random House, 1986.

Matthews, John. *The Elements of the Arthurian Tradition.* Longmeade, Shaftsbury, Dorset, England: Element Books, 1989.

Matthews, John and Caitlin Matthews. *Hallowquest: Tarot Magic and the Arthurian Mysteries.* London: The Aquarian Press, 1990.

McCoy, Edain. *Witta: The Irish Pagan Tradition.* St. Paul, MN: Llewellyn Publications, 1993.

Monroe, Douglas. *The 21 Lessons of Merlyn: A Study in Druid Magic and Lore.* St. Paul, MN: Llewellyn Publications, 1992.

Pachter, Henry Maximilian. *Paracelsus: Magic Into Science.* New York: Schuman Publishers, 1951.

Rhys, Ernest, ed. *Fairy Gold: A Book of Old English Fairy Tales.* Freeport, NY: Books for Libraries Press, 1970 (first published in 1907).

Robertson, R. MacDonald. *Selected Highland Folktales.* London: David and Charles (Second Edition), 1977.

Rovin, Jeff. *The Fantasy Almanac.* New York: E.P. Dutton, 1979.

Sanderson, Ivan T. *Abominable Snowman: Legend Come to Life.* New York: Chilton Co., Publishers (Third Printing), 1963.

Scott, Allan, and Michael Scott Rohan. *Fantastic People: Magical Races of Myth and Legend.* New York: Galahad Books, 1980.

Spense, Lewis. *The Magic Arts in Celtic Britain.* New York: Dorset Press, 1992 (a reprint of an edition which appeared in Britain in the 1950s).

Time-Life Books, The Editors of. *The Enchanted World Series.* Alexandria, VA: Time-Life Books.

Toor, Frances. *Mexican Folkways.* New York: Crown Publishers, 1947.

Wilde, Lady. *Ancient Cures, Charms and Usages of Ireland.* Detroit: Singing Tree Press, 1970 (first published in 1890 by Ward and Downey Ltd. of London).

Zipes, Jack, trans. *The Complete Fairy Tales of the Brothers Grimm.* New York: Bantam Books,1987.

Index